PRAISE FOR PREVIOUS EDITIONS OF
THE COMMON-SENSE MORTGAGE

"One of the best guidebooks to the realty financing jungle."
—*Los Angeles Times*

"Jam-packed with ideas for saving on mortgage costs."
—*Chicago Tribune*

"Intelligently written, logical, and thorough."
—*Kirkus Reviews*

"Lucidly written. . . . This book should have a large audience."
—*Booklist*

"An excellent reference book for home buyers, realty agents, and investors interested in residential mortgages."
—*San Francisco Examiner-Chronicle*

"Virtually in a class by itself."
—*Philadelphia Inquirer*

"His coverage of the mortgage market is so complete as to make this a compact layperson's handbook of the field. . . . A timely choice for business and consumers."
—*Library Journal*

"You won't find a better 'how to get a mortgage' book than this one."
—Robert J. Bruss,
Syndicated Real Estate columnist

PETER G. MILLER

THE COMMON-SENSE MORTGAGE

How to Cut the Cost of Home Ownership by $50,000 or More

CB
CONTEMPORARY BOOKS

Library of Congress Cataloging-in-Publication Data
is available from the United States Library of Congress

Some of the material in this book was previously published in *The Mortgage Hunter*, published by HarperCollins, in 1997.

Cover and interior design by Scott Rattray

Published by Contemporary Books
A division of NTC/Contemporary Publishing Group, Inc.
4255 West Touhy Avenue, Lincolnwood (Chicago), Illinois 60646-1975 U.S.A.
Copyright © 1999 by Peter G. Miller
Printed in the United States of America
International Standard Book Number: 0-8092-2601-4

99 00 01 02 03 04 QV 15 14 13 12 11 10 9 8 7 6 5 4 3 2 1

To Amanda, Sam, and Caroline

CONTENTS

ACKNOWLEDGMENTS

THE MATERIAL YOU now hold has a publication history spanning more than 20 years and would not have been possible to assemble without information and assistance from many people and institutions.

Danielle Egan-Miller, business editor at NTC/Contemporary Publishing, encouraged this project and did much to bring it to market.

Major portions of this book were first printed in the *Washington Post* as part of a weekly column on real estate finance. The sections on timesharing, reverse loans, and equity-sharing mortgages first appeared in *Goodlife* magazine. Sections concerning computers and the searching process and the material on hidden refinancing costs were originally published by *Fact, The Money Management Magazine*. Portions of the material concerning computer services have been rewritten and updated for this edition. Some portions of the book originally appeared in slightly different form via publication in *The Washington Weekly*.

This book would not have been possible without the cooperation and assistance of many individuals and organizations. The author wishes to thank Albert B. Crenshaw, of the *Washington Post*; Bill Winn and Gene-Gabriel Moore, of *Goodlife* magazine; Daniel M. Kehrer and Joseph Lisanti, of *Fact, The Money Management Magazine*; Edward R. DesRoches, editor and copublisher of *The Real Estate Professional*; and Jody Lane, of *Real Times*.

Also, Katherine B. Ulmann and the United States League of Savings Institutions; Bonnie O'Dell, Kevin Hawkins, Alfred King, Eugene R. Eisman, and the Federal National Mortgage Association (Fannie Mae); John J. Coonts, director, FHA Single Family Development Division, HUD; John Flynn and Angelina M. Ornelas, HUD; Victor S. Parra, of the National Timesharing Council; Jerry Karbon and the Credit Union National Association; Phyllis R. Pleasants, of the Mortgage Insurance Companies of America; and Hilda Pena, Erica Greenberg-Lewis, Gerald Ferrance, and the Department of Veterans Affairs.

Thanks also to James Sherman, Talman Home Federal Savings and Loan (Chicago); James J. Hall, James J. Hall Realtors (Silver Spring, Maryland); Douglas M. Bregman, Esq., of Bregman, Berbert, and Schwartz (Bethesda, Maryland); Leon Pomerance, Esq. (Marrietta, Georgia); John Hemschoot, Director of Home Mortgage Standards, and Brad German, with the Federal Home Loan Mortgage Corporation (Freddie Mac); Steven A. Skalet, Esq. (Washington, D.C.); Charles R. Wolfe (Gaithersburg, Maryland); and David Reed with Partners Mortgage (Austin, Texas).

Over the years this book has greatly benefited from the inclusion of materials first published in *The Real Estate Professional* (Suite 4, 1492 Highland Avenue, Needham, MA 02192, [781] 444-4688).

Certain material concerning reverse mortgages first appeared in a weekly column written by Jody Lane, publisher of the online real estate news service Realty Times (http://www.realtytimes.com).

Portions of this book originally appeared in a weekly column written by the author and syndicated nationwide on the online real estate news service Realty Times.

Portions of the material concerning mortgage credit certificates (MCC) financing were originally developed by the author and electronically posted on America Online.

Jeffrey A. Stoltz, CPA, of Bethesda, Maryland, has been a valued source of tax information and ideas for many years. I am grateful to the Bethesda firm of Osterman, Pollack & Moses, LLC, certified public accountants, for their courtesy and assistance.

The author would also like to thank Warren Dunn and the Mortgage Bankers Association of America and Martin Keithline and the

Montgomery County (Maryland) Board of Realtors, who graciously provided amortization statements and other valued information used in earlier editions of this guide. In this edition, amortization statements have been recalculated by the author with the use of a business calculator, commonly available spreadsheet software, and a personal computer.

As always, authors are responsible for content. The assistance provided by various individuals and organizations is a matter of courtesy and does not represent, imply, or infer a recommendation or endorsement of this guide.

INTRODUCTION

THE INFORMATION AGE is here, and the world is now awash with mortgage facts, data, publications, programs, and websites. But so much information has produced a new complexity—the need to sort through a huge number of potential mortgage options to find the one best for you.

Although the mortgage industry has become more consumer friendly over the years, the fact remains that there are still sharks in the waters. While many good loan programs are available, consumers must still shop with care because seemingly minor differences in rates and terms can mean *thousands of dollars in additional costs* for the unprepared and the unwary.

Long ago the *Washington Post* ran a series of columns that had something different to say about real estate financing, ideas that instantly created a following among consumers, brokers, and lenders. Those columns became the core material for a book entitled *The Common-Sense Mortgage*, a guide updated constantly to help borrowers take advantage of new opportunities to save money.

For nearly 15 years *The Common-Sense Mortgage* has been used by armies of borrowers to get the best possible mortgage loans, and you, too, can benefit from the information and strategies it offers. Not puff, not a marketing device for lenders, this book cuts through the clutter to show how loans work, what they really cost, and what questions you must ask to succeed in the marketplace.

This book is written with the view that consumers have rights in the marketplace—but to get the best deals, you must understand how the mortgage marketplace works.

- Mortgage rates, terms, and programs are entirely negotiable—but only if you know the right questions to ask.
- Good consumers let lenders compete for their business—but the most successful borrowers are the ones who understand how best to shop.
- Interest costs can be substantially reduced by pre-paying loans, using loans with shorter terms, and finding the specific loan programs that work best for individual borrowers—but there are cases where quickly paying off a mortgage is not the best financial choice.

This is a book about money, real estate, and choices. The selections you make when financing or refinancing a home can save tens of thousands of dollars—and often a lot more. Designed to serve as a basic reference, consumer aid, and classroom text, this guide stresses the idea that with so many loan choices now available, borrowers can customize home financing options to meet individual needs—and save substantial sums of money in the process.

Today, the battle is to find the right loan in a marketplace flooded with choices. *The Common-Sense Mortgage* exists to provide the ammunition you need to make informed choices, to raise the questions that ought to be asked, and to help you keep the money that you've earned.

DISCLAIMER

THIS PUBLICATION IS designed to provide accurate and authoritative information in regard to the subject matter covered. It is sold with the understanding that the publisher is not engaged in rendering legal, accounting, or other professional services. If legal advice or other expert assistance is required, the service of a competent professional person should be sought.

Figures used throughout the text, in various charts, and in amortization statements are for illustrative purposes only and have been rounded in most cases. Readers should consult with lenders for precise figures when computing mortgage amortization statements and other information.

Names, characters, places, and incidents used in examples throughout this book are fictitious. Any resemblance to actual persons, living or dead, or to actual places or events is purely coincidental.

Phone numbers and Web page addresses were reviewed at the time this book was developed but may change with time.

The term *OurBroker* is a registered trademark owned by Peter G. Miller. Other trademarks used in this guide are the property of their respective owners.

I

THE CASE FOR THE COMMON-SENSE MORTGAGE

FEW OF US ARE so rich that we can give away tens of thousands of dollars, and yet it happens every day. We pay too much for home mortgages, and the money we waste could easily send our kids to college, underwrite retirements, or simply make home ownership more affordable.

Although much attention, debate, and haggling surround home prices, financing is rarely given equal time or study. The result is that enormous sums of money—often amounts as great or greater than the original purchase price of a property—are lost to borrowers.

But why lose the money-making and money-saving advantages that sound mortgage planning can create? Reducing home interest costs is not an activity reserved for the rich. There is nothing illegal, immoral, unfair, or abusive about cutting mortgage expenses. You don't have to be a financial whiz to succeed; there are no miracles involved, nothing difficult to understand, and no tax rules to violate. Getting a good mortgage does not presume that you find a foolish lender or an impractical seller.

What you need is time to study your financial options, perspective to evaluate personal preferences, probing questions to find the best possible deals, and professional assistance from brokers, lawyers, and tax advisers. You'll have to work with lenders to arrange mutually attractive deals, and you'll have to forget the idea that mortgage financing is a once-in-a-lifetime event: it isn't. You can finance and refinance at any time, and the choices you make can put thousands of dollars in your pocket.

What's a Mortgage?

In general terms, a *mortgage* can be seen as a contract between a borrower and a lender. A lender provides money for a borrower under two conditions: first, the lender wants the entire debt re-paid. Second, the lender wants a kind of rent for the use of money, what we call *interest*.

Lenders don't give money to just anyone. Lenders want to make sure that both the original debt (the *principal*) and the interest are re-paid. To protect themselves, lenders require borrowers to meet a number of tests.

Borrowers must have strong credit histories showing they have made full and timely payments to other creditors. This is why lenders require credit reports. Borrowers must have a strong income today and prospects of a strong income tomorrow. Lenders verify employment records and income histories (income tax returns) to measure financial abilities.

Borrowers can have other debt besides a home loan but not too much debt. How much debt is allowed depends on the amount paid down and the specific loan program. Credit reports help lenders measure debt obligations.

Lenders will not provide 100 percent financing. Instead, they will furnish 80 percent financing, and the borrower will put up the rest in cash. But because most people don't happen to have tens of thousands of dollars handy at any given moment, lenders will accept substitutes for all or much of the 20 percent down. Re-payment guarantees from the federal government through the Federal Housing Administration (FHA) or the Department of Veterans Affairs (VA) can be used to offset down-payment requirements. Non-government programs known as *private mortgage insurance* (PMI) can also allow buyers to purchase with 5 percent down and sometimes less.

Lenders not only look at personal financial qualifications; they also want to know about the value of the property. This is important because if a borrower does not re-pay a loan, the property will be sold to cover the debt. Lenders will get an appraisal to show the value of the property, a pest inspection to show it is free and clear of termites and other wood-chomping insects, and a survey to show where the land is located and what's on it.

Lenders want to know not only how much a property is worth, but they also want to know who owns it and whether it is free and clear of other debt. For this reason, lenders insist on title searches and title insurance.

One result of lender requirements is that relatively few mortgages in the United States are *foreclosed*—a situation where owners lose their homes because they have failed to make their mortgage payments. A second result is that to get a mortgage, borrowers must supply piles of paperwork.

Mortgage Overpayments Aren't Small Change

Whether you earn $20,000 or $200,000 a year, you may think that you can't possibly spend an extra $50,000 on home financing. Yet if you've managed to waste "only" $50,000, you're probably doing better than most friends or neighbors. Here's a quick example:

Suppose two home buyers borrow $150,000. Each has a 7 percent interest rate. Over 30 years, borrower Dobson pays $997.95 per month for principal and interest, a total interest expense of $209,262.

The second borrower, Hayes, pays $150,948 in interest—a savings of nearly $60,000.

How?

Each day when he got home, Hayes would take the change from his pocket and set it aside. He would use coupons at the supermarket and place his savings in a small jar. Instead of getting his car washed every two weeks, Hayes would do it himself. At the end of each week, Hayes would have $25, more or less, from his little economies—about $3 or $4 a day.

Saving More than $50,000: A Quick Example

	Dobson	Hayes
Loan Amount	$150,000.00	$150,000.00
Interest Rate	7 Percent	7 Percent
Required Payment	$997.95	$997.95
Extra Payment	$0.00	$100.00
Total Payment	$997.95	$1,097.95
Total Cost	$359,262.00	$300,948.00
Less Principal	$150,000.00	$150,000.00
Total Interest	$209,262.00	$150,948.00
Interest Savings	$0.00	$58,314.00
Loan Term	360 Months	274.1 Months

Then Hayes would take the money he saved, round it off to $100 a month, and add it to his monthly mortgage payment. Each payment included both the $997.95 required by the lender plus a voluntary, optional $100 pre-payment. Instead of taking 30 years to pay off, the Hayes mortgage is re-paid in 22 years and nine months. More than seven years of payments are eliminated.

Pre-payments with bigger loans and higher rates can produce far larger savings. So can the choice of the right loan product for your specific needs.

Cynics will look at this illustration and say, "Aha. Few people keep a loan for 30 years, or even for 20 years, so this example doesn't work."

Actually—as huge numbers of homeowners know—it works very well. If Hayes moves after 10 years, the mortgage is surely not paid off. But less is owed to the lender than would otherwise be the case, which means Hayes gets more cash at closing. That bigger check from settlement means Hayes doesn't have to borrow so much to finance house number two. In effect, the benefits of smart money management pass through to consumers in the form of a smaller new loan or as a bigger check at closing.

We can engineer whatever results we want by choosing the right loan program initially, refinancing and restructuring when it is to our benefit, and using spare dollars over time to reduce our interest cost. If you let someone tell you different, you'll pay . . . and pay, and pay.

In every community, you can find loan plans that slash home ownership expenses. Piggyback mortgages, loans with shorter terms, combo adjustable-rate mortgages (ARMs), mortgage credit certificates (MCC financing), bond-backed mortgages, and buy-downs are just some of the approaches savvy borrowers use to cut interest costs.

Interestingly enough, if you ask the right questions, lenders will often help you develop money-saving strategies. Why? Because although you pay less interest overall, they have less risk, get their money back quicker, and thus can generate additional loans that mean new fees and charges.

Common-Sense Rules for Saving Mortgage Dollars

There is nothing sacred about being in debt for 30 years, especially because *conventional* mortgages—30-year loans with fixed rates and 20 percent down—are rarely the best deals for most borrowers. What consumers must look for today is the one loan that makes the most sense among thousands of choices.

Because everyone's income and needs differ, it follows that no single mortgage format works well for all borrowers. Not only are needs different; needs also change. The conditions that made one loan ideal several years ago may no longer exist. A new job, more or less income, the re-payment of other debts, an inheritance, retirement, or a killing on the stock market may each influence mortgage thinking.

Rather than searching for a particular type of loan with so much down or a certain interest rate, consumers should go into the marketplace with a viewpoint, an idea, a way of looking at real estate debt. In very basic terms, successful borrowers are guided by nine central principles.

First, borrowed money represents *actual* debt that must be re-paid, preferably at discount or with cheaper dollars over time. Interest is a *potential* cost that can be controlled, reduced, or eliminated through sound financial planning.

Second, mortgage rates and terms are not set in stone. Selecting a mortgage should not be viewed as a static, one-time event that ends once property is bought. Borrowers must instead search continually for profitable opportunities to acquire, refinance, curtail, and restructure loans. New mortgage opportunities that lower interest costs, preserve buying power, and raise additional capital can be available at any time, opportunities borrowers will want to consider in light of changing needs, resources, and goals.

Third, when buying or refinancing property, look for loans that offer the lowest possible interest cost. That "lowest possible interest cost" does not necessarily mean the lowest interest rate, say, 7 percent as opposed to 8 percent. Structure counts. For instance, both a 30-year conventional mortgage and a graduated-payment mortgage (GPM) loan may each have a 7 percent interest rate, but the absolute interest cost of the conventional loan is likely to be thousands of dollars higher than GPM financing. How a loan is paid off can be more important than interest rates alone, and the money you save can be spent or invested elsewhere.

Fourth, a mortgage must be seen as an alternative investment choice. Does it make sense to rapidly pay down your mortgage or is your money better spent on retirement plans, stock, mutual funds, or other investments? What about after-tax results and the effect of inflation?

Fifth, reducing mortgage costs should not be seen as an exclusive financial option. There is no reason why an individual cannot have investments, a savings account, insurance, and the best possible mortgage financing.

Sixth, saving interest and earning interest are really two sides of the same coin. One thousand dollars invested today at 8 percent interest will be worth $4,660.96 in 20 years because of compounding. Conversely, small mortgage reductions today produce big savings over time because there is less principal on which to pay interest and less interest to compound.

Seventh, leverage is an important financial tool that can be made even more valuable by cutting potential interest costs.

Eighth, personal decisions are not always economically rational. If it makes you feel good to pay off the mortgage, at least consider that feeling even if higher returns are available elsewhere.

Ninth, you and I can make financial choices that are both different yet equally valid. Our economic decisions will be based on individual needs, incomes, assets, ages, and perceptions, and no single strategy is always "correct." The important points are to have a strategy, to consider alternatives, and to actively take those steps that produce the best financial results.

Inflation and "Wealth"

Over time most people who have held real estate have seen values rise, at least in cash terms. Whether such increases in value are "real" is sometimes difficult to demonstrate.

Suppose Sullivan bought a home for $107,600 in 1985 and sold it for $152,400 10 years later. There is the appearance of a profit, at least in cash terms, but what can Sullivan buy with her extra dollars?

If Sullivan moves into a house of equal size in an equivalent neighborhood, it will probably cost her $152,400 to buy the new property. Why? Because the cost-of-living index between 1985 and 1995 rose from 107.6 to 152.4, according to the Bureau of Labor Statistics. Only if Sullivan's house sold for more than $152,400 will she gain additional buying power, what the world calls *wealth*.

(In fact, local home prices often rise faster than the rate of inflation. As examples, those who bought in Seattle, Las Vegas, and Phoenix did especially well if they held for the period between 1985 and 1995.)

What really happened here is not so much that the value of Sullivan's home rose but rather the buying power of cash declined as a result of inflation. Thus, although Sullivan had more dollars, each dollar bought less than it did 10 years earlier.

Inflation and Loans

Inflation has an interesting impact on loan choices.

With fixed-rate financing, borrowers have a hedge against inflation. If interest rates soar, fixed-rate borrowers just make their monthly payments. Lenders, however, are not so lucky. They finance long-term loans with short-term borrowing. When rates shoot up, lenders can lose money on fixed-rate loans.

Those with ARMs have different inflation concerns. Monthly ARM costs can rise and fall with inflation—more inflation raises interest rates and higher interest rates increase ARM costs. Seen the other way, reduced inflation tends to lower rates.

The effect of ARMs is to shift the risk of inflation from lenders to borrowers. If interest rates rise, ARM rates are also likely to increase and so lenders are protected.

Because ARMs reduce lender risk from inflation, lenders try to market such loans by offering easier qualification standards and lower costs upfront.

Taxes and Profits

In 1997, new federal tax legislation revised the way real estate profits are treated, much to the good fortune of property owners.

The new rules virtually (but not entirely) end federal taxes on profits from the sale of a prime residence. Highlights include:

- You can shelter $250,000 (if single) to $500,000 (if married) in sale profits from taxation.
- In the general case, you must have owned and lived in the property for at least two of the past five years to qualify for this write-off. In effect, you can use this provision once every two years. Special rules may apply in the case of illness, job loss, divorce, etc.
- There is no age requirement or income limit. Every homeowner can take advantage of the residential profit write-offs.
- First-time buyers can obtain up to $10,000 penalty free from an IRA for use as a down payment. The 10 percent penalty is dropped, but regular income taxes may still apply. A *first-time buyer* is defined as someone who has not owned property in his or her own name for the two previous years.

As always with tax matters, speak with a tax professional regarding specifics before buying, selling, financing, or refinancing. Tax professionals include certified public accountants (CPAs), enrolled agents (individuals recognized by the IRS as tax advisers), and tax attorneys.

Taxes and Interest

It is clear that widespread real estate ownership would be virtually impossible without the present tax advantages property owners enjoy. Tax deductions are crucial to homeowners because they reduce effective interest rates. If, for instance, you pay 10 percent interest but are in the 28 percent tax bracket, your true financing cost is 7.2 percent. As tax brackets rise, effective financing costs drop, so the expense of being in debt falls less heavily on the rich.

Combining tax and inflation factors produces an interesting view of true mortgage costs. If Green's mortgage interest rate is 10 percent and he's in the 28 percent tax bracket, his out-of-pocket mortgage cost is 7.2 percent. That is, if Green spent $6,000 on mortgage interest last year, his real cost was only $4,320. The other $1,680 would not have been available to Green because he would have been forced to spend it on taxes.

But if the inflation rate was 10 percent, there was no "real" economic cost for Green's loan because the rate of inflation (10 percent) was greater than his effective, after-tax interest rate (7.2

The True Cost of Green's Mortgage	
Interest Rate	10.0 Percent
Tax Bracket	28.0 Percent
Effective Interest Rate	7.2 Percent
Inflation Rate	10.0 Percent
Interest Cost Corrected for Inflation	−2.8 Percent

percent). In this case, Green's buying power (wealth) actually increased because the after-tax cost of borrowing money was less than the rate of inflation.

Doesn't this illustration suggest that it's best to have the largest possible mortgage and that quickly repaying a home loan is not a good financial strategy, especially if you're in a high tax bracket?

How Taxes Impact Interest Rates		
Interest Rate (%)	Tax Bracket (%)	Effective Interest Rate (%)
6	15	5.10
6	28	4.32
6	31	4.14
6	36	3.84
6	39.6	3.62
7	15	5.95
7	28	5.04
7	31	4.83
7	36	4.48
7	39.6	4.23
8	15	6.80
8	28	5.76
8	31	5.52
8	36	5.12
8	39.6	4.83
9	15	7.65
9	28	6.48
9	31	6.21
9	36	5.76
9	39.6	5.44
10	15	8.50
10	28	7.20
10	31	6.90
10	36	6.40
10	39.6	6.04

Financial Options

To answer the questions above, a mortgage must be viewed as only one of several investment alternatives. A good personal-finance strategy will include not only home ownership, but also the following:

1. Life and health insurance, particularly to protect against catastrophic medical costs
2. The equivalent of three to six months' income in a savings account or money market fund
3. A retirement plan

Once your basic financial foundations are in place—home ownership, adequate insurance, cash on hand, and a good retirement program—you can begin to devise an investment strategy. Just where should you put extra dollars?

Does it ever make sense to pay down your mortgage early? If you are now paying 7.5 percent interest or whatever figure for real estate financing, where else can you get an equal or better rate of return with as little risk? Maybe such dollars are better used to pay off credit cards or high-cost consumer debt. Maybe the money is better spent on education or building a business. Perhaps putting money in a retirement plan or the stock market is a good choice.

Looking at mortgages, taxes, inflation, and real estate, four conclusions stand out:

First, both taxes and interest are expenses.

Second, tax policies reward certain types of behavior. As tax rules change, borrowers need to see how shifting tax requirements impact their interests.

Third, it's always cheaper to pay taxes than to pay excess interest. If you're in the 28 percent tax bracket, it's far better to pay $28 in taxes than $100 in excess interest. Spending $100 on unnecessary interest creates, in this case, a $28 tax deduction. Not spending $100 in additional interest creates a $28 tax debt—but leaves $72 in your pocket. If excess interest costs made sense, then we would have borrowers demanding 9 percent interest in a 7 percent market.

Fourth, when considering financial options, it's important to realize that large numbers of people either do not have savings programs or cannot afford to save more. A few dollars here and there that might somehow be spent each month can be set aside with little pain and used to slowly and gently reduce mortgage debt. Instead of frittering away small amounts of money that add up over time, saving such dollars and investing in one's home is a low-risk financial option that works well for borrowers at every income level.

Leverage

It is commonly argued that borrowers should put down as little cash as possible when buying real estate. Use "other people's money" (OPM) and you'll have leverage and a better chance at big returns. If you can buy property with 10 percent down, that's fine. If you can buy with 5 percent down, that's better. Some argue that no money down is best of all.

There is no conflict between the idea of a common-sense mortgage and maximizing leverage. Whether you put down 5 percent, 10 percent, or 20 percent, you are still financing the bulk of the property, so why not borrow money under the best possible terms and conditions?

A problem arises, however, when the idea of maximum debt is thought to be synonymous with maximum interest. There is no benefit in terms of leverage with steep interest costs. Putting down 5 percent to buy property and having a $100,000 interest bill is likely to be a much better deal than putting down 5 percent and paying interest costs of $200,000. Although the leverage factor is the same, the property's ultimate cost is not.

Investment Real Estate

There are significant distinctions between real estate purchased for personal purposes and property bought for investment. Two identical townhouses in a single subdivision may be physically alike but if one is residential property and the other investment real estate, the financing, taxes, and strategies appropriate for each property will be influenced by different factors.

First, owners of pure residential property—real estate used for no purpose other than personal housing—may not claim deductions for depreciation, maintenance, utilities, repairs, improvements, or condo and co-op fees. Investors can claim deductions for such expenses.

Second, residential owners may move from one personal property to another as often as once every two years and shelter substantial profits. With investment property, selling routinely results in taxation.

Third, the financing available for owner-occupied residential housing with one to four units is substantially different than the loans available for large commercial investments.

Home ownership and investment choices are guided by different philosophies, motivations, economics, and tax policies. These factors mean that strategies which work well for personal real estate may be inappropriate or even harmful when making investment decisions.

How to Profit from This Book

This book has been written to help you both make money and save money. It's a starting point in the search for the best available deal, a guide to the loans that make the most sense for you, and a reference for consumers. It provides information, raises ideas, and poses questions. It creates the opportunity for you to be a better consumer, and it encourages you to aggressively assert your interests in the marketplace.

But although this book is a starting place, it is not a substitute for other actions and activities.

To get the best deal, you must ask questions, speak to mortgage loan officers, talk with real estate brokers, consult with attorneys and tax advisers, and always consider alternative approaches. You'll need a calculator or computer program that can figure interest rates and monthly loan payments and a willingness to study, listen, and explore.

If it seems as though finding the best financing is a lot of work, you're right. But it's also true that a properly structured mortgage can easily save the equivalent of several years' income, a fact few of us can ignore.

2

THE LENDER'S
LANGUAGE

REAL ESTATE FINANCING is more than a matter of interest rates and loan terms. To compete as an equal with lenders, you need to know their language—otherwise, you may pick the most-costly loan from a variety of choices that seem to be the same.

Every trade has its special words, and so it is not surprising that real estate financing has a unique vocabulary.

The most frequent financing words you will encounter are *mortgage* and *trust* or *deed of trust*. Simply stated, mortgages and trusts are both promises to re-pay a loan secured by real estate. The actual loan terms—length, interest rate, size, and so forth—are found in a separate document, the *note*. For the general purposes of this book, the terms *mortgage*, *loan*, and *trust* are used interchangeably.

On a more technical basis, mortgages and trusts are different. A mortgage represents a direct arrangement between lender and borrower. If I loan you $100,000, I am the lender and you are the borrower.

A deed of trust is a triangular affair in which there is a borrower, a lender, and a trustee selected by the lender. If we have a deed of trust and I lend you $100,000, I am the lender, you are the borrower, and the note will be administered by the trustee. If you fail to make adequate or timely payment, the trustee has the right to foreclose on the property. In many jurisdictions, foreclosure is faster with a deed of trust than with a mortgage.

Some aspects of a trust arrangement favor borrowers. For instance, what happens if the loan ends and the lender is on a two-year trip to Nepal or was hit by a bus and is now comatose in a hospital? You cannot sell or refinance the property as long as your debt to the lender is outstanding. Who can provide all the papers needed to show your debt has been paid? With a deed of trust, the trustee is there to handle the paperwork.

Words You Need to Know

In the next few pages you can learn the basic terms and phrases necessary to understand much of the lending system. There's nothing fancy or formal here, just some terms that are likely to emerge from discussions with lenders and a capsule explanation of what they mean.

• **Adjustable-Rate Mortgage (ARM).** Adjustable-rate mortgages (ARMs) are loan products characterized by monthly payments, interest rates, and final loan costs, which are all subject to change. This means a monthly payment of $500 now could be $535 next month, and that an interest rate of 7 percent this month might change to 8 percent in the future. It is equally possible that a current monthly payment of $500 might decline to $475 and that a 7 percent interest rate could fall to 5 percent.

Generally, ARMs have low introductory (teaser) rates and low monthly payments. ARM programs also tend to have liberal qualification standards when compared with conventional fixed-rate financing.

• **Amortization.** As payments are made to a lender each month, the mortgage debt (or principal) declines in most cases. This process is called *amortization*. Also, *see* "Negative Amortization" and "Self-Amortization."

• **Amortization Schedule.** A table that shows how each monthly payment is divided into principal and interest and also the starting loan balance for the month and the remaining balance after the payment is made. For a level-payment, 30-year $100,000 loan at 7 percent interest, monthly payments will total $665.30 and an amortization schedule will look like this:

Payment	Interest	Principal	Balance
1	583.33	81.97	99,918.03
2	582.66	82.44	99,835.59
3	582.37	82.93	99,752.66
4	581.89	83.41	99,669.25

• **Annual Percentage Rate (APR).** The rate of interest for a loan over its projected life, say, 30 years. The APR may be different than the nominal interest rate. For instance, a "7 percent loan with 2 points" will have an APR over 30 years of 7.2 percent. (A *point* is equal to 1 percent of the mortgage amount.) Why is the APR higher than the nominal loan rate? Because points are a cost of financing.

• **Arrears.** In the usual case, mortgage interest is paid "in arrears," the opposite of "in advance." This means the mortgage payment made December 1 pays for interest earned by the lender during the month of November.

• **Balloon Payment.** A large remaining balance that must be paid in full with one payment when a loan ends. Balloon payments may be necessary when

  • monthly payments are not large enough to cover the combined value of the principal balance and interest
  • monthly payments cover principal and interest, but there are not enough payments to re-pay the debt in full
  • a home is sold or refinanced before the end of the loan term. In this case, money from the sale or refinancing is used to re-pay the old debt.
  • a borrower has an interest-only loan. Here, the balloon payment at the end of the loan term will be equal to the original amount borrowed.

Second trusts often feature balloon payments because they tend to be short-term obligations, usually 2 to 10 years in length.

• **Blanket Mortgage.** A single mortgage secured by several properties.

• **Bridge Loan.** Financing placed on one home and used to purchase a second home. The first home is typically for sale. As soon as the first home sells and settles, the bridge loan is re-paid in full at closing. Many bridge loans are interest-only loans that require no monthly payments. Many bridge loans last only a few days or weeks.

• **Closing.** *See* "Settlement."

• **Community Reinvestment Act (CRA).** Federal legislation that encourages lenders to provide mortgages and other services in areas historically underserved by financial organizations such as banks and savings and loan associations. CRA regulations do not require lenders to make imprudent loans or to lower lending standards; rather, CRA urges lenders to assist marginal borrowers by acting in a flexible manner, by creating community programs, and by locating offices in underserved communities.

• **Conventional Mortgage.** Generally, a fixed-rate loan without government insurance or guarantees that last 30 years, is self-amortizing, has equal monthly payments, and requires 20 percent down. The amount you can borrow with a conventional loan is limited to a given number of dollars, a figure that changes each year. Loan amounts above conventional loan limits are called *jumbo* mortgages. Speak with lenders to find the current conventional loan limit.

• **Cram Down.** A less-than-charming expression that means someone cannot pay all that is due from them in a bankruptcy, so creditors must accept whatever is available (i.e., "Take this offer or the bankruptcy court will cram it down your throat").

• **Curtailment.** A payment that shortens or ends a mortgage. For example, if you have a $15,000 balance on your mortgage and pay off the entire debt, the loan has been curtailed.

- **Deferred Interest.** *See* "Negative Amortization."

- **Entitlement.** A right due to an individual. Used with VA mortgages. For instance, a $36,000 entitlement will mean that a vet can borrow that sum from a lender and the VA will guarantee its re-payment. Since lenders usually want a 1:4 ratio between the value of an entitlement and the loan amount, having a $36,000 guarantee will allow a borrower to get a $144,000 loan—$36,000 backed by the VA and $108,000 secured by the borrower's credit and the property's market value.

- **Equity.** The cash value of property, less marketing expenses, after all claims (such as mortgages) have been paid off.

- **Escrow.** When money is held by one party for another, it is usually placed in an escrow, or trust, account. For example, if you give a real estate broker a $10,000 deposit to purchase a house and those funds are placed in an escrow account, the broker in most states (if not all) cannot use that money (commingle) for his or her own purposes.

- **Fixed-Rate Mortgage.** A mortgage with an interest rate and a schedule of payments established in advance where the total payment for principal and interest is equal each month during the entire loan term.

- **Gotcha Clause.** *See* "Weasel Clauses."

- **Installment Sale.** A transaction in which the buyer pays the seller in whole or in part after title has been transferred. For example, Wilson buys a house from Davis and pays $100,000 for the property. Davis receives $20,000 at settlement and $20,000 a year plus interest for the next four years. The advantage to Davis is that his profit is spread over several years, and thus he may enjoy a reduced tax rate.

- **Junior Lien.** Much like shoppers in a supermarket, lenders line up to be paid when a property is foreclosed. The order of re-payment is established by the loan documents recorded in local government offices. The lender with the first recorded claim has the first mortgage or first trust, the lender with the second recorded claim holds the second mortgage or second trust, etc. If a loan is not recorded first, it is a *junior* lien.

Junior liens have a higher interest rate than first loans because they represent more risk. The reason is that if there is a foreclosure, the first loan must be paid in full before any money goes to a junior lien.

• **LAPP Lender.** Under the VA loan program, a LAPP lender—a lender who is part of the "Lender Appraisal Processing Program"— can do the appraisal review and underwriting in-house. Because the appraisal and underwriting folders need not be sent to the VA for review, the time to process the loan can be cut from weeks to days.

• **Leverage.** A general investment concept meaning that you borrow funds and thereby use other people's money (OPM). If you buy a home for $100,000, put down $20,000 at settlement, and get an $80,000 mortgage for the balance, then leverage is at work.

• **Liens.** A lien is a claim against property. Not only are mortgages and trusts liens, but overdue property taxes, unpaid repair bills, condo fees, and even water and sewage charges can all be liens. A major purpose of a title search is to be certain that all liens are known as of the day of settlement and paid off as required.

• **Loan-to-Value (LTV) Ratio.** Conventional loans are equal to 80 percent of the purchase price of the property. Comparing the loan amount to the purchase price gives us the loan-to-value ratio, or LTV. The cost not covered by the loan amount must be paid in cash, with a second loan, or a combination of cash and additional financing.

• **Locking In.** Mortgage rates are widely advertised, but the rate you see may not be the rate you get. Borrowers must ask when a rate is *locked in*, that is, guaranteed by the lender. Rates may be locked in at the time a loan application is made; several weeks later, when the loan is approved; or at the time of settlement. If a loan is not locked in at the time of application, then a borrower may pay higher rates if interest levels rise. Some lenders have lock-in programs, which permit a one time re-lock so that consumers can get a lower rate if interest levels fall before closing. With such deals, if interest rates fall between the time of application and settlement, borrowers pay the lower rate.

Caution: some lock-in agreements contain "weasel" clauses, which allow lenders to wiggle out of loan commitments if rates rise. Always read lock-in agreements with care.

• **Negative Amortization.** A loan in which monthly payments are too small to pay for either principal or interest reductions. The result is that the principal balance grows by both the amount of unpaid interest and the interest on the unpaid interest. Example: with a 30-year $85,000 loan at 7 percent interest, a self-amortizing loan will require monthly payments of $665.30. If monthly payments are only $600, negative amortization will develop.

Negative amortization will produce a balloon payment when the loan ends in most cases. However, with some formats, such as graduated payment mortgages (GPMs), there can be negative amortization in the loan's first years, but higher payments later in the loan term eliminate the possibility of a balloon payment over the full loan term.

• **Other People's Money** (OPM). Money that you borrow. To get the maximum amount of leverage, you want to borrow the largest possible amount of money and have it work for you.

• **Package Mortgage.** A single mortgage used to acquire not only a house but personal goods as well, such as a car or boat— or, more commonly, furnishings.

• **Par Pricing.** The interest rate quoted for a loan without points. Example: a mortgage offered at "7 percent plus 0 points" is available at par pricing. The same loan might also be available at "6.750 percent plus 2 points" and "6.875 plus 1 point." Over 30 years, the cost of each loan is roughly similar, but a borrower might prefer a higher rate and no points if the property is only going to be held a few years or cash is tight.

• **Points.** A point, or loan discount fee, is an amount equal to 1 percent of the mortgage. This sum is paid or credited to the lender at settlement. The purpose of points is to raise the lender's yield. (For more information about points, see Chapter 4 and the material concerning "Yield and Points.")

• **Principal, Interest, Taxes, and Insurance** (PITI). The four basic costs of home ownership that most concern lenders. For example, a lender might say that only 28 percent of your gross monthly income can be devoted to PITI if you are to qualify for financing.

• **Refinance.** A situation in which new financing is placed on a property. The addition of a second trust is a *partial refinancing*. Replacing one loan with another is a *total refinancing*.

• **Restructure.** A mortgage that remains in place but with new terms. If you increase your monthly payments by $25, you have restructured your loan. By making the additional payments, you will reduce the principal debt at a faster rate than originally planned, so you will pay less interest and have fewer payments. For example, if you have an $85,000 loan at 7 percent interest, it will take 30 years to re-pay the loan with monthly payments of $665.30. If the monthly payment is raised $25 to $690.30, the loan can be re-paid in less than 27 years.

• **Self-Amortization.** When monthly payments for principal and interest allow a loan to be re-paid over its term without any balloon payment, self-amortization has occurred. *See* "Amortization Schedule" for illustration.

• **Settlement.** Settlement, or closing, is nothing more than an accounting of who owes what to whom as a result of a real estate sale. Not only must the buyer pay the seller, but the seller may have to pay off old loans, brokerage fees, and so forth. It is at settlement that transfer taxes, points, adjustments between buyer and seller (for such items as oil in the furnace or prepaid taxes), title insurance, and other costs are first collected from buyer and seller and then paid out or credited as required. In some states, settlement is called *going to escrow* or *escrow*.

• **Take Back.** An expression used in real estate to mean that a loan has been made directly to a purchaser by the seller, as in "seller Conklin will take back a $30,000 second trust from buyer Hastings."

Caution: both buyer/borrowers and seller/lenders should be aware that owner financing may not be regarded as a loan. The logic is that no cash has been advanced and that instead the owner is merely receiving part of his or her equity over time. If an owner take-back is not a loan, then possibly it is not subject to usury rules and other regulations.

Because owner take-backs may occupy an odd financing niche, both sellers and buyers are best advised to speak with an attorney before accepting such financing.

• **Usury.** In many jurisdictions, there is a maximum rate of interest permitted for certain types of loans. If the interest rate is above the limit, this is *usury*. The usury limit varies not only between jurisdictions, but according to loan types—for instance, there can be one usury limit for first loans and another rate for seconds.

• **Weasel Clauses.** Contract language, also called "gotcha clauses," which seem harmless but actually hide conditions and terms that can substantially hurt one party to a sales agreement or mortgage. Weasel clauses are one very good reason to have real estate papers reviewed by an attorney *before* signing. It is important to know that legal language often contains terms and expressions which have precise meanings in law, and which may not mean what they appear to say to those without legal training.

3

WHO MAKES LOANS, WHO HELPS

PICK UP THE LOCAL phone directory or search the Internet, and you can find huge numbers of lenders who offer mortgage financing.

That there are so many choices is generally good for borrowers. Competition tends to hold down prices—at least for informed consumers.

But not every name under *mortgages* is actually a lender—a person or company lending their own money. Most "lenders" today are actually middlemen (and -women) who find investor dollars and make that money available to borrowers.

Knowing the Players

The great number and variety of loan sources raises a frequent question: Is one type of lender better than another? In a word: no.

Money is money. Whether a loan comes from a gigantic national firm, a company with a big advertising budget, or a local lender makes no difference—providing the lender you choose can deliver the best loan program for your situation with the best available rates and terms.

So where do you find mortgage money? Here's a list of the leading loan sources.

• **Savings and Loan Associations.** S&Ls are specialized financial organizations and a traditional source of residential mortgages.

Historically, S&Ls have been able to attract savings from the general public because governmental regulations once gave them the right to pay slightly more interest than commercial banks. Federal rules also guided the use of those savings: to get maximum tax benefits, S&Ls were forced to invest most of their available funds in mortgage loans.

Rule changes during the 1980s allowed S&Ls to venture outside their historic area of expertise. The results were devastating: many S&Ls proved they did not understand how to finance commercial office buildings and other major projects, and institutions failed in many states.

Today's S&Ls are a source of financing that should not be ignored, especially by those who maintain accounts with such institutions.

• **Commercial Banks.** Commercial banks provide checking accounts, business loans, and related services.

Although mortgages are not generally seen as a core commercial banking service, most banks offer mortgage financing, especially to depositors with whom a bank wants to develop a relationship. By *relationship*, banks mean individuals who have business accounts, maintain high-dollar personal accounts, and borrow money for commercial purposes.

Also, commercial bankers have become increasingly active in the mortgage field in recent years as a result of the Community Reinvestment Act (CRA). Commitments to finance home purchases in historically underserved areas are now fairly routine, in part because banks need regulatory approval to open new branches and such approval is often tied to CRA compliance.

• **Mutual Savings Banks.** Owned by depositors, mutual savings banks are thrift institutions that specialize in mortgage financing. There are several hundred mutual savings banks nationwide, with most located in New England.

• **Life Insurance Companies.** The nation's insurers are a substantial mortgage resource and often provide financing for office buildings, apartment complexes, shopping malls, and single-family homes.

While some insurance firms deal directly with the public, most make residential loans through mortgage bankers and mortgage brokers. For this reason, it is possible to have a home financed with insurance dollars even though the loan seems to come from another source.

• **Credit Unions.** Credit unions have been a growing source of mortgage financing for many years. Because credit unions are nonprofit entities, they are often a good reservoir of low-cost financing—but only for member depositors.

• **Mortgage Bankers.** Individuals and institutions who use their own capital as well as money from such sources as pension funds, insurance companies, and savings and loan associations to create mortgages. Mortgage bankers locate borrowers who meet standards established by investors and often service the loans they make. *Servicing* means collecting monthly payments from borrowers and, if necessary, foreclosing.

• **Mortgage Brokers.** Individuals and institutions that match those who need money with those who have it, such as commercial banks, S&Ls, insurance companies, and pension funds. Mortgage brokers today are nationwide and provide a large percentage of all home financing.

• **Real Estate Brokers.** For many years, real estate brokers dealt in real estate, lenders provided loans, and no one crossed into the territory of the other. In recent years, however, an increasing number of real estate brokers have begun to originate loans.

Real estate brokers today often have in-house mortgage companies, and a growing number now offer loans from CLOs—computerized loan origination services.

In the competition with other loan sources, brokers have a unique advantage in that they are present at the point-of-sale, the very moment when a home purchase is being negotiated. This means that brokers instantly know who needs a mortgage.

The entry of real estate brokers into the lending field means there is an additional mortgage source for borrowers to consider.

Given that competition tends to hold down costs, this is good news for borrowers who shop around and compare rates and terms.

• **Sellers.** There are always a few deals available in which sellers act as lenders and hold financing. The attraction of seller financing is that it likely requires less paperwork and may be available at a lower cost than other mortgages—at least when an owner really needs to sell.

But relatively few sellers are willing to take back loans (because they need cash from the sale to buy their next home), and not all seller financing is attractive—an overpriced house with seller financing is still an overpriced house. As always, it pays to consider all loan options and to be aware that a good loan is not a substitute for a bad deal.

Secondary Lenders: Who They Are and What They Do

Anyone who has applied for a mortgage is familiar with *primary lenders*—local lenders with nearby offices who make loans and collect monthly payments. Less well known are *secondary lenders*, multi-billion-dollar organizations that play a key role in the mortgage financing system.

Suppose a local lender has $5 million available for mortgages. Fifty home buyers, each in need of a $100,000 loan, apply for financing, and every loan application is approved. This is great news for the first 50 people, but what about future borrowers? Has the primary lender run out of money?

If the local lender holds on to the 50 mortgages it originated, then yes, it is out of the lending business until more dollars come in. But what usually happens is that the local lender does not keep the 50 loans. It sells some or all of them in the national secondary market. By selling the loans, the local lender now has more cash, it can make more loans, earn more fees, sell the new loans, and recycle its money over and over.

To have a national mortgage market, investors must be able to buy, sell, and trade standardized loan products, the value of which can be measured against alternative investments. Secondary lenders have created such products by developing guidelines that define which mortgages they will accept from local lenders.

To have an acceptable, conforming loan that can be re-sold, primary lenders will tailor their lending practices to meet the standards established by secondary lenders. In practical terms, this means that when you apply for a loan, you will have to fill out standardized documents and meet benchmarks largely dictated by the secondary market.

For instance, one guideline may suggest that no more than 28 percent of a borrower's gross monthly income can be devoted to mortgage principal payments, mortgage interest payments, taxes, and insurance, what is known generally in the real estate industry as PITI. Such a guideline might then have a series of exceptions that allow local lenders some flexibility.

Who buys loans from local lenders? Insurance companies and large pension funds. However, the main buyers are three huge organizations: Fannie Mae, Freddie Mac, and Ginnie Mae.

• **Fannie Mae.** Originally a governmental agency that was spun off to the private sector, Fannie Mae buys conventional, FHA, and VA mortgages as well as second trusts and adjustable-rate mortgages. The company gets its money by selling mortgage-backed securities that can be purchased and re-sold by investors.

• **Freddie Mac.** A part of the Federal Home Loan Bank Board, this regulatory agency oversees federally chartered savings and loan associations. Freddie Mac purchases conventional, VA, and FHA loans and finances such purchases through the sale of mortgage-backed bonds.

• **Ginnie Mae.** Part of the Department of Housing and Urban Development (HUD), Ginnie Mae assembles and guarantees pools of FHA and VA mortgages. Ginnie Mae gets its money from investors who purchase "pass-through" certificates on which they receive monthly payments for both interest and principal. Ginnie Mae then uses the money from the certificates to buy more loans.

In addition to the three major secondary lenders, there are smaller firms as well. The advantage of having a variety of players in the secondary market is that each is likely to have somewhat different loan standards. Local lenders can then have more flexible loan policies than might otherwise be possible because a mortgage that does not conform to the requirements of one secondary lender may be acceptable to another.

The national mortgage market collectively created by these secondary lenders has profoundly influenced the entire process of real estate financing. Here's why.

First, the existence of a national mortgage market allows money to readily move from capital surplus areas to regions that require additional funding. A national mortgage market prevents a situation where mortgages can be available in one region or state but not others, or where rates are significantly higher in one place or lower in another.

Second, the guidelines established by secondary lenders for conventional loans have proven to be in the public interest. Financial qualification standards, for example, protect borrowers, sellers, lenders, and mortgage investors alike, since they assure that loans will be made only to financially-able purchasers.

Third, a national marketplace creates an element of liquidity for local lenders, the ability to quickly convert mortgages to cash at a reasonable value. Without a national marketplace, a common ground to buy and sell standardized products, it would be far harder and more expensive to finance or refinance a home.

Fourth, a national mortgage marketplace allows local lenders to view their mortgage portfolios as potential profit centers, because loans may be regarded as a commodity to be bought, sold, or held advantageously. Moreover, primary lenders can also reap profits by servicing the loans of others—collecting monthly payments for a fee, perhaps three-eighths of a percent of the remaining principal balance. The servicing business can be highly profitable, and in some cases local lenders may offer loans at especially attractive rates to build service portfolios.

To make matters more interesting, there are also some large lenders with so much capital they do not need to sell all their loans in the secondary market. These "portfolio" lenders are important because they may have financing available with more liberal standards than can be found with conforming loans. Loans from portfolio lenders are typically available from the lender directly and from mortgage brokers and mortgage bankers.

4

More than Interest

For most borrowers, the cost of mortgage financing—and the lender's income—can be measured in terms of interest. But interest is only one mortgage expense; there are others, and they greatly influence the cost of financing.

Yield and Points

Mortgage rates are described with both a nominal rate, say, 7 percent, and the APR, or annual percentage rate, a figure generally higher than the nominal interest cost, perhaps 7.2 percent in this case. The difference between the nominal and APR figures is the result of loan costs in addition to the rate of interest, especially *points*, or, as they are also known, *loan discount fees*.

A point is equal to 1 percent of a mortgage and is paid or credited to the lender at settlement. The purpose of points is to raise the lender's yield. Suppose you get a $100,000 loan at 7 percent interest. The lender charges one point, or $1,000, and effectively has loaned only $99,000. Alas, the lender expects you to repay the full face value of the loan, $100,000—plus interest.

In terms of interest rates, a point is usually valued at one-eighth of 1 percent over the 30-year term of a conventional mortgage. Using this figure, one might expect that if a lender is making one loan at 7 percent and another mortgage at 6 percent interest, the lower rate note will require the payment of eight points.

As a practical matter, however, loans do not last 30 years. Most loans are re-paid within 8 to 10 years, in large measure because people routinely move or refinance far more frequently than once every 30 years.

The result is that to lower the interest rate by 1 percent, lenders will surely ask for less than eight points, perhaps three or so.

But suppose there are two lenders in town and you have a choice: you can get a 30-year $100,000 loan at 7 percent interest and pay no points or you can pay 6.75 percent interest and pay one point. Which is the better deal?

The answer depends on how long you own the property. The difference between an interest rate of 6.75 percent and 7 percent is $16.70 per month ($665.30 monthly versus $648.60 for a 30-year loan). It will take almost 60 months to pay out $1,000 at the rate of $16.70 monthly, plus you will lose any possible interest or investment income from the point paid at closing.

Points Versus Interest		
	Loan 1	**Loan 2**
Loan Amount	$100,000	$100,000
Interest Rate	6.75	7.00
Monthly Payment	$648.60	$665.30
Number of Points	1	None
Cash Value of Points	$1,000	None
Extra Monthly Cost	None	$16.70

The bottom line: if you intend to own the property much more than 60 months—five years—consider paying the additional $1,000 charge up front. If you intend to own the property only for a shorter time, then the higher interest rate is a bargain.

This example also illustrates something else: if a point equals interest worth one-eighth of a percentage point over 30 years, the lender in this case is charging a lot for points—1 point for a .25 percent reduction in the interest rate (7 percent versus 6.75 percent) for a loan that is likely to last less than 30 years. Given such pricing, borrowers would do well to at least check with other lenders to see if better pricing is available for the same program.

The general rule is that the longer a property is held, the cheaper the one-time cost of points. Borrowers will need to "run the numbers" and calculate the actual cost of various combinations of points and interest. In most cases, deciding whether to opt for a higher interest rate or more points—when such options are available—is a function of time.

Since points are a cost of financing, it would seem that they are an expense which "should" be borne by purchasers, but this is not necessarily the case.

- If you're the buyer, you can present an offer that has the seller paying all points. If unacceptable, try splitting points. Another approach is to create an offer where the seller pays a set amount to you at closing— say, the first $3,000 of your closing costs or whatever figure might be appropriate.
- If you're a seller, you too have a right to negotiate. From your perspective, you will certainly argue that points are an expense to be borne exclusively by the purchaser or that you'll pay points only if the buyer will accept a higher purchase price. In effect, the buyer pays such costs over the term of the mortgage.

Because points are a payment for the use of money—interest— they should be tax deductible. Points paid for the purchase of a prime residence are fully deductible by the purchaser in the year in which they are paid—even if paid by the seller. Points paid to refinance a home, however, must be apportioned over the loan's life.

Suppose you have a property bought many years ago, and today it's mortgage free. You want to raise money and refinance the property with an $85,000 mortgage. The mortgage has a term of 30 years and you pay two points, or $1,700, at settlement. The points in this case must be deducted over the mortgage's 30-year life at the rate of $56.67 a year.

But what if the $85,000 loan is paid off in 20 years? The remaining deduction can be taken in a single lump sum, $566.70 in this case ($56.67 × 10 years).

For the latest information and rules regarding points, be sure to check with your tax adviser.

Questions to Ask

Can you pay fewer points in exchange for a higher interest rate?

Can you pay more points in exchange for a lower rate of interest?

How long must you own the property to justify a high-interest mortgage with few points?

How long must you own the property to justify a low-interest loan with more points up front?

Can you deduct points charged when purchasing a personal residence?

Can you deduct points charged for refinancing from federal taxes?

Special Points Rule Cuts Home-Buying Cost

The history of federal taxes has largely been associated with rising rates and falling deductions. Thus, a special tax rule regarding the treatment of points is a stunner: home buyers can deduct points paid by sellers—and so can sellers!

Under a special rule (Revenue Procedure 94-27), points are deductible under a variety of situations when a property is purchased for use as a prime residence:

- If a buyer pays points to acquire a personal residence, the points are deductible in the year paid.
- If a *SELLER* pays points to help a buyer acquire a personal residence, the seller has an additional expense that reduces any profit from the sale of the property.
- If a buyer purchases a personal residence where the seller has paid points, the *BUYER* can deduct the points paid by the seller. When the buyer sells the property, the value of the points paid by the seller must be added to the buyer's profit.

The result of this rule is that home buyers get a tax benefit when sellers pay points. The seller deducts the cost of points when figuring the tax basis of the property because points are a selling expense. The buyer obtains a deduction up front for the points paid by a seller but later has to add the value of seller-paid points to profits when the home is sold.

The special points rule creates both an immediate write-off for buyers as well as an accounting item that increases a buyer's profit when a home is sold. In reality, however, because of the huge capital gains tax exclusion, most people will never pay a tax when it comes time to sell.

For details, speak with a tax attorney, CPA, or enrolled agent to see how you benefit under the special points rule and related guidelines.

Escrow Waiver Fees

In some areas of the country, borrowers may encounter something called an *escrow waiver fee*. Like points, this fee may impact interest levels. It works like this:

When you borrow with 20 percent down or less, the lender maintains an escrow (trust) account on your behalf to pay property taxes and home insurance costs. This account is funded by monthly payments in addition to money collected for mortgage interest and principal.

If you borrow with more than 20 percent equity, you are not required to maintain an escrow account. But some lenders argue that loans without escrow accounts are more risky than loans with such collections. Because loans without escrow accounts are regarded as more risky, lenders charge more for the loan, what is sometimes called an escrow waiver fee. Conversely, if you have the right to avoid an escrow account but set one up, the lender charges less interest for the loan.

Bottom line: if you are borrowing with more than 20 percent down, ask about escrow waiver fees, if any.

5

Paperwork Games

If there is a single matter most borrowers find both harrowing and harassing, it is the mountain of papers and documents sought by lenders to justify loan decisions.

Although not a huge problem for the salaried worker with good credit buying a single-family home, paperwork under most loan programs is a major headache for the self-employed, those with credit dings, individuals with real estate holdings, and folks with multiple income sources.

Full Documents Versus Reduced Paperwork

One way to overcome the paper challenge is to have necessary documents in hand when first applying for a loan. The loan application checklist provided in the next few pages should show you how to address most lender needs.

But another approach is to look for mortgage programs that offer not only attractive rates and terms, but also fewer paperwork requirements.

Just in Case

There are millions of real estate closings each year, and virtually none involve closing agent fraud. But every so often a closing does involve some kind of theft, and the results can be devastating because the usual protections are missing. For instance, if title insurance has not been paid, how can you claim coverage? If property taxes have not been paid, will the government forgive them?

A few phone calls might save a lot of hassle.

- Under the Real Estate Settlement and Procedures Act (RESPA), you have the right to see closing papers 24 hours before settlement. Call the party that will conduct closing a few days or weeks in advance (or have your attorney call) and tell them you want to have the papers in advance for review. Keep notes showing with whom you spoke and when.
- Call your old mortgage company a few days after closing. Has your loan been closed?
- When you speak to your old mortgage company, ask about a refund for any money remaining in your escrow account. If money is owed, when can you expect a check?

Lenders are sometimes willing to "trade" the need to prove employment, deposits, and such for larger down payments. The theory is that if prospective borrowers put more equity into a property, the lender's risk is reduced and therefore the need for extensive paperwork declines.

In general terms, one might define mortgage paperwork requirements under the following basic categories.

• **Full Documentation.** Loans issued under full documentation guidelines require underwriters to verify virtually every fact and figure asserted by prospective borrowers.

• **Alternative Documentation.** Less rigorous than full docs, alternative docs require fewer verifications, a trade-off that can produce faster processing. For example, under some alternative documentation programs, if borrowers provide their three most recent original bank statements, lenders will not seek written verification of the account from a bank. (Note that a growing percentage of loan applications no longer require a written employment verification—a phone call to an employer will satisfy many loan programs.)

• **Low Documentation.** Under typical low-doc programs, much paperwork is eliminated, especially for those who are self-employed or derive income from partnerships and corporations.

• **No Documentation.** You may have heard about no-doc financing, but in absolute terms such programs do not exist. All loan programs require some paperwork; happily, no-doc programs require far less documentation than others. With no-doc financing, lenders will require large down payments to offset risk and will often use credit report information to confirm borrower data rather than separate verifications from employers, lenders, banks, stockbrokers, and so forth.

Pitfalls and Cautions

Through substitute documentation programs, borrowers can often avoid many hassles and complications. However, as good as substitute documentation programs may sound, there are several issues that should concern prospective borrowers.

• There is no general agreement on how terms such as *alternative doc*, *low doc*, and *no doc* are defined. Different lenders have different definitions, even for programs that seem to have the same description. In other words, the standards for one low-doc mortgage may be entirely different from those of another low-doc program.

• Even with reduced documentation, underwriting standards still apply. For example, suppose Green needs $6,000 a month to qualify for a given loan. Suppose further that his monthly income is $5,000. Without an "exception" from an underwriter—that is, unless typical loan rules and requirements can be ignored—he will not get the loan.

• Low-doc and no-doc loans rely on borrower data rather than verified information, but now many lenders are requiring certified statements from borrowers declaring that the information supplied is correct and complete. This is not an additional verification, just another piece of paper for lenders to use in the event of fraud or material misrepresentations.

• Many lenders now ask borrowers to sign IRS Form 4506. This form allows you or someone else to obtain a copy of your tax returns for the past four years.

Lenders want access to past tax forms, even after a loan has been closed, to assure buyers in the secondary market that the loan application is correct and also to review the loan application in the event of foreclosure.

However, borrowers need to complete IRS forms with care. If line 5 is left blank—the line used to show who is authorized to obtain your information—then the lender or anyone else holding the form can obtain access to your tax records. If line 11 is not completed, then whoever has the form can ask for the return from any year. And if the signature lines are not dated, then the IRS requirement to receive the form within 60 days of signing can be moot.

• No-doc loans are less and less common. No-doc mortgages— loans where few facts are checked—suggest big fees, little work, and lots of risk for lenders, suggestions causing many lenders to back away from no-doc financing.

• Loans are complex transactions and it's entirely possible that some borrowers may encounter even more paperwork than the basic items mentioned on the following checklist. If additional verifications are required, make a point of getting needed information to the lender as quickly as possible to speed the application process.

Mortgage Application Checklist

The best way to make lenders happy is to be credit-worthy and prepared. Lenders routinely require various papers, account numbers, and tax forms, and so the best approach is to have all paperwork in hand when first applying for a loan. The list below suggests what most lenders will require in various situations; however, each loan is unique, and requests for even more paperwork are entirely possible.

(Note: "ST" = Sometimes; "NA" = Not Applicable; "VC" = Verify via Credit Report)

Requirement	Full Docs	Alt Docs	Low Docs	No Docs
BASICS				
Appraisal	Yes	Yes	Yes	Yes
Personal Credit Report	Yes	Yes	Yes	Yes
Ratified Final Sales Contract	Yes	Yes	Yes	Yes
Standard Application Form	Yes	Yes	Yes	Yes
Termite Report	Yes	Yes	Yes	Yes
Insurance Coverage (by Closing)	Yes	Yes	Yes	Yes
Land Survey	Yes	Yes	Yes	Yes
IRS Form 4605	Yes	Yes	Yes	Yes
DEPOSITS				
Receipt for Deposit	Yes	Yes	ST	No
Bank Statements (Three Months)	Yes	Yes	ST	No
Stock and Bond Accounts	Yes	Yes	ST	No
Mutual Fund Accounts	Yes	Yes	ST	No
MORTGAGES				
Account Number	Yes	Yes	ST	VC
Current Balance	Yes	Yes	ST	VC
Payment History	Yes	Yes	ST	VC
If Divorced				
Final Settlement	Yes	Yes	Yes	Yes
If Gift Is Provided				
Irrevocable Gift Letter	Yes	Yes	Yes	NA
Evidence of Donor's Ability to				
Make a Gift	Yes	Yes	ST	NA
Show Relationship (i.e., Not Seller)	Yes	Yes	Yes	NA
Donor Name and Address	Yes	Yes	Yes	Yes

(cont.)

Requirement	Full Docs	Alt Docs	Low Docs	No Docs
If Current Home Must Be Sold				
Evidence of Sale, or	Yes	Yes	Yes	Yes
Copy of Current Listing or				
Marketing Effort	Yes	Yes	Yes	Yes
If Employed				
W-2 Forms (Two Years)	Yes	Yes	No	No
Pay Stubs (Last 30 Days)	Yes	Yes	No	No
Verification of Year-to-Date Income	Yes	Yes	Yes	No
If Self-Employed				
Business Credit Report	Yes	Yes	Yes	ST
Tax Returns (Two–Three Years)	Yes	Yes	No	No
Form 1099 for Commissions	Yes	Yes	Yes	No
YTD Profit and Loss Statement	Yes	Yes	No	No
Current Balance Sheet	Yes	Yes	Yes	No
If Partnership Owner				
Form K-1 (Two–Three Years)	Yes	Yes	NA	NA
Partnership Return (if Available)	Yes	Yes	NA	NA
Personal Tax Return (Two–Three Years)	Yes	Yes	No	No
If Corporation Owner				
Personal Tax Return (Two–Three Years)	Yes	Yes	No	No
Form 1120 (Two Years)	Yes	Yes	No	No
If Rental Property Is Owned				
Current Lease (if Any)	Yes	Yes	No	No
Personal Tax Return (Two–Three Years)	Yes	Yes	No	No

Pre-Approval Versus Pre-Qualification

Pre-approved and *pre-qualified* are terms commonly used to suggest that a consumer has met with lenders and has some idea of how much he or she can borrow.

The general idea—and it's a great idea—is that home buyers should know how much they can borrow and which loan programs work best for them before looking at houses. This makes enormous good sense because those who rush out and purchase the home of their dreams are likely to find that they have signed a purchase agreement that requires them to qualify for a loan within a week to 10 days.

In this short period, buyers are expected to find the best possible mortgage—or at least a mortgage that will allow them to purchase the home, even if the costs and terms are not so great.

Knowing what you can afford before entering the marketplace has two huge advantages for buyer/borrowers:

1. You won't look at houses you can't buy.
2. When you make a purchase offer, you can include a lender letter showing how much you can borrow.

The letter you get from a lender is most likely *NOT* a firm loan commitment. Within the real estate industry, such forms are generally known as "hand-holding" letters—they are evidence that you spent time with a lender and have some general sense of what you can borrow.

But, are such letters a firm loan commitment? In the overwhelming number of cases the answer is no. Hand-holding letters typically say

> We have reviewed the financial standing and credit report of Harry and Helen Homebuyer and determined that they can borrow as much as $100,000 under our "Happy Debtors" program, subject to a final credit report, property appraisal, and related verifications.

In other words, there is no loan commitment. There is no promise to show up at closing with a check for $100,000—the lender can always say the credit report, appraisal, or other documents are not satisfactory and "decline" the loan.

Then why go through the pre-approval process?

You want a lender to review your finances—especially your credit report—several months before you have a serious financing or refinancing interest. You may find a negative credit item that is wrong or out-of-date. Catch such credit dings early enough and you can complain to credit reporting agencies and have them removed from your report before applying for a loan. Or, if the negative item is legitimate, you can write out why it happened, knowing that lenders will likely ask for a written explanation.

Pre-qualifying is also good for another reason: when buying a home, sellers and their brokers like to make sure that you have the resources and credit to purchase. They can ask for a financial qualification statement because if an owner accepts an offer from an unqualified buyer, the property will be under contract, and offers from better-qualified buyers may be lost.

Although you can understand the seller's need, you have needs too. If you complete the financial qualification statement, it may show that you have the ability to pay more than you are offering.

Rather than reveal all with a financial qualification statement, it is much better to have a letter in hand from a lender saying you have the ability to borrow a certain number of dollars and not more than you need. For instance, let's say you have the ability to borrow $150,000 but only need a loan for $100,000 to buy a property. If you qualify for $150,000 then you surely qualify for $100,000. Have the lender give you a hand-holding letter for $100,000—that way, the sellers know you can borrow the $100,000 needed to make the deal work but they do not know that you could readily offer more.

It's sometimes argued that there is a difference between the terms *pre-approval* and *pre-qualification*. Because there is no standard definition for either term, this is a debatable matter. I would argue that the definition of each term is determined by a specific lender, that the "pre-approval" process at Jones Lending may be the same as a "pre-qualification" session with Smith Mortgage, that neither is an absolute loan commitment, and that—in any case—definitions are less important than sitting down with a lender and getting some sense of how much you can borrow.

Quickie Loan Programs

Sometimes lenders will combine computer processing and perceived needs to offer instant financing.

"Go with us," says lender Smith, "and we'll have your loan ready in 15 minutes."

Are quickie loans a good deal?

Maybe yes, maybe no—but ask these questions:

- Is this an absolute loan commitment? Or are you looking at a glorified hand-holding letter subject to an appraisal, final credit check, and other verifications?
- Is the interest rate for a quickie loan the same rate you would pay if you wanted the identical loan and went through the regular processing system?
- Does the rate quoted include both interest and points?
- What is the cost to apply under a quickie loan program? What is the cost to apply with a regular loan application?

Lock-Ins

In a world where interest rates constantly rise and fall it would be nice to have some assurance that mortgage financing is available at a given interest cost. There is such assurance, a process known as a loan *lock-in*, *rate lock*, or *rate commitment*.

At first it would seem that a lock-in is a fairly straightforward matter. If 30-year financing is available at 8 percent, a lender could promise, "If we accept your application, we'll finance your deal at 8 percent." This sounds good and seems to make much sense, but we are instantly headed in the wrong direction.

In the example used here, the lender's "commitment" is oral, which means it is difficult and perhaps impossible to enforce. And, as we saw earlier in the book, the cost of a loan is not just interest— it also includes other expenses, particularly points. The lender in this case has said nothing about points, so we don't know if this loan is available at 8 percent and 0 points or 8 percent and 3 points—a huge cost difference.

And, not to be overlooked, we have a lender willing to provide money at 8 percent, but what if rates fall to 7.5 percent? Perhaps 8 percent is not such a good deal.

Certainly, the lender is not offering to provide 8 percent financing forever; but if not eternally, then how long? The lender's promise does not explain.

A *lock-in* is best defined as a lender's commitment to provide financing at a given cost for a particular period of time. This promise is made in response to market conditions, including some not generally seen by borrowers.

Mortgage money comes from various sources—insurance companies, investors, savings and loan associations, banks—what we can call *investors* or *funding sources*.

Funding sources are enormously important because local lenders commonly do not have cash in a vault to make your loan. Instead, they have a commitment from a funding source to provide the cash that will become your loan—providing it produces a given yield and meets investor standards. (Some local lenders have a different approach—they do not have a funding commitment at all. Instead they play the interest marketplace. They might lock in your loan at a given rate and points and then gamble that they can get a better rate and points in the market when it comes time to settle your loan. If they are right they make a profit; if they are wrong they take a loss.)

Because of the way in which the lending system works, lock-ins are not a casual event to local lenders. If you have a lock-in to receive $100,000 at 8 percent interest and no points within 60 days, that means the local lender must be able to deliver this loan to a funding source. In most cases, a loan lock-in means that a local lender has a commitment from a funding source to provide the money you need.

Now let's go back to our definition of a *lock-in*. The definition says a lock-in is the "lender's commitment to provide financing at a given cost for a particular period of time." This definition does not create any borrower obligation to accept the loan. You could have a lock-in with Wompus Mortgage to provide a loan and ultimately borrow from Flambe Funding.

The problem is that if you have a lock-in with one lender and borrow from another, the first lender has likely made a promise to provide a loan with a given yield to a funding source. If you are not borrowing, the local lender must find other ways to provide the promised loan, most likely by coming up with another borrower.

What the lender wants to avoid is a situation where the funding source does not receive the promised loan. If the funding source does not get its loan, it will have trouble meeting its obligations to investors and depositors and that will make the folks who run the funding source very unhappy. In the future, when the local lender comes to the funding source for loan commitments, those managers will refuse such business. The result is that the lender will be unable to offer as many loan choices as competitors or offer only choices at a higher cost. And if the lender habitually fails to deliver loans, funding sources will quickly dry up and the firm will be out of business.

So far we have seen that a lock-in is really the tail end of a fairly tangled process. We have also seen something else: because interest rates go up and down, there is risk in the marketplace. Funding sources, lenders, and borrowers are all struggling to get the best possible deals and to hold down risk. Everyone is competing with everyone else to get the best rates and terms.

Sorting through this maze, we now come to the one person who is not in the mortgage market every day—you, the borrower.

How do you effectively lock in loans and protect your interests? Let's go through the baseline issues you need to consider.

• **What is being locked in?** There are numerous forms of lock-ins, including the following formats:

1. Lock-ins with set rates and points. This is a true lock-in, one where—no fooling—the terms quoted are the terms you get.
2. Lock-ins where interest rates are set but points float. Here you might find financing at 8 percent, but the cost for points can rise or fall, effectively changing the loan's cost.
3. The conditional lock-in. With this lock-in, the lender promises to provide financing at a given cost, providing the marketplace—or some aspect of the marketplace— remains stable. This lock-in provides the illusion of commitment because marketplace conditions are always changing.

4. Lock-ins with a "float-down" option. In this situation the borrower locks at a given rate (and points, we hope) but has the one-time right to lock at a different rate (and points, we still hope) prior to closing.

• **How long is the lock-in period?** Lock-ins can range in length from a few days to several months, but 30 to 60 days is typical. From the borrower's perspective, longer is better because more time than originally anticipated may be needed for inspections, repairs, loan processing, and so forth.

Conversely, a short-term lock-in at a terrific rate may be useless. If you have a lock-in at 7 percent in an 8 percent market, that's great. But, if the lock-in must be used within 10 days and you cannot settle within this time period, you cannot take advantage of the rate.

Some lenders provide lock-ins as part of the pre-approval process. This can be attractive, providing the lock-in term is sufficiently long. If the lock-in period is short, it may not be possible to find and settle on a home within the allotted time frame.

• **What does the lock-in cost?** Many lenders offer lock-ins without charge. This is possible because such lenders have a large number of loans and thus little trouble meeting commitments to funding sources. Such a policy is also a good way to attract business.

In many cases, however, there is a lock-in charge—anywhere from .25 percent of the loan amount to a full point. In general, one would expect to see lock-in fees for longer lock-ins, say, 60 days or more.

A small lock-in fee may actually be a bargain. If the fee is .25 percent, that's a cost of $250 to borrow $100,000 at a given rate. Such an expense may be worthwhile to avoid marketplace swings. In this case, if borrowers can avoid a rate rise of just one-eighth of a percent, the $250 cost will be saved within two years. Conversely, if rates fall, at least there is a ceiling on loan costs, not a bad way to sleep better at night.

• **When are lock-in fees collected?** Lock-in fees can be collected at the time of application, upon acceptance of the loan, or at closing.

• **Are lock-in fees ever rebated?** Yes. The lender's goal is to have the borrower go through with the loan so that commitments to funding sources can be met. Some lenders charge for a lock-in fee, but then give back the lock-in fee to borrowers at closing. In other words, if the borrower goes through with the loan transaction, the fee is returned. If the loan is not closed, then the lender keeps the fee.

Why does a lender rebate a lock-in fee? Because from the lender's perspective it is better to close loans than to collect lock-in fees.

• **Are lock-in fees ever a bad deal?** If the fee is too high or rates are clearly falling, then a fee may not be attractive.

• **Are there situations where a lock-in fee may be worthwhile even if better rates are available?** Yes. Let's say a loan is locked in at 8 percent and you have paid a $500 fee to hold the rate and points for 90 days. Rates fall, and now financing at 7.875 percent is available. For a $100,000 loan over 30 years, your monthly cost for principal and interest would drop from $733.76 to $725.07. If you switch loans, you save $8.69 a month. But, because you would lose the $500 lock-in fee, you would have to keep the property for almost five years (58 months) to get back the $500. You would also have to obtain a new loan application and probably pay for a new credit check and appraisal as well.

If you switch lenders during the application process, it may be possible for the second lender to re-use the appraisal ordered by the first mortgage source. However, this does not usually happen because not all lenders use the same appraisers. If the appraiser is not "approved" by the second lender, a new appraisal may be required when switching lenders.

• **What if I pay a lock-in fee and the lender goes bankrupt?** Lenders are in business, and not every business succeeds. In this situation, the lock-in fee can be seen as debt if the loan is not originated and thus the borrower becomes a creditor of the lender. See an attorney for details.

• **Suppose I have a 60-day lock-in, rates go up, and the lender purposely delays processing my application so that I cannot settle within the lock-in period?** This is a serious matter because lenders control processing arrangements and have the ability to delay completion of the loan package. However, it should be said that most lenders will honor commitments because that is the only way they can stay in business.

But, just in case, the way to defeat this problem is to be a model borrower. Have all paperwork available at the time of application. Respond immediately to any lender requests for additional information. Be in touch with the lender on a regular basis, at least weekly. And most importantly, keep notes showing dates and times for each lender request and the delivery of each requested item.

By being a model borrower, if you do run into a problem, you will then have a complete record showing what was done and when.

State laws and court decisions may well view a lock-in agreement as a contractual obligation that the lender must fulfill. For details regarding lender delay issues, contact a legal clinic, real estate attorney, or the state attorney general's office.

6

THE HIDDEN WORLD
OF UNDERWRITING

FIGURING OUT WHAT makes credit good or bad is a subject that perplexes vast hordes of borrowers. No mortgage topic seems to arise more frequently nor is any loan subject viewed with such trepidation.

To set hearts and minds at rest, let us start with the proposition that lenders do not require perfect credit, that you can get a mortgage even if you have debt, and that the one late payment you had five years ago will not doom your mortgage applications for the next decade.

Lenders need to make loans. If we accept this concept, then we can see that if credit standards are too stiff, lenders will go out of business. Because lenders want to stay in business, it follows that credit standards must include some element of flexibility and common sense.

"Good" credit need not be flawless. Lenders would like to see an effort, attempt, and desire to maintain perfect credit, but a late payment here or there does not automatically demolish mortgage applications. Some general standards follow:

- Lenders are most interested in credit activities during the past two years. Older credit events have less impact and often none.

- Two credit card payments more than 30 days late in the past year can be acceptable. Payments 60 days late are not acceptable.
- One car payment or other installment payment 30 days late in the past year can be acceptable. Installment payments 60 days late are a no-no.
- Late mortgage or rental payments in the past year are taboo.
- Disability income, if non-taxable, is likely to be "grossed up" 125 percent. In other words, if you receive $500 a month, most lenders will add $625 to your qualifying monthly income. If taxable, disability income is treated like other income.
- Outstanding credit items such as unpaid bills (charge-offs) need to be paid or otherwise resolved to the lender's satisfaction.
- It's OK to have credit card and other debt, but borrowers should avoid having a mound of credit cards, cards charged to the hilt, and a large total debt load. It may make sense to consolidate credit debt to lower rates, cut monthly costs, and spread payments over a longer term—but only if borrowers adopt a budget and rip up excess cards.
- Treat the application process as a business matter. Have all papers and data available when first meeting with loan officers.
- If you have late payments or other problems, be prepared to explain them to lenders truthfully and in writing. For example, if asked about a late payment and the payment was late, say so.
- No, lenders will not count income not reported to Uncle Sam. The theory is borrowers who are not honest with the IRS will not be honest with lenders.
- Yes, lenders can read a tax return and understand the economics of a small business or partnership.
- If you have gone bankrupt, you *can* get a mortgage. In the usual case, lenders will want two years of sparkling

credit following a bankruptcy. (However, in recent years lenders have increasingly wanted to know if the bankruptcy was within the borrower's control; that is, could financial care—fewer big cars or trips to Rio—have prevented the bankruptcy? If yes, what is to prevent reckless spending in the future?)

- If you have a history of good credit and went bankrupt, it is sometimes possible to get a mortgage a year after the bankruptcy is resolved. For instance, if you had a medical emergency or unfortunate career development (the plant closed)—events not of your causing—then you may well be able to quickly re-establish credit and obtain a mortgage.

- If you have had a foreclosure or a short sale on a prime residence, figure three years of impeccable credit. But also figure that exceptions can be made if the foreclosure was caused by an exceptional event—the death of a wage earner, illness, downsizing, or a local economic decline.

- If you have had an investment property or vacation home foreclosed, exceptions are unlikely to apply. The theory is that such properties could have been sold to cover the debt.

- You generally have 60 days to obtain a free credit report if your mortgage request is rejected. Speak with your lender immediately if a loan is rejected. More importantly, don't get in this position. Instead, have lenders review your credit several months before entering the buying or refinancing marketplace. See if there are factual errors or outdated items. If yes, complain. Credit bureaus will check with credit sources—mistakes must be corrected within 30 days. Then, when you do apply for a loan, you will have the cleanest possible credit report.

Caution: If someone says you can get a new credit report without any of the problems on the current one, watch out. You may be dealing with a "credit substitution" program, where someone opens a business tax ID for you and then claims lenders won't know the difference if you use the new number as a credit reference. Lenders will notice and they will reject such applications out of hand.

You can see that those with a troubled credit history are not forever excluded from the mortgage process. But borrowers with credit problems also have a great need to find competent loan officers and underwriters who know the rules and understand how they apply.

A real problem arises when someone who had a bankruptcy several years ago re-establishes good credit, and is then told that the only financing available is some exotic mutant loan with sky-high rates and 16 points. In such situations the borrower is best advised to keep looking—there is no shortage of lenders who want your business. No less important, in the age of toll-free numbers and limitless websites, competent lenders and sane mortgage programs are now more accessible then ever.

Credit Scoring

The latest lending idea is a no-brainer—at least in the human sense. Using computer models and statistical analysis, lenders can now evaluate your credit-worthiness in a matter of minutes.

This is good news if you are a standard-issue human with the requisite income, the right number of credit cards, and a sound payment history. A computer merely whips through your credit report, tallies your score, and—hopefully—you have a loan approval.

If it happens that the computer casts a gloomy electronic "nyet" on your application, that's not a final turn-down. Your application is then shunted off to the reject pile for further inspection and review by an actual mortal and perhaps approval.

Welcome to the new world of *credit scoring*, the logical mating of actuarial analysis and credit reports, speedy loan approvals, and growing unemployment among mortgage underwriters.

The reasoning and mechanics behind the credit-scoring movement make great sense in the general case. Borrowers have been screaming for years about lengthy loan reviews, and credit scoring is surely efficient, fast, and impartial.

Or is it?

One concern with credit scoring is that like all computer-based processing, what you put in determines what you get out. If a credit report is faulty, than credit scoring will not work. More than ever, buyers and those seeking to refinance should review their credit files before speaking with lenders.

A second issue concerns those who do not have credit in the traditional sense.

Lenders in recent years have begun to modify qualification standards to account for the millions of people who do not have credit cards or savings accounts. Such individuals have often been denied loans because lenders could not document credit and payment histories.

The catch to such credit standards is that they were (and are) often tinged with implicit racial and ethnic distinctions. In low-income, minority neighborhoods, for example, residents may not have nearby banks in which regular deposits can be made and they may not receive daily invitations to open accounts with credit card firms. Immigrants from some other countries often avoid banks because such facilities are associated with repressive governments and the ruling elite back home.

Many lenders and loan programs now have policies in place that recognize these issues. FHA, perhaps typically, now allows down payments from cash saved at home (mattress money) and private savings clubs—as long as the accumulation of such assets can be reasonably explained.

As to credit scoring, FHA explains that "artificial intelligence systems may be used for loan approvals only; loans rejected by an artificial intelligence system must be reviewed by a human underwriter.

"Underwriting," says FHA, "remains more art than science and requires that the underwriter carefully weigh the many aspects of the mortgage. While we specifically recognize several compensating factors as described in the mortgage credit analysis handbook, we also are aware that each loan is a separate and unique transaction and that there may be other factors that demonstrate the borrower's ability and willingness to make timely mortgage payments."

With credit scoring, it might even be possible to quickly qualify applicants over the phone. A plausible scenario might work like this:

"Good morning. Thank you for calling Wompus Mortgage. Please enter the PIN number supplied previously by mail."

A few clicks and dots later, the computer asks for the caller's name, address, and social security number. This is really performance art, because once the computer has the PIN number, it can automatically obtain the caller's address and everything else needed to start the loan process.

When the buyer supplies the property address, the computer looks for the estimated home value it already holds for that specific property. Comparing the property value with the loan amount, the loan-to-value ratio is automatically calculated; the loan approved, conditioned upon verification, title, and survey work; and a good faith estimate generated, stuffed, and mailed.

Think it can't happen?

About every two weeks a lender is kind enough to write me with an offer of home equity financing. What makes this particular offer different is that the lender is prepared to make a loan based on the "known" value of my property, even though no appraisal has been conducted.

I don't need a new loan, but if I did this lender would certainly have my interest. After all, it's nice to know that I can get a mound of cash over the phone in just a few minutes. If only they could make those pesky re-payments as painless . . .

Loan ABCs

You may hear lenders refer to "*A* paper," "*B* paper," "*C* paper," and sometimes even "*D* paper." There are no universally accepted definitions for these expressions, but in rough terms here's what they mean:

• *A* **Paper.** A loan application by someone with stable employment, good income, excellent credit, an acceptable down payment, and a property that appraises for the full sale price—or more. Such applications, called *cookie-cutter deals* because they instantly meet general standards, result in speedy loan processing and acceptance.

• *B* **Paper.** Situations where the loan applicant has a blemish or two, such as more late credit card payments than lenders like to see or too much debt. Such applications are marginally harder to process but usually obtain financing.

• **C Paper.** A "financially impaired" applicant, someone with miserable credit, little income, or perhaps a recent bankruptcy. Lenders generally like to see two years of good credit following a bankruptcy, so this credit standard can be overcome with time and prompt bill paying.

• *D* **Paper.** An application from an individual with rotten credit, no income, and no prospects to do better. A very unlikely loan candidate, but if financing is available, it will be at sky-high rates and with lots of points.

Front and Back Ratios

Lenders often use a shorthand expression to describe what they want in terms of qualifying income. For instance, they might say that up to 28 percent of your gross monthly income can be used for basic housing costs. They might also say that up to 36 percent of your income can be devoted to housing costs plus ongoing expenses such as monthly auto loan costs and required credit card payments.

These percentages are known to lenders as *front and back* ratios. For example, a 28/36 loan would require a front ratio equal to 28 percent of an applicant's monthly income and a back ratio equal to 36 percent. Here's how the numbers work in greater detail.

• **Gross Income.** Your income before taxes. This is a fairly clear figure in most cases, but it may require some adjustments for bonuses, overtime, rental property depreciation, etc.

• **Front Ratio.** The percent of monthly income that can be applied to mortgage principal, mortgage interest, property taxes, and property insurance (PITI). For example, if the monthly mortgage payment for principal and interest is $500, insurance is $30, and taxes are $50, then PITI equals $580. If a lender allows you to allocate up to 28 percent of your monthly income for PITI, then you need a monthly income of at least $2,071 to qualify for this loan.

• **Back Ratio.** The percent of monthly income that can be applied to mortgage principal, mortgage interest, property taxes, and property insurance (PITI) and recurring credit costs. For example, if the monthly mortgage payment for principal and interest is $500, insurance is $30, and taxes are $50, then PITI equals $580; and if monthly credit card and auto payments are $200, then total monthly costs are $780. If a lender allows you to allocate up to 36 percent of your monthly income for PITI and recurring debt expenses, then you will need a monthly income of at least $2,167 to qualify for this loan.

Appraisals

What is the worth of a given property? It may seem as though a sales price, determined by informed buyers and sellers in an open market, is the best index of value.

Yet this is not always the case as far as lenders are concerned. Although buyers and sellers may look at a property as a home or an investment, lenders see the very same real estate in different terms. To lenders, property is security—the ultimate recourse in the event a borrower fails to re-pay a mortgage. In this sense, lenders must know real estate values to limit their risk.

Consider what would happen if a lender valued a real estate parcel at $150,000 and made a $120,000 mortgage based on that judgment. If the mortgage is not repaid, the lender will sell the property at foreclosure, a costly and time-consuming process. But if the property can be sold for only $100,000 or any value less than the mortgage balance and the cost of foreclosure, the lender will have a loss.

To limit such risks, lenders want a precise but conservative estimate of value before making a loan. To determine the right numbers, an appraiser satisfactory to the lender will be hired to evaluate the property as part of the lending process.

The worth of a particular property is represented by more than bricks and mortar. Here are the major factors appraisers use to determine real estate values:

- **Transition.** Property values that fluctuate as a result of zoning changes, growth patterns, and other factors must be noted. Most instances of transition are evolutionary, but in some cases there can be dramatic value fluctuations. In one situation, an appraisal was changed from $15,000 to nearly $500,000 because a property was zoned and incorporated within a rapidly developing urban area.

- **Predominant Value.** Housing prices tend to be bunched at given values. Homes worth $100,000 are in $100,000 neighborhoods; $150,000 properties are in $150,000 areas, etc. For appraisers, it is important for properties to be within the general pricing patterns of their neighborhoods because over-valued homes, even though they may have exceptional features, are difficult to sell at full market price.

Buyers, it is said in the real estate industry, *"seek the least expensive property they can find in the most expensive neighborhood they can afford."* A home with a pool and five bedrooms in a neighborhood of three-bedroom homes will be difficult to market at full economic value, and therefore a lender will want to limit the size of a loan made against such property.

- **Facilities.** The existence—or lack—of community improvements, such as sewers and sidewalks, will influence property values.

- **Improvements.** Anything other than raw ground, such as houses, apartment buildings, garages, pools, and so forth, is regarded as an *improvement* in real estate. An appraiser will evaluate each improvement in terms of its age, condition, and modernization. The improvement's remaining economic life will be estimated. Extra value will be given for modernized baths and kitchens, additions, and energy-efficient items such as enhanced insulation, wood-burning stoves, and even landscaping that reduces energy usage.

Once all the variables have been considered (the items above are but part of a far longer list), an appraiser will calculate a property value using one of three systems.

1. With the *market data approach,* an appraiser will compare the subject property with other neighborhood sales. This

is the most common form of appraisal for residential property.

2. The *income system* can be used to determine values for investment properties. Here the analysis is based on revenues and rates of return.

3. A third approach, *replacement cost valuation*, estimates the value of materials and labor needed to erect a similar improvement on comparable property. This form of appraisal is valuable for specialized structures, such as churches and synagogues.

Using one or more forms of analysis, an appraiser will provide an estimate of value to the lender. Given this valuation, the lender will provide a loan for a portion of the property's value, say 80 percent, and the purchaser will put up the balance in cash, as a second trust, or both. For the lender, a limited loan commitment plus the buyer's equity contribution both have the effect of reducing risk.

Not everyone can put up sufficient cash or secondary financing for a property purchase. In such situations a lender may provide more than 80 percent financing when there are promises of re-payment by a third party, such as the VA, FHA, or a private mortgage insurer.

In recent years there has been an effort to broaden the appraisal process. Appraisers, we are told, should now check for specific physical flaws when evaluating homes.

In theory this is a great idea. While the appraiser is at the property, he or she may as well flush the toilets and flip some switches.

But in reality, appraisers are not trained as home inspectors. They do not climb on roofs, open electric service boxes, or poke flashlights into furnaces.

To state the matter plainly: appraisers are not home inspectors, and an appraisal is not a home inspection. Do *NOT* think that an appraisal can be a substitute for a home inspection.

Evolving Lender Standards

The loan guidelines established by Fannie Mae, Freddie Mac, Ginnie Mae, and even internal lender standards are not absolute. Exceptions are permitted, but many lenders prefer to interpret guidelines with literal precision, much to the detriment of borrowers.

The reason local lenders are often so hard-nosed is that if loans purchased in the secondary market are later found to violate general guidelines, the local lender can be forced to buy back the offending mortgage. Sticking to basics, not taking a chance, limits lender risk.

A major problem with lender guidelines is that as society evolves, so do financial considerations. The nation is no longer composed—if it ever was—of nuclear families with a working Dad, a homemaker Mom, and two adorable children. The result is that guidelines are evolving to meet newly emerging conditions.

- As part of the effort to meet Community Reinvestment Act (CRA) standards, lenders may allow liberal standards for certain borrowers. For example, instead of requiring 5 percent down, a buyer might put up 3 percent and the lender can then supply the additional 2 percent.

- Related persons who have lived together for at least a year can pool funds to buy property.

- The value of sweat equity—up to 2 percent of the purchase price—can be credited toward the down payment under certain loan programs.

- Even though a neighborhood has a fair or poor rating, according to Freddie Mac, mortgages can still be made as long as a viable housing market exists.

- Because minority and low-income communities have often been underserved by lenders, many individuals do not have checking or savings accounts. They instead have loose cash, money that has traditionally been banned from use as a down payment or for closing costs. (In fact, a 1997 study published in the *Federal Reserve Bulletin*, "Family Finances in the U.S.: Recent Evidence from the Survey of Consumer Finances," shows that 13 percent of all households do not have savings or checking accounts—or accounts with stockbrokers or mutual funds.)

Lenders can allow cash on hand, says Fannie Mae, "if the borrower customarily uses cash for expenses and that usage is consistent with the borrower's profile and financial status." Freddie Mac says cash is acceptable, as long as the source can be verified.

• Seasonal income can count, as long as the same work has been done for the past two years and is likely to continue.

• Lenders used to penalize consumers for the crime of mortgage shopping. When you shop for a loan and a lender pulls your credit application, that was regarded as solicited credit inquiry, and too many requests for credit made lenders nervous. Now all mortgage inquires made during the past 30 days will be regarded as a single inquiry that will not reduce credit scores. In effect, consumers will no longer be penalized for loan shopping.

• With regard to credit ratings, Fannie Mae states, "We emphasize that excellent credit does not have to be a perfect or spotless credit record since certain circumstances that are beyond a borrower's control can affect his or her intent to have excellent credit.

"Generally," Fannie Mae says, "a history that consists of a minor, isolated instance of poor credit or a late payment can be considered as meeting the intent of excellent credit—as long as it is satisfactorily explained and the borrower has other credit accounts with excellent payment records."

• Alternative credit references may be developed by showing the payment of utility bills, telephone charges, and rental costs.

• For many years co-signing borrowers have encountered substantial problems when seeking mortgages. Borrowers are entirely liable for the full and complete repayment of notes they have co-signed. But—as a practical matter—borrowers often have a paper liability without a real financial obligation.

Now major lenders (but perhaps not all lenders) have determined that if a borrower has co-signed a note but the other borrower has made all payments for at least the last 12 months, the note will not be considered a debt for qualifying purposes. This may be particularly important in divorce situations, where one spouse gets the house but both names remain on the mortgage. Speak with lenders for details.

• There is substantial debate regarding the issue of how many people can occupy a property. Landlords, for instance, sometimes set occupancy restrictions to limit property wear and tear.

But when *occupants* are defined by age (children versus adults) or in terms of personal relationships (married individuals versus non-married), fair housing issues arise. Rather then get involved in such matters, lenders now accept applications from entire households, ignoring numbers and requiring only that all applicants actually live at the property.

• As part of the appraisal process, lenders want to ensure that homes are not only safe and habitable, but also in reasonable condition. In some cases this concern has been used by local lenders to require cosmetic repairs in older homes and lower-income properties. Now, however, lenders have determined that cosmetic makeovers are outside the scope of the lending process and will no longer insist on repairs without clear health and safety values.

7

ONLINE MORTGAGE MARKETING

THE PAST FEW YEARS have seen the growth of a new communication medium—online services and the Internet. The volume and diversity of information online is enormous. There are millions of websites, and a single website may well lead to thousands of Web pages. Not only are there a huge number of websites, the number grows daily.

All of which brings us to a central issue: can I use the Web to obtain mortgage data and information?

Not surprisingly, the Web has lots of electrons devoted to lending. Use a search engine, look up the term *mortgage*, and you can find tens of thousands of websites with loan information.

But no one wants to go through thousands of websites, so the first step to finding online gold is to look for more than the term *mortgage*. As examples, try these search concepts (without quote marks):

"Mortgage and Ohio" for someone searching in Ohio.

"Home and mortgage and Arizona" for someone searching in Arizona.

"FHA and mortgage and Los Angeles" for someone seeking an FHA loan in L.A.

An Online Example

A lender quoted a rate of 7.75 percent with 3 points to a borrower a month earlier. The rate was not locked in, but now with closing looming in a week the lender was sticking to the same quote even though rates had sharply dropped.

The borrower turned to the Internet, went to the lender's site, and found that the lender was offering a lower rate online. The consumer printed out the Web page and faxed a copy to his loan officer. The result: a new and lower rate as well as fewer points.

"VA, mortgage, and Oregon" for someone searching for VA loans in Oregon.

Once you've found mortgage information sites, the next step is to consider the value of the information presented.

• **How inclusive is the site?** Does it describe many loan programs or just a few? A site with a few programs can be worthwhile if those are the programs you need. But a site with more programs is advantageous because it presents more options to the borrower.

• **Who produced the site?** Was the site created by a single lender? If yes, does it include a large variety of loans?

• **Is the site specialized?** You may well find websites that only address certain types of loans—say home equity financing or 203k loans. (Search for "203k and Nevada," for example.) These sites may have a wealth of information regarding particular forms of financing.

• **Is the site interactive?** Many sites allow visitors to contact lenders by e-mail. This can be handy if you want additional information because contact is then between your screen ID and the lender, thus preserving one's privacy because screen IDs can be anonymous.

• **Does the site have mortgage calculators?** A number of sites have online mortgage calculators that can show monthly payments, total interest costs, amortization statements, etc.

• **Is the site well designed?** This is a practical issue. In the same way that an attractive magazine makes content easier to digest, a website can be enormously more helpful if it is merely well organized and intelligently designed.

For example, a site with fancy graphics may take a very long time to upload. A site with lengthy material concerning a single subject may take 19 screens to read, if a user is willing to spend that much time in front of a monitor.

Online Cautions

A growing number of online sites provide loan pricing information. Generally, there is little doubt that more information is inherently better for consumers, especially where mortgage issues are concerned.

For instance, what about privacy? What happens to the information you enter into forms and online calculators? Is it collected, sold, re-sold, or exchanged? Be certain to read privacy statements and site notices before providing information you may wish to keep confidential.

If a site with rates is not continually updated, the value of such information will be close to nil. Rates change constantly, so if current rates (today's) are not available, send e-mail to the lender for an update. (In fact, lenders would probably be well-advised to send a daily rate via e-mail to anyone requesting such a service.)

Generic mortgage information that explains how programs work and includes underwriting guidelines can remain online for months at a time and still hold value. Such background information sites can be readily bookmarked for ongoing reference, saved, or printed out.

Many lenders now take basic loan applications online. More will do so in the future.

The idea of online mortgage applications makes great sense in terms of convenience and speed, but as is always the case when disclosing private information, care should be taken to ensure that personal financial data will be held in confidence.

It makes sense to check any online lender before providing confidential information to be certain that they are who they say they are, in business, active, and alert to your concerns. At least call lenders at their business location and speak to whoever handles their online processing. If you are not familiar with the firm, it may be prudent to ask several questions:

- Is the firm now licensed to do business in your state? Unfortunately, not all states license mortgage brokers and mortgage bankers.
- Is the current e-mail address correct? You do not want to send confidential information to someone now at another company or perhaps no longer in the mortgage business.
- Will your name, e-mail address, or any other information you supply be sold, exchanged, or given to any other lender or non-lender without your express written permission?

Keep notes showing with whom you spoke, the number called, what was said, and the time and date.

Be aware that *orphan* sites exist on the Internet, sites put up by companies and individuals no longer active online. There does not seem to be an automatic mechanism to delete such sites, a problem in that information, links, and e-mail addresses may be incorrect.

Lastly, when you see offers and opportunities that look really good ("Make big money *NOW*. Partner wanted. Earn 15 percent per month . . . "), be careful.

Online sites should pass the same regulatory and common-sense tests as a lender or broker with a physical office setting down the street. Unfortunately, we are at an early point in the development of the Web and there is some question as to who has jurisdiction over what.

Although the Securities and Exchange Commission, a federal agency, can step in when investment abuses involve stocks or bonds, and although the Postal Service can examine offers such as chain letters that "touch the mail stream," real estate is regulated at the state level. Because a website is not anywhere, physically, it may be difficult to determine who has jurisdiction over goofy claims and outright electronic frauds.

This means that "buyer beware" must be an online mantra. As a guide to the perplexed, consider the following warning signs when looking at online offerings.

- For a fee, someone offers to take title to your home and negotiate a "short sale" with a lender. But doesn't the outstanding debt to the lender still remain the responsibility of the original borrower even if the title changes hands? Are taxes owed on *imputed* income—any money not repaid to the lender but reported to the IRS? Such matters, and others, surely require careful review by legal counsel and a tax professional.

- For a fee, someone who is not a lender offers to re-pay your loan on a bi-weekly basis. This "service" is about as necessary as a spare gall bladder. You can achieve the same results without sending your mortgage money to a third party by just increasing regular monthly payments when permitted without penalty. Speak to your lender for details.

- Someone offers "no-cost" or "zero-cost" financing. In the usual case, such loans merely move up-front fees into higher rates or larger principal amounts. In other words, there *is* a cost—it is merely delayed or moved elsewhere. There is no such thing as a loan without cost.

- While rates for VA and FHA loans are at 8 percent and no points, someone offers the same loan at 7 percent. Because money is a commodity with a given price, loan rates for common products should be tightly grouped. A rate that is wondrously low (or absurdly high) should be considered only with great caution.

- At a discount, someone offers to buy, sell, or broker mortgage notes. If you are selling a note, what is the discount and what is the total check you will receive after all costs? If you are buying a note, how strong is the security for the note and the borrower's credit?

- Online tax information should be seen as generic and perhaps not applying to your situation. For specifics, be certain to consult with a CPA, tax attorney, or enrolled agent, as appropriate.

- "Legal advice" and information that looks like legal advice should be seen as generic information. For specifics, consult a knowledgeable attorney. Be keenly aware that rules and concepts that apply in one jurisdiction may be inappropriate elsewhere.

- "Standard" sale and lease forms should be regarded cautiously. The Web is awash with sale agreements and lease forms, but use care.

Generic documents are often void or voidable if they lack required local wording or clauses. For example, in my community a sale agreement must include information relating to helicopter landing sites. Without an appropriate clause, a sale agreement in my area can be unenforceable. If you see a nice form agreement online that you're allowed to use, consider it a starting point, something to be perfected by a local attorney or broker, as appropriate.

It is not quite fair to look at online sites and infer that they somehow deserve a level of caution not appropriate or necessary for local lenders and brokers. Prudence is required in all business dealings, and sites online are simply more places to do business.

In fact, sites online may well offer a powerful consumer benefit. Because they provide so much information, online sites represent a standard against which local lenders can be judged.

If you live in a small community or a rural area, you no longer need to depend on the only lender in town. And if you live in a big city or suburban area, you can readily see what is going on around the country.

The Web now represents a national marketplace. Everyone everywhere must now compete with everyone else, no matter where they are located.

In terms of mortgage financing, we know that secondary lenders such as Fannie Mae and Freddie Mac have the effect of homogenizing wholesale loan rates nationwide—the cost of financing to a lender in Oregon is the same as the cost to a lender in Alabama. With the Web, the same principle now applies to retail loan costs.

Is this a good thing for borrowers?

You bet. More information, additional loan choice options, and an ability to ask questions by e-mail—and quickly receive written responses in return—are all positive changes in the mortgage marketplace. No less important, there is no reason why lenders cannot update rates with great frequency, say three or four times a day.

What we are now likely to see are nimble lenders (and nimble folks in many other fields, as well) who use the Web not only for marketing, but also as a transactional medium to conduct business and as a communications device to speed the exchange of news, data, and information.

Those who will lose out in this process are lenders not willing to be open with consumers, lenders who are not responsive, and lenders who offer products and rates that are simply not competitive.

Sites to See

My experiences online began in 1992 when I established the original Real Estate Center with America Online. At the time the service had 120,000 members—less than 1 percent of today's membership. The area was an enormous success; *NetGuide* magazine described it as the best of its type online, "bar none."

Later I created a consumer information site on the Internet for those with an interest in real estate and mortgage matters at http://www.ourbroker.com. This site has been described as one of the 10 "best spots on the Web for financial info and advice," by *Verge* magazine. Other winners included sites operated by *Money* magazine, E*Trade, and organizations of equal quality.

Today I am often asked for the names of online sites that I find especially useful, and so here are a number of locations that should be valuable. Please note that I provide content to various online sites, including some of those listed here.

General Sites

Realtor.com (http://www.realtor.com). By far the largest source of home listings online and one of the largest sites on the Internet.

HSH.com (http://www.hsh.com). An exceptional site. HSH is a financial publisher and not a lender; thus, the information provided here is not posted with an intent to generate loans. The site features current loan rates, background information, and calculators.

National Association of Home Builders (http://www.nahb.com). An excellent source of new home information.

Realty Times (http://www.realtytimes.com). The leading real estate news source, found on most major portals as well as Realtor.com. (I write a column each Tuesday for Realty Times.)

Smart Consumers Services (http://www.sconsumer.com). A site to assist consumers with ownership and maintenance issues.

Federal Sites

VA (http://www.va.gov/vas/loan)

FHA MIP Insurance Refund Information (https://entp.hud.gov/cgi-bin/websql/idapp/html/hicostlook.hts)

FHA Loan Limits (http://www.hud.gov/fha/sfh/sfhhicos.html)

Federal Trade Commission Home Information (http://www.ftc.gov/bcp/menu-home.htm)

IRS (http://www.irs.ustreas.gov)

Secondary Lenders

Fannie Mae (http://www.fanniemae.com)

Freddie Mac (http://www.freddiemac.com)

Ginnie Mae (http://www.ginniemae.gov)

Credit Reporting Agencies

Experian (http://www.experian.com)

Equifax (http://www.equifax.com/consumer/index.html)

Trans Union (http://www.tuc.com)

Useful Sites

Association of Real Estate License Law Officials (ARELLO)
(http://www.arello.org)

Community Associations Institute (http://www.caionline.com)

Fair Housing Network (http://www.fairhousing.org)

Fair Isaac (Credit Scoring Information)
(http://www.fairisaac.com)

Mortgage Bankers Association of America
(http://www.mbaa.org)

In addition to the core sites listed here, I maintain links
to several hundred real estate and mortgage sites on my
Web location (http://www.ourbroker.com).

8

FINANCING AND OWNERSHIP

WHEN LOOKING AT real estate we often associate a form of property with a type of ownership. Townhouses, for instance, are frequently seen as condominiums when they can be cooperative units or part of a planned unit development (PUD).

For lenders, and consequently for owners, buyers, and investors, ownership is a central financial issue. It is entirely possible to have two identical apartments in two identical buildings in a single city, each worth $100,000, yet because one is a condominium and the other a co-op, the ability to readily finance or refinance each property will vary dramatically. *Different forms of property ownership mean more or less risk for lenders and thus higher or lower interest rates—if lenders are willing to finance a particular form of ownership at all.*

The ownership of real estate can be compared to a shopping basket of rights, and the biggest shopping basket is associated with the outright possession of property, real estate held in *fee simple* ownership, or *severalty*. Basic rights associated with fee simple ownership include:

- You can sell your property to anyone at any time.

- You have the right to finance your property in any manner you choose, refinance at any time, or pay off all liens and own the property free and clear.
- You pay property taxes directly. If a neighbor does not pay his or her taxes, there is no possibility that your property will be foreclosed.
- You can rent all of your property or you can rent a part of it.
- You can paint the front door puce and your neighbors have no right to complain (though they do have a First Amendment right to snicker).
- You can sell individual rights, such as mineral rights or a right-of-way.
- You can have pets or children or both.

What you can't do is violate *zoning codes*, public policies established for the benefit of the general community. If you live in a suburban area, for example, you may own the backyard but you can't turn it into a shooting gallery.

Fee simple ownership does not necessarily require that only one person holds title. Fee simple ownership, as well as other ownership interests, may be held by several people or by entities such as partnerships or corporations. Ownership groupings can include

- one individual
- husbands and wives as *tenants by the entirety*, a form of ownership reserved exclusively for married couples. With this form of ownership, there is an automatic right of survivorship; that is, with the death of one spouse, title to the property automatically passes to the other.
- unmarried individuals. There are times when unmarried individuals wish to own property with a right of survivorship, and they can do so in many states by establishing a joint tenancy with a right of survivorship. In the event of death, title to the property can pass automatically to the surviving owner.
- general owners. A *tenancy in common* can be formed in those cases where joint ownership is merely a

business deal. Each owner has an undivided interest in the property, which can be sold, exchanged, or willed. There is no automatic right of survivorship.

- entities. Property rights can not only be held by people, but by entities as well. Real estate can be owned by partnerships, corporations, and trusts. Thus, it is entirely possible to have 20 people or 20,000 people through a single corporation owning real estate on a fee simple basis.

Additionally, an endless number of ownership combinations—corporations and individuals, partnerships and trusts, trusts and corporations—can join together to form syndicates organized to buy, sell, and manage real estate generally and joint ventures established for a specific real estate deal such as the construction of a particular shopping mall or the ownership of an apartment complex.

Holding title is an intricate matter made more complicated by the fact that ownership rules vary in each jurisdiction. Because holding title to real estate is complex, and because real estate ownership is related to a variety of other matters such as taxes and estates, consult with an attorney about any title questions you may have.

For example, what happens if husband and wife die simultaneously in a car crash? Who gets the property if there are no children? The husband's relatives? The wife's relatives? The state? A correctly drawn will is necessary to properly resolve such potential issues, which, as odd as they may seem, do occur. Speak to your lawyer for complete information regarding wills and living wills.

Although fee simple ownership is the ultimate form of real estate possession (because it gives owners the largest number of rights), it's not the only way to own property. You can also possess property through other ownership formats: condominiums, PUDs, cooperatives, and timesharing are each forms of ownership with unique characteristics and thus separate financing requirements.

Condos

Thirty years ago few people ever heard of condominiums and almost nobody owned one. Today, the situation is different. Condos are everywhere, and what had once been a wrinkle in the marketplace is now an accepted and popular alternative to fee simple ownership.

What is condominium ownership and what makes condos unique in the eyes of a lender?

- Condo ownership means that you possess a specific unit within the condominium project plus an interest in the common areas—possibly the land under the condo, the pool, the hallways, etc. You may also have an interest in certain limited common elements such as a balcony or patio. Limited common elements are owned by the condominium association but their use is reserved exclusively for a particular unit owner.
- There is a separate recorded deed for each condo unit. This means the property can be used to secure a loan.
- Condo units are bought, sold, taxed, financed, and refinanced independently. This is important to lenders because the failure of one condo owner to make mortgage payments will not cause the foreclosure of other units.
- All unit owners are voting members of the condominium association, often called the "council of unit owners," and may be elected to the association's board of directors.
- The condo association as well as all common costs are funded by a monthly condo fee levied against each owner. Failure to pay this fee can result in foreclosure.

Although a condo owner does have exclusive title to and possession of a given unit, condos do not offer the same basket of rights as fee simple ownership. To ensure the comfort and safety of all owners, there must be certain rules, understandings, compromises, and financial allocations that govern the condominium "regime," information contained in these key documents:

- **Declaration.** Describes the condo and how it works, including such matters as the location of units and the definition of common areas. Shows how voting will be conducted, usually "one unit, one vote" or votes based on the square footage of each unit—the bigger the unit the bigger the vote. Once in place, matters established in the declaration are almost impossible to change. The declaration is usually packaged with an engineering report, paid for by the developer, that describes the physical characteristics of the improvements being sold.

- **By-Laws.** Outline the condo's general management; for example, how often the board of directors is required to meet. By-laws can usually be changed by majority vote.

- **Rules and Regulations.** Directives established by the board of directors, items such as how long the pool will be open and how much the monthly condo fee will be increased next year.

- **Budgets.** A condo budget is developed each year to show projected expenditures based on past projections and experience. Included in the budget is a reserve fund, money set aside for future capital needs such as the repair of a cracked pool or leaky roof.

- **Public Offering Statement** (POS). When a condo is first offered for sale to the public, the developer must provide a *public offering statement*, a lengthy document that usually includes the declaration, by-laws, a projected budget, the terms of any maintenance or management agreements, and an engineer's report describing the project's condition and estimating future repair and replacement requirements.

Even though condo units are owned and financed independently, lenders generally view condos as representing more risk than fee simple ownership. You may be a wonderful person and well entitled to a mortgage, but what about other condo members? Will a lender be able to get full value for your unit at a foreclosure if the condo association decides to save money and defers needed maintenance? What happens if a large portion of owners rent out their units? Will investors want to allocate association money for elective expenses such as fixing up the tennis courts or redecorating the lobby? If there is a large portion of investor-owners, is the lender then making a loan for residential or investment property? Investments represent more risk to the lender than owner-occupied units.

Investment condos greatly trouble lenders. Many won't make residential condo loans if investors own 30 percent or more of the units in a given project. A related policy provides that when investors own many units, owner-occupant financing is available only when buyers put down 25 percent of the purchase price. This is a huge resale barrier, one that lowers unit values and makes owner-occupied units in "investment" condos more difficult to sell.

By any standard, certain lender policies create difficulties for owner-occupants who merely want to finance or refinance their units but who live in projects that have attracted investor interest. These policies may also complicate refinancing for those who live in condos and then decide to move elsewhere and rent their old units. Refinancing in such situations may not be available.

If you buy a condo (or a PUD or a co-op, for that matter), in the lender's eyes you will have fewer dollars to support a mortgage.

Suppose you can afford monthly mortgage payments of $800 for a single-family house. At 8 percent interest that $800 can underwrite a 30-year conventional mortgage for $109,000. But if you buy a condo, there may be a monthly condo fee, which is a lien against the property. If the condo fee is $100, lenders might figure that you can only set aside $700 a month for mortgage interest and principal. In turn, $700 will only underwrite a 30-year 8 percent mortgage worth $95,400.

Condos also present another dilemma for lenders: all those documents. Is there something in the by-laws or rules that will reduce the lender's security? The only way to find out is to have the papers reviewed by the lender's attorney—an additional loan application cost for a lender who has not financed a unit at the property.

Resale unit buyers can eliminate the documents problem by talking to lenders who previously financed units at the project. Such lenders have already reviewed the basic papers, so there is no need for an additional review. Real estate brokers and condo association officers can name those lenders who have made loans at the project.

All forms of financing can be used to finance condos, but borrowers may find that processing is more complex than with fee simple properties. Get a list of lenders who already have made loans to unit owners because they will be familiar with the property, but don't hesitate to contact other lenders who may offer better terms and rates.

The additional cost of an application for a new lender must be viewed in context. If it costs an extra $100 to process a loan but you can save one-fourth of a percent interest, it pays to spend the additional $100 to get financing from a new lender. With a 30-year $50,000 loan, the difference between a 7 percent rate and a rate at 7.25 percent is $8.44 per month, a difference that means that the $100 extra fee will be saved in a year.

PUDs

A second type of ownership is a planned unit development, or PUD, a cross between condo and fee simple ownership with these characteristics:

- With a PUD you may own a townhouse, condo, or single-family home.
- You and the other project members belong to an owners' association that takes care of mutual needs such as the mowing of common areas, snow removal, pool management, etc.
- PUD units are taxed and financed separately.
- Because PUDs are owned separately, they typically have separate utility meters.
- The level of financial risk represented by a PUD unit is usually equated with that of a condo.

PUDs have proven popular in many suburban areas because they often combine planned growth with a variety of housing styles. Some PUDs are actually entire "new communities" where the owners' association is nearly the equivalent of a town government. Other PUD projects are quite modest—maybe just a few townhouses.

Co-Ops

Co-ops are generally perceived as a more restrictive form of possession than fee simple, condo, or PUD ownership.

If you own an interest in a co-op, you do not own real estate directly. Instead, you own stock in a corporation and that corporation owns the entire project. In addition to stock, you also have an exclusive right to the use of a particular unit as well as a right to use all common facilities.

Because it is an organization rather than an individual that actually owns the property, the co-op has great power over the project's day-to-day operations.

A co-op—much like a selective country club—has the right to ensure that new members are compatible with current owners. New buyers must be approved by the co-op board, a process that can be tinged with highly subjective criteria. Thus, to sell a co-op one must not only find a purchaser who is ready, willing, and able to buy the property, but one who is also acceptable to the co-op. Conceivably, if no buyer is acceptable to the co-op, one's interest in a co-op will not be marketable. Co-ops also have these unique features:

- The sources of authority in a co-op include the articles of incorporation of the cooperative association, the association by-laws, and the house rules. These documents should be reviewed by prospective buyers to determine how the co-op is organized.
- Co-op projects are financed with an "underlying," or "blanket," mortgage. For instance, a single project may be built with 200 units and financed with a $10 million mortgage. Assuming all units were the same size, each unit will then have a $50,000 mortgage obligation. If the underlying mortgage is not paid, the entire project is in default, in which case all units can be foreclosed.
- Co-op units are not taxed individually. The co-op project, because it is a corporate entity, receives a single property tax bill. If this bill is not paid, the entire co-op is in default and all units can be foreclosed.
- Because co-op ownership is in the form of stock, co-op buyers and sellers may be able to avoid property transfer taxes when they buy or sell units.

- If the co-op conforms with IRS regulations, deductions for mortgage interest and property taxes may be passed through to individual unit owners.

In terms of financing, lenders—except for those in the New York area and a few other metro locations where co-ops are widely accepted—have not been rushing to make resale co-op loans. Here's why:

If you are a lender and someone applies for a condo or PUD loan, it is clear that a definable property will be pledged as security for the mortgage. The actions of other unit owners, such as the nonpayment of taxes, will rarely, if ever, affect the unit you finance.

With a co-op the situation is different. If some co-op members—maybe even a small percentage—do not pay their taxes, then ownership of the entire project is threatened. Because a lender has no right to check the credit of other unit owners, there is no way of knowing the overall financial condition of the shareholders as a group.

The borrower is pledging a stock certificate rather than real property as a security for the loan, a certificate bound to the fortunes of the entire corporation.

Co-ops also present interesting financial questions when re-sold.

Suppose you buy a unit when a building is first erected or converted to co-op status. Your unit costs $55,000 and of that amount $50,000 is represented by the underlying mortgage. Five years later your unit is worth $85,000 and you want to sell your interest. What do you do about financing? Because the underlying mortgage is for all the units at the project, your buyer cannot simply get a new first loan.

One approach is to have the buyer assume the unit's underlying mortgage and to then pay you the difference between the underlying mortgage and the sales price in cash. But this is not a great choice for buyers who may not have such cash.

A second choice is for you to become a lender, to take back some financing above the value represented by the underlying mortgage. However, if you take back financing from a buyer, where will you get the cash to buy a new residence for yourself?

So-called share financing, essentially a second mortgage option for co-ops, is also available. If a unit is worth $100,000 and the underlying mortgage has a $60,000 balance per unit, then with a

$20,000 share loan 80 percent financing is available; a $30,000 share loan will give 90 percent coverage.

Share loans are attractive because lenders can sell them to investors in the secondary market. For information, write to the NCB Savings Bank, SFB, 1401 Eye Street NW, Washington, DC 20005. The phone number is (202) 336-7700.

Another approach to co-op financing has been through the use of "recognition agreements." With recognition financing, ownership documents are assigned to lenders, who then have certain rights in the event borrowers default or the unit is sold. Check to see if a co-op in which you are interested has recognition agreements.

Lastly, borrowers might ask about the FHA 203(n) program, which can be used to insure co-op loans for individual units. This program is so obscure, and so complex, that there is not one known example of an individual unit financed under this program in recent years. Still, it's on the books.

Critical Issues to Review

Because of their corporate nature, condos, PUDs, and co-ops raise a variety of questions that in many cases would not be asked when buying or financing fee simple real estate.

• **What is being sold?** In some cases, certain parts of the property, such as pools or underground parking spaces, have been retained by developers, and the result is that these facilities are available only at extra cost.

• **What is the current fee?** Condo fees are subject to change and normally go up over time. Look at past budgets and see if there have been radical fee increases from year to year. If so, it may be that the budget is not well planned.

• **What is the current co-op fee?** Note that the co-op fee will include a payment for the underlying mortgage. With a condo or PUD unit, monthly fees and mortgage payments are paid separately.

• **If you are considering a new project, how was the condo, PUD, or co-op fee estimated?** What other projects has the developer completed? Visit past projects and speak to unit owners there. Has the developer made a good-faith effort to keep all promises? Has all promised work been completed? What would the unit owners do differently?

• **Are any major capital repairs expected within the next two years?** If so, are adequate reserves being built up to handle repair costs? Be aware that public-offering statements contain a wealth of information regarding potential repairs. For instance, an engineer's report may say that unit air-conditioning systems have a projected life of 15 years. If the building is 12 years old, you can expect to make replacements fairly soon.

To cite another example, a public-offering statement may show that a roof has a life expectancy of 20 years, and the building is 23 years old. In such cases the developer has honestly and openly declared where a potential cost may be found. In the event of a claim against the developer because of roof leaks, the developer can justly say that the problem was disclosed and that the units were bought by buyers who had the opportunity to make an informed decision. The moral: it pays to read documents closely.

• **Have reserves been set aside?** Check the budget to ensure that reserves are being collected for future repairs and improvements. The alternative to reserves are *special assessments*, possibly huge, budget-wrecking fees charged to each unit owner when an emergency repair must be funded. Failure to pay a special assessment can result in foreclosure.

• **Has there been a special assessment in the past two years, and are any expected within the next two years?** If you are a buyer and a large special assessment looms in the near future, you should adjust any purchase offer downward.

• **How are utility bills paid?** In some condo and co-op projects utility costs are included in the fee. The problem with paying utilities as a group is that individual unit owners are not directly responsible for their gas and electric costs, and utility expenses at such projects tend to be far higher than at condos or co-ops with separate meters for each unit. Also, it invariably happens that while you are willing to conserve fuel, a neighbor runs a sauna or model steel smelter 24 hours a day. Resolve the problem before it develops by avoiding projects without separate meters.

• **How large is the unit?** The size of a unit is generally expressed in terms of square feet but the definition of a unit may vary. Some developers measure from the middle of one common wall to the middle of the next common wall, while others measure wall to wall. Some developers include balconies and patios in their calculations.

• **What is standard?** Are the appliances in the model the ones being sold with the unit or are they extra-cost options? What about carpets, tiles, kitchen floors, and cabinets? Do they come with the unit or are they extra-cost options? Items sold with the unit are items that will not have to be bought or upgraded later.

• **How much parking is available?** Are spaces assigned? Do you pay extra for parking?

• **If you are buying a co-op unit, is the sale contingent on the board's approval?** If so, what criteria are used to evaluate prospective buyers?

• **Are there any new lawsuits or judgments currently outstanding against the condo association, PUD, or co-op?** If so, what is your potential responsibility as an owner?

• **Are there now or have there been any lawsuits by the condo association, co-op, PUD, or individual owners against the developer?** Suits can arise for many reasons, not all of them justified, but in many cases they concern allegations that may be of interest to prospective borrowers because they may require special assessments if not settled.

• **Is there an alteration or improvement to the unit that violates the condo declaration, master deed, by-laws, rules, regulations, or insurance coverage?** For instance, has the current owner added a built-in barbecue to the balcony or changed the electrical wiring?

• **Are there any outstanding building or health code violations against either the unit or the project?** In particular, ask whether pools have been shut down for health code violations.

• **Is the unit now leased?** If so, what are the lease terms? Leases remain in effect even when ownership changes, unless the lease provides otherwise. If the property is in an area governed by rent control, does the tenant have an automatic right of first refusal to purchase the property? Consult with an attorney when buying leased property.

• **Are many units rented?** Are large blocks of units owned by investors? This can be a serious problem, because resident owners may be more willing to make repairs and improvements than non-resident investors. Also, lenders may not be overjoyed by the prospect of making a loan in projects with a large portion of investors, a factor that may reduce resale values.

• **Is the project on a land lease?** With a land lease the ground under the project is leased for a given term, perhaps 75 or 100 years. At the end of that period, title to the improvements on the property—the entire project—reverts back to the owners of the land lease. With land leases, the landowners may typically renew or not renew at their option. In all cases, the unit owners—the land lease tenants—face the possibility of new costs and the loss of their lease and thus their unit.

A land lease may be attractive initially because acquisition costs are reduced—you are buying a unit but not the ground under it. The problem is that as time goes by there is less and less incentive to maintain the project. After all, why repair the roof 10 years before the reversion date? Also, a land lease is much like an apartment rental. When the rental period ends, not only may you be required to leave, but you will have no equity in the property.

Much can also be learned about condos, co-ops, and PUDs by speaking with past and current owner association presidents and treasurers. Also, why not speak to prospective neighbors? They will certainly have an interest in meeting a potential owner, and it's a good opportunity to evaluate the project on an informal basis.

Timeshares

Few of us vacation year-round so why own or pay for resort property 52 weeks a year or hassle with ever-increasing resort rental costs? That basic question is behind the large and growing time-sharing concept.

Until recently most property was sold on a fee simple basis; you bought a home or vacation property and owned it outright. Within the limits of zoning and public safety, you can rent it or keep a dog the size of a heifer and answer to no one about your taste or style.

As choice locations in both urban and resort areas grew in value, condominiums increasingly replaced fee simple ownership. Although people paid more per square foot for condo units than for fee simple property, condos had fewer square feet and thus cost less per unit.

One result was that condos made the ownership of real estate more affordable for buyers who were otherwise unable to purchase. Higher prices per square foot also generated more dollars per project to developers, an economic factor not to be overlooked.

Timesharing goes a step further. A timeshare project is not only a condo, but it is a condo where multiple owners have access to a given living space, albeit at different times. With the timeshare concept, what you get is the use of a furnished condo unit for a specific period of time, say the first week of February in Miami or the second week in December in Aspen. Units are available year-round, however, so prices for timeshares in a single project can vary extensively.

The timeshare concept raises four central questions: What are you buying? How do you pay for it? What happens if you can't use your unit? Are timeshare units a good investment?

Timeshare units are sold in two formats. Many projects sell units on a fee simple basis—that is, the full ownership of a condominium interest. These units represent a recorded, legal interest that can be sold, rented, traded, or willed.

Timeshare units are also marketed on a right-to-use basis, where purchasers are not actually buying real estate. Instead, they receive one of three types of right-to-use leases, including club memberships, which allow for the use of facilities but are generally not easy to re-sell; vacation leases, which can be sold or rented; and vacation licenses, which cannot be sold but typically give access to hotel facilities. Right-to-use programs generally have a set time frame, say 12 to 40 years, after which the unit reverts back to the developer.

If you're interested in purchasing a timeshare unit, don't expect to get a mortgage from your nearby friendly lender. Timeshare financing is typically in the form of a personal loan.

The catch with funding a timeshare purchase with a personal loan is this: mortgage interest is usually tax deductible; interest on personal loans is not.

A second catch concerns rates. Mortgages are generally viewed as among the most safe and secure loans that can be made. Personal loans are less secure and therefore rates are higher. Combine higher rates with a lack of write-offs and the true cost of timeshare financing is substantially greater than a home loan.

For instance, if someone has a 7 percent mortgage and their combined federal and state tax rate is 33 percent, for each $100 they spend on mortgage interest, their tax bill declines by $33. Viewed another way, the true out-of-pocket cost of this loan is $67 after taxes.

With a personal loan the numbers work differently. First, the rate is likely to be higher than interest levels associated with mortgages, perhaps 12 or 13 percent rather than 7 percent. Second, pay $100 for personal interest and there is no deduction.

In many cases, timeshare units are purchased on an installment loan or land contract basis; that is, ownership in the property is not conveyed until all or most of the loan has been paid. Conceivably, if a single payment is missed, the loan can be in default; but most developers, according to industry sources, have a liberal late payment policy.

The "advantage" of the installment loan system, at least to developers, is that lengthy foreclosure procedures are avoided. This is necessary because a single timeshare project may encompass thousands of interval units, each with a relatively small mortgage balance. For instance, a project with 50 units can sell 2,500 intervals (50 units × 50 weeks)—as many transactions in a single building as may occur in small cities!

Foreclosure in such circumstances is costly and impractical, so installment sales are often used to reduce the developer's financial risk. If a buyer won't pay the mortgage, at least the developer can re-sell the unit without too much difficulty. Foreclosure may also result if annual maintenance fees are not paid. This is a charge for management and upkeep, cleaning between intervals, etc.

Because the developer will be managing the project and providing financing, many states require developers and sales organizations to be registered and bonded. For more information about a particular developer, contact such authorities as consumer affairs offices, real estate commissions, and state attorneys general.

Because timeshare units provide rights only during specific time periods, they may seem useless if you are not free for a given week. However, units may be exchanged, a unique timeshare concept. It works this way:

You register your unit with an exchange service at least 90 days before you use your interval. They will then suggest possible units for which you can trade, units that may be in different parts of the country or even overseas. In general, like units are traded for like units but it is sometimes possible to trade an inexpensive unit in one location for a prime unit elsewhere. In addition, many units are exchanged within projects.

Whether or not timeshare units are a good investment is a matter of opinion, and the view here is that right-to-use units have little profit-making potential and are best viewed as a hedge against future vacation costs.

As the timeshare industry has grown, the number of units that have become available for resale has also increased. If timesharing seems attractive, prospective buyers should consider resale units typically available at a substantial discount when compared with new units. Although resale units represent the same financial and ownership considerations as new ones, they may offer the advantage of far lower prices, sometimes as much as 50 percent below new timeshares. To find the latest timeshare resale prices, check the classified ads in your local newspapers and magazines, Internet sites, and national publications such as USA Today.

The website operated by the American Resort Development Association (http://www.arda.org) includes useful consumer information concerning timeshares.

Questions to Ask

What form of timesharing ownership is being sold?

If a lease interest is for sale, how many years are left on the lease?

Are there any resale intervals available in addition to intervals available through the developer? If so, at what price and at what terms?

How is the interval unit financed?

If installment financing is used, what happens if a payment is late? Is there a penalty or does the loan automatically terminate?

Will your local lender, or a lender where the project is located, provide a personal loan to cover the unit's cost?

What is the current maintenance fee?

What is included with the unit (furniture, dishes, etc.)?

Does management have an in-house exchange program? If so, is there a fee to unit owners? How much? Are resale units available? If so, look for discounts.

Have there been complaints to the Better Business Bureau, local consumer offices, or the state real estate commission concerning either the project or the developer? If so, what are the complaints about and how have they been handled?

How is timeshare financing interest treated for tax purposes? Ask a CPA, enrolled agent, or tax attorney for current tax information.

9

THE STRANGE
WORLD OF ESCROW
ACCOUNTS

IF YOU BUY A HOME with less than 20 percent down, the lender undoubtedly has two basic requirements: first, that you obtain insurance or a guarantee from the VA, FHA, or a private mortgage insurer to make up for the smaller down payment. Second, that you establish an escrow (or trust) account with the lender to ensure that all property tax and insurance payments will be made.

(If you put more than 20 percent down, you will not be required to establish an escrow account. However, you may still want to have the lender collect money from you each month to avoid lump-sum tax payments and insurance bills. Although this may not be the best financial choice because of lost interest and investment opportunities, it may still be a good idea if it is not easy to save regularly. Also, see the escrow waiver fee material in Chapter 4.)

For instance, if your property tax is $1,000, then a lender will want to collect $85 a month—plus as much as a two-month cushion to guard against sudden tax increases. In addition, the lender will want money to pay for fire, theft, and liability insurance coverage.

The money you pay to the lender not only ensures that property taxes and insurance bills are paid, but the money also provides a steady income for the lender. While the money must be placed in escrow, separate and apart from the lender's funds, it can earn interest—money that traditionally goes right into lender accounts rather than your pocket. This may not sound like a big deal, but one lender settled escrow overcharge claims in 12 states by paying roughly $100 million to more than 350,000 borrowers.

Escrow accounts require minimal management and administration, but when there are problems they can severely impact homeowners. For instance, if a lender fails to pay a property tax bill, you are still obligated to pay the debt, and it's a lien against your property. Or, suppose that local taxes go up by $500. The money isn't in the escrow account, so the lender says pay up now or you'll be in default. If you don't happen to have $500 immediately available, then you've got troubles.

A more subtle problem works like this: you owe $750 a month to the mortgage company and you pay $800. Rather than reducing your debt and thus lowering interest costs, the lender instead credits the pre-payment money to the escrow account, where it draws interest for the lender. (To avoid this problem many, if not most, lenders have monthly forms that allow borrowers to specifically designate that additional payments are to be credited toward principal. If your lender does not use such a form, be certain checks indicate that extra dollars are to be applied to principal. Speak with lenders for details.)

An escrow account should be seen as an asset for borrowers, one that requires careful supervision. To ensure that no problems arise, or to deal with a lender if problems develop, take the following steps.

1. Check your escrow balance yearly to be certain that all payments and credits are shown. Lenders must provide an annual statement showing your monthly payments, the amount held in escrow, total escrow payments during the past year, and the money paid out for taxes, insurance, or any other approved purposes.

2. If you pre-pay your mortgage, clearly show that the pre-payment is to be credited against the loan's principal balance and not simply added to the escrow account or held in escrow for 30 days.

3. Watch the cushion rules. Federal regulations generally allow lenders to maintain a two-month cushion, but not all lenders are federally regulated. Also, FHA and VA loans only permit a one-month cushion.
4. Even if you find an error, keep up all payments; otherwise, you can set off a chain reaction of late charges and default notices. Work with the lender by phone and letter to resolve the problem; most lenders will be helpful. If the lender is uncooperative, contact the state attorney general in the jurisdiction where the property is located.
5. If you have a choice, and if you have the discipline, forget escrow accounts and pay your own taxes and insurance. The money set aside can then earn money for you.
6. When you refinance or pay off a loan, be certain the lender returns or credits all escrow funds as quickly as possible. The money in an escrow account is yours, and lenders have no justification for holding it once the debt has been retired.

Escrow Rules

Lenders have historically been free to enact a variety of accounting and collection practices that swell escrow accounts and the interest that lenders earn on such money. Now, however, federal rules prohibit a variety of old and odd escrow accounting practices.

- Lenders must place all escrow monies in a single account. By using two or more accounts, lenders were able to keep more money on hand than was necessary.
- New borrowers must receive a disclosure statement at closing showing how much will be required each month for escrow costs.
- Lenders can maintain as much as a two-month cushion in addition to required escrow monies.
- Borrowers will receive an annual statement showing the status of their escrow account and projecting escrow payments for the coming year. Read this statement with care and keep it with your mortgage records.

- Anything above a $50 account surplus must be returned to the borrower.

In essence, if you owe $1,000 in property taxes and $200 for property insurance, a lender will collect $100 a month for your escrow account, $200 up-front for an escrow cushion, and as much as $50 extra. Anything more should raise questions.

10

How to Pick the Right Mortgage

THE MOST DIFFICULT problem in real estate financing is not in finding a mortgage. Real estate financing is always available in every market and in every community—if you are willing to pay the price. Simply stated, there is no shortage of people and institutions that will gladly loan all the money you need at premium rates and terms.

The real dilemma is choosing one loan from among the essentially limitless number of financing options available at any given time. The issue here is not confined merely to interest rates and monthly payments; rather, there is the broader problem of finding the best financial package within the context of your needs, income, assets, financial potential, and personal goals.

Many of the questions regarding loan selection are academic in the sense that borrowers often have few realistic choices. It might be great, for instance, to have a zero-interest loan, but if you don't have the up-front cash, such financing is out of the question. (Yes—there really is a zero-interest loan! But only for those willing to pay a huge purchase price premium.)

Because we must each work within the bounds of our financial positions, the best way to find a loan is to see which mortgage format best meets our needs. If we lack cash we will want financing that requires little money down. If we lack income we will want financing with small monthly payments. If our financial position is stronger we can opt for a loan with a low interest cost but high monthly payments. Here is how common lending forms can be divided according to borrower requirements.

• **Benchmark.** Since borrowers are going to compare loan rates and terms, we need a standard against which mortgages can be measured. The best benchmark is the *conventional* loan, financing that features a 30-year term, self-amortization, market interest rates, 20 percent down, and level monthly payments.

Although conventional financing is the most consistent benchmark, FHA ARM loans are useful when comparing adjustable rate mortgages because they offer uniform terms nationwide. Rates and fees, of course, may differ.

• **Low Down Payment.** Many buyers cannot afford to make a 20 percent down payment, so there is a need for financing that requires few dollars up front. Such loans include FHA, VA, mortgage credit certificates, and loans backed with private mortgage insurance (PMI), as well as loans through such plans as Affordable Gold or the Community Home Buyers Program. Pledged-account mortgages (PAMS) and reserve-account mortgages (RAMS) do not require much cash in the form of a down payment, but someone, possibly the buyer, must deposit funds with a lender.

• **Lots of Cash Up Front.** If you have big savings you have more loan options. All-cash deals mean 100 percent of the purchase price must be paid up front. Zero-interest loans usually require one-third down. But the important point is that buyers with cash can put down additional dollars with any loan program, thus making them more desirable to lenders.

• **Low Initial Monthly Payment.** As monthly payments drop it becomes easier to qualify for financing, and several loan formats— adjustable rate mortgages (ARMS), graduated payment mortgages (GPMS), and buy-downs—all have low initial payments. ARMs usually feature low monthly costs at first, but, unlike the other loan formats in this category, which have programmed monthly increases, future ARM payments may rise or fall in a random manner.

• **Variable Payments.** ARMs have monthly payments that can rise or fall, so they require more budget planning than loans with set monthly costs.

• **Low Rates and Terms.** *Blend* loans feature below-market interest rates. Assumed loans often have both below-rate interest and shortened terms. Second trusts and wraparound mortgages can have both low rates and good terms, depending on the particular deal and market conditions.

• **Low Interest Cost.** Low interest "cost" does not necessarily mean a low interest "rate." Instead these are loans that over their terms require relatively few dollars for interest expenses. Zero-interest plan loans (ZIPs) have—not surprisingly—no direct interest expense. Second trust and wraparound loans, depending on individual rates and terms, can often cut interest costs significantly.

• **Short Loan Terms.** If 30-year financing is a "standard" loan term, then shorter mortgages include 15-, 20-, and 25-year loans and virtually all second trusts. Wraparound loans have terms of less than 30 years, depending on the remaining term of any existing financing. In the usual case, shorter loans mean higher monthly payments but lower interest costs.

• **Assumable Loans.** ARMs and FHA and VA financing can be assumed by qualified borrowers in most cases. Loan assumptions are sometimes available at below-market interest rates, often a good deal for borrowers.

• **Balloon Payments.** Balloon payments are a common feature of second trusts and short-term loans. Some graduated-payment mortgages are also balloon notes. Short-term loans with balloon features are not recommended.

How to Compare Loan Formats

Because needs differ there is not a single, magical mortgage formula that will somehow resolve loan problems for all borrowers. Different strategies work well for different people, and it is therefore necessary to have a sound selection process before one can have a sound financing choice.

Variety has always been part of the real estate financial system because conventional loans simply don't work for all purchasers. Conventional loans require too much down for most borrowers, initial monthly payments are too high, and total interest costs are too great. To get around these problems, and in many instances to simply make a better deal, buyers routinely use alternative mortgage formats.

Just because a mortgage is not a standard-issue conventional product does not suggest that the loan is "abnormal" in some way. Alternative mortgages are perfectly legitimate forms of financing. In the right circumstances, alternative mortgages can cut interest rates, reduce monthly payments, lower down payments, and drop overall mortgage costs.

The fact that alternative loans are different from conventional financing does not imply that such distinctions are necessarily negative. All loans are merely financial tools that are useful in some cases and inappropriate in others. Deciding whether or not to use a particular loan format depends on the needs of the buyer or refinancer and the facts and circumstances in each situation.

Loans should be compared individually—the second trust of one lender versus the second trust of another—as well as format against format—zero-interest mortgages versus graduated-payment loans. Here are the central comparison points to consider.

• Does the loan require fewer dollars down or more dollars down than other mortgage formats? Small down payments mean maximum leverage—the use of OPM to finance as much of the property as possible. Unless mortgage rates are "high" relative to other investments, it pays to seek leverage when buying. Once a loan is in place you can then look at restructuring and refinancing opportunities. FHA and VA loans are examples of financing that require few dollars up front.

• Are monthly payments subject to change during the term of the loan? If changes occur, are they pre-planned or random? How often are changes permitted? Pre-planned changes, such as monthly payment increases found in graduated-payment loans, allow borrowers to budget their incomes. Random changes, such as those associated with ARM financing, are more difficult to project.

• Are the initial monthly payments larger or smaller than other mortgage formats? The lower the initial monthly payments, the easier to qualify for a loan of any given size. Graduated-payment loans are attractive because they often feature significantly lower initial payments than would be required for conventional financing. In many cases loans offering below-market interest rates initially also feature lower monthly payments upfront—at least until the low-ball promotional rate ends.

• Are monthly payment changes limited? Is there a cap on the amount your monthly payments can rise, say, not more than 7.5 percent annually?

• Is there a cap on the maximum amount of interest that can be charged? Is there a minimum? If there is no interest cap, rates can rise with the market. If increased interest costs are not passed through to borrowers through higher monthly payments or occasional cash injections, is negative amortization permitted?

• Is negative amortization allowed? If negative amortization occurs early in the term of the mortgage is it automatically corrected later with higher scheduled payments, that is, without additional infusions of cash?

• If negative amortization occurs, can the loan term be extended? With adjustable rate loans there is often a provision to extend the loan term from 30 to as many as 40 years. This provision benefits the borrower in the sense that it is not necessary to refinance the property if any loan balance remains after 30 years. It also means larger interest payments and slower amortization over the life of the mortgage.

• If interest payments are related to an index, which index is used? The longer the span of events being measured, the better the index from the borrower's perspective.

• Can the loan be assumed at its original rate and terms by a qualified purchaser? This may be of value in the future when today's borrower becomes tomorrow's seller.

• Can the loan be pre-paid in whole or in part at any time and without penalty? This is a key question because if a loan can easily be pre-paid in part and without penalty, then the borrower can unilaterally restructure the loan at any time.

• What are the tax consequences of the loan? Speak to a CPA, tax attorney, or enrolled agent for specific advice.

• When all factors are considered, which loan format is best within the context of your needs today?

• Which loan format will best meet your needs five years from today? Ten years? Will your income decline as a result of retirement or a job change? If so, be wary of loans with rising monthly costs, such as graduated-payment mortgages, or loans that may have random monthly increases, such as adjustable rate mortgages.

Basic Mortgage Checklist

What is the specific name and product number (if any) for this loan program?

Name: _____

Number: _____

What is the maximum loan amount under this program?

$_____

What is smallest required down payment?

$_____ (_____%)

What is today's interest rate?

_____%

How many points, if any, are required to borrow at today's interest rate?

_____

What is today's interest rate without points (par pricing)?

_____%

Are monthly payments subject to change during the term of the loan?

Yes ❑   No ❑

How often are payment changes permitted?

Monthly ❑   Semi-annually ❑   Yearly ❑   Bi-annually ❑
Never ❑   Other ❑

Is there a cap on monthly payment changes?

Yes ❑   No ❑

If there is a monthly payment cap, how much is it?

_____%

Are initial monthly payments larger or smaller than other mortgage options?

Larger ❑   Smaller ❑

What is the maximum interest rate that can be charged during the life of the loan?

_____%

Is there a minimum interest rate?

Yes ❑   No ❑   If yes, what is it? _____%

(cont.)

Is negative amortization allowed?

Yes ❑   No ❑

If negative amortization occurs, can the loan term be extended?

Yes ❑   No ❑

If interest payments are related to an index, which index is used?

Name of index: _____

Can the loan be at its original rate and terms by a qualified purchaser?

Yes ❑   No ❑

Is there an assumption fee?

Yes ❑   No ❑   If yes, how much? _____

Can the loan be prepaid, in whole or in part, at any time and without penalty?

Yes ❑   No ❑

If there is a penalty, explain: _____

_____

Source: _____

Title: _____

Company: _____

Phone number: _____

Date information provided: _____

II

CONVENTIONAL LOANS

UNTIL THE MID-1930s, the most common form of real estate financing was the *straight*, or *term*, mortgage—a loan with a five-year life and semi-annual interest payments. Straight loans were attractive years ago because interest rates were low and plenty of cash was available for refinancing.

But the Depression and harsh weather in the Midwest—the Dust Bowl—brought out the worst features of the term loan system. People who were unemployed could not make semi-annual interest payments, farms where crops no longer grew were not acceptable collateral for new financing, and many lenders failed, shutting off valued sources of community cash and credit. The inevitable result was a rash of foreclosures and calls for a new system of home financing.

That new system arose in the 1930s when the Federal Housing Administration (FHA) popularized the long-term, self-amortizing home loan, a concept we today know as *conventional* financing.

Conventional loans are the benchmark against which all other mortgage concepts are measured because they have standard features, can be found nationwide, and have been around for decades. Conventional loans are distinguished by several central features:

- **Set Monthly Payments.** Each month the borrower makes payments that are substantially equal during the life of the mortgage.
- **Set Interest Rates.** The interest rate is established at the time the loan is first created and remains unchanged during its life.
- **Fixed Loan Term.** Conventional loans are designed to be re-paid over 30 years.
- **Self-Amortization.** Conventional financing is arranged so the entire loan, including all interest costs and principal repayments, will be completely re-paid when the mortgage ends. As a result there are no *balloon payments*—huge sums of money due at the end of the loan term.
- **No Refinancing Required.** Once you have a conventional loan, it need not be refinanced unless you want a new loan to obtain a lower rate or better terms.
- **No Re-Qualification Required.** Once you have a conventional loan, a lender cannot come back and demand that you re-qualify in the future.
- **Loan-to-Value (LTV) Ratio.** Conventional loans are equal to 80 percent of the purchase price of the property.

With these factors in mind, a conventional sale might look like this: buyer Stevenson purchases a new home for $100,000. Of this amount, $20,000 is represented by the cash down payment paid by

---

Conventional Loan Limits

Each year, in December, the new conventional loan limits are announced by Fannie Mae and Freddie Mac. For 1999, the conventional loan limit for a single-family, owner-occupied house is $240,000. Loans above this level, so-called jumbo mortgages, are somewhat more expensive.

Speak with local lenders and brokers for the current conventional limit.

Stevenson at settlement, and the remaining $80,000 is in the form of a 30-year mortgage from a local lender. At the end of 30 years, Stevenson owns the property free and clear of any mortgage debt.

Conventional loans are appealing to lenders because such financing means limited risk. The buyer's down payment creates a deep cushion that protects the lender in the event of foreclosure. With the $100,000 home above, for instance, the buyer has invested $20,000, leaving the lender with less risk than if the home was bought with $5,000 down or nothing down. If the house must be foreclosed, the lender's interest will be completely protected if the property sells for $80,000 plus foreclosure costs. Because $80,000 is considerably below the property's market value, the lender has only the most limited financial exposure.

Conventional loans are a useful index against which other mortgage options can be compared. Unlike other forms of financing, conventional mortgages are commonly offered by all community lenders, and because the terms and conditions of conventional loans are standardized, it's an easy matter to determine which lender has the best available rates and terms.

How Much Can You Borrow?

In most cases, to qualify for a conventional loan borrowers must have 28/36 front and back ratios. Using these ratios it is easy to provide a *conservative* estimate of borrowing power.

For example, payments for a 7.5 percent $100,000 mortgage will be $699.15 per month. If insurance is $25 per month and taxes are an additional $75, then we know the total cost for principal, interest, taxes, and insurance—*PITI*—is $799.15. If lenders qualify borrowers by allowing 28 percent of our gross pre-tax income for *PITI*, then to afford a monthly cost of $799.15 we need an income of $2,854 a month, or $34,250 per year. (In this example, we divide $799.15 by 28. That equals $28.54. We then multiply $28.54 by 100 to get our *gross monthly income*—income before taxes.)

We also know that if the back ratio is equal to 36 percent of our gross monthly income, then in addition to housing costs we can

The Conventional Loan	
Sale Price	$125,000.00
Cash Down	$25,000.00
Loan Amount	$100,000.00
Loan Term	30 Years
Interest Rate	7.5 Percent
Interest Type	Fixed
Monthly Payment	$699.15
Balloon Payment	None
Total Payments	$251,694.00
Total Interest	$151,694.00

spend as much as $228 on credit card debt, auto payments, etc. We obtained this figure by multiplying $2,854 by 36 percent. The answer is $1,027. If we subtract the amount of money allowed for housing expenses ($799.15), we are left with $227.85 ($1,027 less $799.15).

Is a 30-year loan the best mortgage format? For some portion of all borrowers, conventional loans remain the best deal in terms of interest rates, monthly costs, and down payments. But for many borrowers, conventional financing is far from the best arrangement. Other mortgage formats, as we shall see, feature less money down, smaller initial monthly payments, and interest savings that can top $100,000 for loans of comparable size. Although conventional financing may have been a great idea before World War II, it's not always the mortgage of choice for people today.

Questions to Ask

What is the current rate of interest for conventional financing? (This question should be asked when considering any loan format, because it provides a baseline from which to measure alternative mortgages.)

What portion of the home can be financed with a conventional loan?

Can I get conventional financing if a second trust is used to finance a portion of the purchase?

In addition to the current interest rate, how many points are being charged, if any?

In general terms, how much income will I need to qualify for a conventional loan of X dollars?

12

First-Time Buyer Programs

Each year about 40 percent of all home sales are made by first-time buyers, a marketplace fact that means loans for such purchasers are enormously important. The programs found here and in the following chapter typically allow buyers to purchase with 5 percent down or less—great news for all buyers.

And who is a first-time buyer? The definition is probably wider than you would expect. A first-time buyer clearly includes those who have never before held title. But a "first-time buyer" is also defined under many state-backed mortgage plans as someone who has not owned property in the past three years—which means that some "first-time" buyers are actually former property owners. And to make matters more interesting, there is now a provision in the federal tax rules that allows the use of IRA funds to assist individuals buying a first home. Under the rules for this program, a "first-time buyer" is someone who has not owned property for at least two years. See a tax pro for details.

Affordable Gold

The Affordable Gold program requires 3 to 5 percent down in the usual case. But under the 3/2 option, buyers need only 3 percent down, providing that another 2 percent is supplied as a gift, grant, or unsecured loan by an outside party such as a government agency, family member, non-profit group, employer, or even the lender.

In addition to a tiny down payment, up to 3 percent of the purchase price can come from the owner in the form of a *seller contribution* (money from the seller), which can be used to reduce closing costs. With a $100,000 home, for example, a buyer would have to put up $3,000, and an additional $2,000 could be offset with an unsecured loan from the lender. As to closing costs, in this example they could be reduced by as much as $3,000 should a seller accept such an arrangement.

Low down payments and minimal out-of-pocket cash costs are not the only attraction of the Affordable Gold program. Qualifying guidelines are liberal. Unlike conventional (28/36), FHA (29/41), or VA (41/41) financing, the Affordable Gold program has ratios of X and 40. As much as 38 to 40 percent of a borrower's income, and sometimes even more, can be used for monthly debts. At the same time, there is no guideline for monthly housing costs. This means that borrowers who hold down monthly credit bills can stretch their financing ability. Presumably, a borrower with no credit card or auto payments could use as much as 40 percent of his or her income for housing costs under the Affordable Gold program.

Income limitations can apply. Affordable Gold is directed toward those whose wages are generally equal to or less than the median income of the local community. However, there can be exceptions such as when the property is located in a central city, when the property is located in a census tract where median family income is 80 percent or less than the local area median, when the property is located in census tracts where minorities comprise 50 percent or more of the population, or where agreements have been negotiated with housing groups and governmental agencies.

Sifting through the requirements and exceptions, the Affordable Gold program can work well for many first-time borrowers. The program is widely available, and it is one to consider if little down payment and liberal qualification standards are important. Speak with lenders for the latest standards and requirements.

Questions to Ask

What is the current interest rate for conventional financing?

Does the lender offer the Affordable Gold program?

What are the rates and terms sought by the lender?

Is the lender willing to provide an unsecured loan for as much as 2 percent of the purchase price?

If you are in a pro-buyer market, will the owner make any "seller contributions" to cinch a deal?

Gifts

The use of gifts is fairly common in real estate, especially for first-time buyers. The National Association of Realtors reports that 25 percent of all first-time buyers and 7 percent of repeat buyers obtained family gifts.

The help of friends and family in a real estate deal most often comes in the form of cash or the extension of credit, acts of generosity that must be viewed with some care.

For the protection of buyers, sellers, and lenders, a *gift* should be seen as something more than a passing oral comment by Uncle Willard or whoever to come up with $15,000 if you ever purchase real estate. A gift commitment is truly a gift when it is:

- **Irrevocable.** A gift that can be taken back is not a gift.

- **Free of Consideration.** A gift that requires interest, where re-payment in whole or in part is expected, or where other valued consideration is anticipated is not a gift.

- **Available.** A gift not in hand by settlement may cause the forfeiture of a deposit because the deal cannot be completed.

• **Binding.** What happens if a gift commitment is made and the donor dies before the gift is delivered? Gift commitments should be binding on heirs, executors, administrators, successors, and assigns.

• **Contingent.** A purchase dependent on the delivery of a gift should be structured so that if the gift is not received by a given time and date, the sale is off and the deposit of the purchaser must be returned in full. Conversely, if it is the intent of the donor to provide a gift for the purchase of a particular property, that gift should be returned if for some reason the specific property cannot be purchased.

• **Acceptable to Lenders.** Lenders will want evidence that a gift is really a gift, not a secret loan, and also that promised funds are available. For this reason, donors will be asked to sign a *gift letter*, a statement saying that the money being provided is, in fact, a gift, and that no interest, re-payment, or other consideration is required. Lenders may also want evidence such as bank or mutual fund statement showing that donors actually have the money in hand.

• **Carefully Thought Out.** Sizable gifts may involve significant tax questions that should be reviewed by a CPA, enrolled agent, or tax attorney prior to making a commitment. For instance, will the donor be forced to pay a gift tax? Is there an estate impact? Is an outright gift the best approach for the donor? Rather than handing over a check up front, perhaps the donor is better off providing a mortgage which is then forgiven in part each year.

• **Donated by an Individual with Legal Capacity.** Not all prospective donors can be regarded as capable individuals. The ability of habitual alcoholics, the legally insane, those with certain drug dependencies, minors, senile individuals, and bigamists to make gifts may be subject to future challenge even when such personal difficulties are not immediately apparent. Be certain to obtain advice from an attorney in the event of capacity questions.

Questions to Ask

Can you reasonably expect a gift from any friend or relative? If so, are there any conditions?

Is the donor willing to sign all requisite forms?

When will you get the money?

Does the donor now have the money in cash or securities?

What are the tax implications of a gift? Speak to a tax professional for specific advice.

Are there any concerns regarding the capacity of the donor to provide a gift?

Co-Signers

There are buyers who have managed to accumulate enough cash for a real estate purchase but lack sufficient income to qualify for a mortgage. In such situations, it may be necessary to find a co-signer before a lender will provide financing. Rather than borrowing cash, you are instead "borrowing" credit.

Co-signing is great for buyers and a serious responsibility for those who accept such liability: co-signers are responsible for repayment of the entire debt, not just a part of it.

In many instances, lenders will not only want a credit-worthy individual to be a co-signer, but they will also want the co-signer on the deed as a co-owner. The possible problem with a co-signer as co-buyer is that this is not truly the relationship many families or friends envision. Also, a co-signer on the deed may endanger the ownership of the property—and the lender's interest—if the co-signer goes bankrupt or is forced to pay a liability claim.

With a co-signer as a co-owner, both buyer and co-signer would be wise to have an attorney draw up an appropriate agreement outlining the relationship between the parties. In addition, each co-owner should have a will and living will made or updated at the time of closing.

As with gifts, sales that depend on co-signatories should be made contingent on performance; that is, there's no deal if the co-signer refuses to sign documents, provide credit information, or take such other steps as may be required to complete the sale. In addition, the actions of co-signers should be binding on heirs, executors, administrators, successors, and assigns.

Questions to Ask

Will lenders require co-signers to also be co-owners?

If co-signers are co-owners, how will title be set up? Speak to an attorney about title issues.

Do you and the co-signer have wills and living wills?

As with gifts, are there questions regarding the capacity of the co-signer to enter into a contract? See an attorney for specifics.

Flexible Loans

The two biggest barriers to home buying are poor credit and deep pockets. It takes time to establish credit, and not everyone has cash for a down payment, closing costs, and reserves.

But suppose we looked at the mortgage business differently and say that most people, most of the time, make their mortgage payments regardless of how much they put down. Both FHA and VA loans have offered loans with little or nothing down for decades, both programs have created housing opportunities for millions of buyers, so why not a parallel program in the private sector? In other words, if we get rid of the down payment barrier, we are left with a large pool of people with good credit who want homes.

The Flexible 97 program from Fannie Mae is directed toward people with solid credit and limited cash. Under Flexible 97, you can buy with more liberal qualifying ratios than required with conventional loans and you only need 3 percent down—or perhaps a lot less.

For instance, suppose you want to buy a $150,000 home. Three percent down means you need $4,500 plus closing costs. But what if you don't have $4,500? Or, what if you have $4,500 but would rather hold on to the money?

With the Flexible 97 program you get rewarded for good credit. The 3 percent down payment need not come from you—it can come from a variety of sources:

- a gift from family or friends
- a personal loan
- a grant from an employer, non-profit group, or government agency
- a second loan
- a loan secured with CDs, a 401K account, cash-value life insurance, stock, etc.
- sellers may provide up to 3 percent of the loan amount to cover closing costs and up-front fees

As with all loans that require little or nothing down, some caution is advised. If you buy a home with little down, monthly loan costs will be higher than for purchases with more down. This problem can diminish over time as income rises.

If you buy that $150,000 home with few dollars down at closing, what happens if property values fall and you need to sell? There is no home buyer counseling requirement under the Flexible 97 program. Even though the program is plainly aimed at those with good credit, perhaps counseling should be required so that borrowers fully understand their obligations and the penalties for default.

Flexible 97 Versus Conventional Financing

	Conventional	Flexible 97
Loan Amount	$150,000	$150,000
Interest Rate	7.5 Percent	7.5 Percent
Front Ratio	28 Percent	33 Percent
Back Ratio	36 Percent	41 Percent
Amount Down	20 Percent	3 Percent
Requires Private Mortgage Insurance	No	Yes

Questions to Ask

Is the Flexible 97 program available in your area?

Are alternative programs similar to the Flexible 97 program available?

What is the interest rate for conventional financing?

What is the interest rate for the Flexible 97 program?

Given your income and credit, how much can you borrow with a conventional loan?

Given your income and credit, how much can you borrow under the Flexible 97 program?

What is the monthly cost of private mortgage insurance (PMI)?

HomeStyle Financing

The Fannie Mae HomeStyle program features seven basic loan choices, including options with little down, loans for investors, and loans for properties with up to four units. Some programs can be used for purchasing and some for refinancing.

This is a clever program first-time borrowers should look into because it has more liberal qualification standards than many loans and also because it offers financing choices with unique options.

For instance, suppose you like the Flexible 97 program but want to buy a home that needs substantial repair. Like the regular Flex 97 program, the HomeStyle version allows owner-occupant purchases with 3 percent down and 33/41 ratios. Up to 30 percent of the as-completed value can be allocated for repairs and upgrades.

This means you may be looking at a property that costs $100,000 but would be worth $140,000 if repaired and fixed up. If the repairs cost $25,000, you would get a loan for $121,250—

Conventional Versus HomeStyle Financing

	Conventional	HomeStyle
Property Cost	$100,000	$100,000
Repair Expense	$25,000	$25,000
Total	$125,000	$125,000
Down Payment	$25,000	$3,750
Amount Financed	$100,000	$121,250
Second Loan Required	Yes	No

$125,000 less a 3 percent down payment. Of the $125,000 borrowed, $100,000 be used to acquire the house and $21,250 would be held in escrow and released as improvements are completed.

If you look carefully at this loan, you can see some financial magic. You get financing to acquire a property and you get money to fix it up. Although there would usually be two loans in such situations—one to buy and one for repairs—in this case there is just one loan, one application, and one closing. Having one closing means that the usual costs of an extra settlement are avoided, big money when you count title searches, taxes, legal fees, title insurance, and other expenses.

Questions to Ask

What is the conventional interest rate?

What is the interest rate for a single HomeStyle loan as opposed to a first and second loan combo? How do closing costs compare?

How is repair money disbursed? Some programs give out money at closing; others require lenders to set up an escrow account from which money is disbursed in draws as the work is completed. Because there is a cost to pay out money after closing to assure that work has been completed, such loans likely have a higher cost.

What is the cost of private mortgage insurance?

Is some of the loan set aside for contingencies? Ten or 20 percent of the rehab cost may be held by the lender for repair over-runs. Not a bad idea, but if it happens that the work is done within price estimates then what happens to the money held in reserve? Can the excess funds be used to immediately reduce principal without penalty? If yes, can monthly payments be reduced? (Not likely for a fixed-rate loan product, but not a bad idea . . .)

What is the mortgage insurance cost? Can the use of private mortgage insurance be terminated once an owner has 20 percent equity? How is this done?

Is the use of funds restricted to certain items? Federal programs have traditionally limited repair options, while private programs likely allow a wider range of up-grades, including so-called luxury items.

Does the program require a list of repairs and estimates as part of the application process?

Is there a time frame in which repairs must be completed?

Does the loan require the use of certain repair companies? One can understand the requirement to use professionals from a general construction category, say licensed electricians as opposed to unlicensed firms, but not the obligation to choose Smith & Jones or the lender's nephew.

IRA Down Payment Assistance

You don't hear much about one of the buried treasures found within the tax reform legislation of 1997. It's the opportunity to take penalty-free money from an IRA to help first-time home buyers.

Given that 4 of every 10 home purchasers are first-timer buyers, and assuming that few spend weekends buffing their yachts, it follows that more cash for closing would help a lot of people buy a first home. The tax bill provides such help in the form of a new right to penalty-free IRA withdrawals.

You'll want to speak with a tax attorney, CPA, or enrolled agent for specifics before anyone is committed to anything, but in general the program looks like this:

- Under the rules, a *first-time home buyer* is defined as someone who has not owned property in his or her own name for at least two years. This is a markedly liberal definition; most state-backed mortgage programs require three years of title-free living to qualify for first-time status.
- The IRA can be owned by a purchaser or a purchaser's spouse, parents, grandparents, siblings, or "ancestor" (perhaps an aunt or uncle).
- The money can come from one or more IRA accounts.
- Buyers can receive more than $10,000. For example, Mom can donate $10,000, Dad can give $10,000, Grandma can chip in $10,000, and Grandfather can also provide $10,000.
- The money must be used within 120 days after withdrawal.
- Not more than $10,000 can be withdrawn from a single IRA account, say $2,500 apiece if the donor has four first-time buyer children.

But there's a rub. Getting money from a family member often raises a wide array of personal, financial, and psychological issues. Whether such barriers can be overcome or should even be considered is a matter each borrower will have to review individually.

And there's another concern: Although the 10 percent penalty for an early withdrawal will be waived, money taken from the account may still be subject to regular income taxes. See a tax professional for details.

Employer Assistance

Employer-assisted financing is designed to resolve a major problem: attracting workers. Many companies and other entities (such as colleges, charities, etc.) are finding that high salaries are not enough to attract qualified employees. Benefits are important, and home-buying programs provide a powerful incentive, the possibility of ownership with little down.

There are several approaches to employer-assistance programs:

• **Direct Grants.** With a direct grant the employer provides an outright gift that can be used to pay a portion of the down payment, closing costs, or additional points up front. By paying additional points, for instance, the interest rate will be reduced and monthly costs over the life of the loan will be cut.

• **Forgivable Loans.** The probability is that few employers will elect to make direct grants because once a grant has been issued, there is nothing to stop the employee from leaving the company. An alternative is to create a forgivable loan. As an example, Emory might receive a forgivable loan tied to the length of employment— if she works for the company for three years, then the entire loan and all interest will be forgiven, if she quits or is fired before the three-year term ends, then some or all of the loan is due and payable, as well as accrued interest.

• **Loans.** In this case the firm simply makes a loan to the employee for use as a down payment—perhaps with little or no interest. In practice it might be possible to re-pay the loan over time with a payroll deduction.

• **Monthly Payment Assistance.** The employer provides a monthly supplement paid directly to the lender. The idea is to reduce the employee's monthly housing cost (principal, interest, taxes, and insurance) to the point where it is less than 28 percent of gross monthly income. Payment assistance can also be in the form of a loan, money that is re-paid to the employer once employee housing costs fall below 28 percent of gross monthly income.

• **Loan Guarantees.** Under this option the employer promises the lender that the mortgage will be re-paid. Given a sufficiently strong employer, it seems probable that such a guarantee could produce a somewhat lower interest rate and thus a smaller monthly housing cost.

• **3/2 Funding.** A company, working in concert with a local government agency or non-profit group, can help arrange 3/2 financing for an employee. Income limitations may apply under this option.

Questions to Ask

What is the current interest rate for conventional financing?

What assistance can you get—down payment help, closing assistance, monthly supplements, or all three?

If the employer's program requires you to re-pay a loan, what rates and terms are required?

If an employer loan is forgivable, under what conditions is forgiveness available?

What happens if you get employer housing assistance and then leave your employer at an early date?

Equity-Sharing

Equity-sharing agreements are not mortgages in the usual sense but still can be seen as a form of financing for first-time buyers. And regardless of how they're defined, they may interest families who want to buy property together or investors who want to share risks and management.

Equity-sharing is an arrangement in which at least two people hold title to a given property. One, the *equity (money) investor*, puts up part of the cash or credit needed for acquisition but does not live on the property. The second person, the *resident owner*, uses the property as his or her principal residence.

Here's how it works:

Imagine that the Franklins and their son, Franklin Junior, agree to purchase an $85,000 townhouse. A $10,000 down payment is required, of which the Franklins contribute $8,000 and their son pays the remainder. The son also agrees to reside at the property and pay a fair market rental. The ownership of the property is then divided equally in this case.

The property has a fair market rental of $1,000 per month. The cash costs of the property are also $1,000 for mortgage payments, taxes, etc. Here's how the deal works:

1. Franklin Junior pays $500 per month to his parents as rent, because they own 50 percent of the property. He also pays $500 per month directly to the lender for the mortgage and taxes.

2. The Franklins receive $500 per month from their son. They then pay the lender $500 per month.

3. At the end of the year the Franklins report a taxable rental income of $6,000 (12 × $500). They also deduct all costs for which they are liable and that they actually pay, including mortgage interest, taxes, repairs, and condo and co-op fees. In addition, they get a depreciation credit. The result is a significant tax deduction.

4. Franklin Junior claims deductions for the mortgage interest and taxes he actually pays and for which he is liable. However, because he resides on the property he cannot claim depreciation, repair, or condo or co-op deductions.

5. The investors' equity in the property increases as they make monthly mortgage payments. Hopefully, their equity will also increase as a result of rising values.

6. When the property is sold, the profits are divided according to the ownership interest of each party.

Equity-sharing rules were devised to help families buy property together. However, it's not difficult to envision a situation in which potential residential investors such as young families, retirees, college students, and others will seek non-family investors to assist in a real estate purchase.

Indeed, one can see real estate brokers putting equity and resident investors together and then selling them suitable properties. Not only are the tax shelter possibilities attractive, but the problem of rental management is neatly resolved because there is no need to search for a tenant.

In considering the issue of financing for equity-sharing deals, borrowers should be aware that many lenders will not make equity-sharing loans. Others will make such loans but only with conditions. For example, lenders are likely to require that the resident owner must put up some cash to make the deal work, perhaps 5 percent or 10 percent; the equity-sharing arrangement must be between people and not corporations, partnerships, or trusts; the property seller cannot retain a property interest as an equity-sharing owner; and there can be no agreement to sell the property in less than seven years.

Equity-sharing arrangements should be seen as more complex than simple partnerships. For instance, in addition to requiring a resident-owner and a fair market value, regulations also mention that equity-sharing co-owners should intend to own their properties for at least 50 years. The 50-year requirement apparently conflicts with the seven-year buy-out clause found in many equity-sharing deals, but a knowledgeable real estate attorney can explain how to resolve the problem.

Whether an equity-sharing arrangement is a family affair or a pure investment, it is clear that a written understanding between the parties should be developed by a knowledgeable attorney. In addition, because equity-sharing arrangements represent tax issues, the services of a CPA, enrolled agent, or tax attorney should be used.

Questions to Ask

How much cash down is required from each party?

What is the percentage of ownership of each party? (The percentage of ownership does not have to be related to the cash contribution of the equity investor.)

What are the responsibilities of the resident partner in terms of maintenance and upkeep?

How much notice must the resident investor give before moving out?

How will a fair market rental be established? How will rent increases, if any, be determined?

How are disputes to be resolved? Many business agreements contain a binding arbitration clause so that in the event of conflict, a neutral party can resolve the issue without going to court.

What rights will each party have to buy out the other?

Do all parties to the agreement have current wills and living wills?

13

First-Time Buyer Help from State Governments

THERE IS NO LIMIT to the artful ways in which tax policies can be written. At this time we have a system that provides subsidies for some industries but not for others, a tax break for those over 65 but not over 61, and a deduction for the blind but not the lame.

In this maze of exemptions, deductions, exceptions, interpretations, rulings, codes, and court cases are benefits that greatly favor property ownership. Without tax exemptions for mortgage interest and property taxes, the number of residential property owners would be greatly reduced—as would the number of construction workers, real estate brokers, mortgage loan officers, appliance manufacturers, lumberjacks, and all manner of jobholders.

Municipal (Bond-Backed) Mortgages

One tax exemption of some interest is the right of governmental bodies such as cities, counties, and states to issue tax-exempt bonds to finance the construction of dams, roads, industrial parks, or whatever.

Issuers like tax-exempt bonds because they can cheaply fund projects that produce local employment and other benefits. Investors like such bonds because they often produce a higher after-tax income than alternative investments.

Suppose tax-exempt bonds are now paying 4 percent interest. A bond buyer in the 28 percent tax bracket will have to earn 5.56 percent from a taxable investment to have the same net return after taxes. Because not all investments of equal risk pay 5.56 percent in the current market, and because private securities are not backed by a governmental entity, tax-exempt bonds are attractive to investors looking for good yields with little downside exposure.

Tax-exempt bonds can be used to build factories and roads, and they can also be used to underwrite home mortgages, the theory being that cheap mortgages create additional local employment and a larger property-tax base. Here's an illustration:

South County sells bonds worth $75 million that pay 4 percent interest to investors. The money from the bonds is then used to underwrite 6 percent mortgages for local home buyers at a time when conventional rates are at 7 percent. The principal and interest home buyers pay is used to pay off the bondholders, and so South County will not raise taxes to repay the $75 million debt—a politician's dream. In some cases, as in this example, the issuing jurisdiction actually profits by charging homeowners more interest than bondholders receive.

Bond-Backed Mortgages at a Glance

Q. Who buys bonds?

A. Investors, pension funds, etc.

Q. Why are bond returns so low?

A. Interest on bonds issued by governmental agencies is generally exempt from federal taxation and represents little risk.

Q. Are bond-backed mortgage rates lower than conventional financing?

A. Yes, in virtually all cases.

Q. Are bond-backed mortgages always available?

A. No. Bond-backed mortgages are not available in every jurisdiction at every moment, in part because funding is usually limited. If you're interested in bond-backed financing, be certain to keep up with the latest developments in your community.

Q. Who qualifies for financing with bond-backed mortgages?

A. Standards vary but low-to-moderate-income individuals buying a first home generally qualify.

Q. If I qualify for a bond-backed mortgage, are there any restrictions?

A. In some programs there may be restrictions against renting property and selling with a profit.

Although tax-exempt bonds can bring millions of mortgage dollars into an area, that money is not available to everyone. There can be limits related to income, residency, and past ownership—most state programs define someone who has not owned property in the past three years as a *first-time buyer* and thus qualified to borrow with state-backed financing.

Bond-backed mortgages are a good deal but the number of loans available in each state is limited. The result is waiting lists, lotteries, and all-night vigils outside lender offices. In a sense, part of the qualification process for these loans may include luck and physical stamina as well as how many dollars you earned last year.

When considering bond-backed mortgages, potential borrowers should be aware that such financing often contains specialized provisions:

- Bond-backed mortgages are generally unavailable to current property owners and investors.
- If you borrow with bond-backed financing, you may be prohibited from renting the property. The logic is that

bond-backed mortgages are designed for owner-occupants.

- The loans may be only be assumed by individuals qualified to participate in the program.

Information about mortgages backed with tax-exempt bonds is available from real estate brokers, local lenders (who often service such loans), home builders, community groups, and governmental officials. Because this type of financing is often snapped up the day it becomes available, borrowers should obtain program information and forms in advance. With prepared applications and supporting documents in hand, you'll have the best shot at bond-backed mortgages when they are announced.

Questions to Ask

What is the current rate of interest for conventional financing?

Are bond-backed mortgages available in the jurisdiction where the property is located?

What is the current interest rate for bond-backed mortgages?

What are the income, family size, and residency requirements, if any, associated with bond-backed mortgages?

Can you obtain bond-backed financing if you have owned a property in the past three years?

Is the definition of a *first-time buyer* different for those divorced in the past three years?

How much cash down is required?

When will bond-backed mortgages next be available? Is there a waiting list? If so, how do you get on it?

Can you get a bond-backed mortgage from a local lender? If so, what are the proper application procedures?

Are you required to live in the property for a certain period, say 5 or 10 years?

Are you allowed to rent all or part of the property once you have obtained bond-backed financing?

Is the mortgage assumable? If it is assumable, must the buyer be qualified to participate in the program?

Can the loan be pre-paid in whole or in part without penalty?

Mortgage Credit Certificates (MCCs)

Bond-backed mortgages may be a great financing tool for borrowers, but they present problems for Uncle Sam.

One concern is the reduction of federal tax revenues. When states issue bond-backed mortgages, there is no tax on the interest paid to investors—and thus the federal government collects fewer tax dollars. The result is that although bond-backed mortgages are great for individual states, they are not so great for the federal government.

A second issue involves fairness. The federal government limits the amount of bond-backed mortgages each state can issue. States with more people can sell more bond-backed mortgages than states with tiny populations. This is fair because if there was no limit, then states would issue as many bonds as possible to raise capital. The loser would be Uncle Sam's dwindling treasury.

Because the purpose of bond-backed mortgages is to help entry-level buyers, and because the thought of tax-exempt income for investors bothers some people, there is a second state-level program to encourage home ownership, *mortgage credit certificates,* or MCCs.

MCCs and bond-backed mortgages are tied together by common limits.

Imagine that the federal government allows states to issue tax-exempt bonds for mortgages and MCCs worth a total of $1 billion. Suppose as well that Montana has the right to issue tax-exempt bonds worth $50 million this year. But rather than just issuing bonds, the state instead creates MCCs worth $12.5 million and bond-backed mortgages worth $37.5 million. In other words, once states have an allocation of tax credits from the federal government, they can issue either tax-exempt bonds, MCCs, or a combination of bonds and MCCs.

To make bond-backed mortgages work, states need to sell securities to investors. The act of selling requires someone to find investors, and the result is that if Montana sells bonds worth $37.5 million, the state gets something less because of underwriting fees paid to brokers.

With MCCs there are no bonds and no brokers, just a straight deal between the government and those who need assistance.

MCCs create a tax shelter for qualifying home buyers. For example, if Rogers has a $50,000 MCC mortgage at 7 percent interest with a 20 percent tax credit, he will have a first-year interest expense of roughly $3,500. Twenty percent of this amount, $700, can be used as a tax credit, and the balance, $2,800, is a regular itemized deduction.

It may seem that $700 is not much money in the context of a home purchase, but those who buy with MCC assistance typically have entry-level incomes, which means a tax rate of 15 percent or less.

If the tax rate is zero, then the benefit of the tax credit is also zero. But if taxes are owed, the MCC tax credit can be very important.

Rogers's MCC	
Amount Borrowed	$50,000
Interest Rate	7 Percent
Interest in Year One (Approx.)	$3,500
Mcc Tax Credit	20 Percent
Tax Benefit	$700
Itemized Deduction	$2,800

Suppose there are four people in the Rogers household and suppose as well that there is a deduction of $2,500 per person. Rogers is thus able to shelter $10,000.

In addition, because he now owns a home, Rogers has itemized deductions, perhaps $2,800 in mortgage interest, $500 in property taxes, and $300 in state income taxes, a total of $3,600. In effect, Rogers can earn up to $13,600 ($10,000 + $3,600) before paying federal income taxes.

Because he has a $700 credit, however, Rogers's taxable income does not begin at $13,600. Instead we take $700 (the amount of Rogers's tax credit), divide by 15 (as in the 15 percent tax bracket), and the result is $46.66. Multiply by 100 and the result is an additional $4,667 that can be sheltered from taxes. Add $13,600 and $4,667, and the result is untaxed income worth $17,667 to Mr. Rogers.

Under the MCC program, states are allowed to vary the tax credit for individual loans; however, the tax credit is limited to 20 percent of the loan amount in most cases.

MCCs are available only to those who meet the standards established for mortgages funded with tax-exempt bonds. The standards—outlined in Sections 25 and 143 of the Internal Revenue Code—include income limitations, purchase price requirements, non-ownership status for a three-year period prior to buying, and the purchase of property in targeted areas, in some cases.

Although MCCs can be an attractive form of mortgage financing, it may not be easy to obtain such loans.

• Because MCC loans are in demand, they may not be available when you need them—say, late in the year. Try to find out as much as possible about MCC financing in your state before looking at houses.

• Within some state programs is a *recapture provision*, which says that MCC borrowers who sell their property within a given time, say, 10 years, and for a profit, must pay back some or all of the taxes they saved by using the MCC program.

The purpose of this provision is to prevent low- and moderate-income families from profiteering through the use of governmental programs—a concept that obviously does not apply to the wealthy and well-connected.

• Those with MCC mortgages cannot generally refinance their property and retain their tax credits. Thus, if someone has an MCC deal at 9 percent and he or she can now get a loan at 7 percent, the MCC tax benefit stops the moment he or she refinances. Although it can make financial sense for an MCC owner to refinance, the program does not encourage refinancing and thus the reduction of tax write-offs.

The bottom line with MCCs is that they are an attractive, valuable program for those with specific financing needs, but such loans are not attractive for everyone. MCCs offer low-cost, low-rate financing with substantial tax benefits—but only for a limited number of borrowers in each state.

Questions to Ask

What is the current rate of interest for conventional financing?

Are MCC mortgages *now* available in the jurisdiction where the property is located?

What is the current MCC interest rate?

What are the income, family size, and residency requirements, if any, associated with MCC financing?

How much cash down is required?

When will MCC financing next be available? Is there a waiting list? If so, how do you get on it?

Can you get MCC financing from a local lender? If so, what are the proper application procedures?

Are you required to live in the property for a certain period, say 5 years or 10 years?

Is the MCC mortgage assumable? If it is assumable, must the buyer be qualified to participate in the program?

Can the loan be pre-paid in whole or in part without penalty?

What percentage of your loan interest can be claimed as a tax credit if you obtain an MCC loan?

What interest rate will you pay with MCC financing?

Is there a recapture provision if you sell the property? If there is a recapture provision, how long must you hold the property to avoid recapture rules?

Can you avoid recapture rules if you sell to an MCC-qualified buyer?

Does MCC financing restrict your right to rent the property?

14

HELP FROM UNCLE SAM

IN MANY INSTANCES buyers do not have enough cash for a 20-percent down payment, and even when they do purchasers would often prefer to buy with less down. There are a number of programs to help buyers purchase with little down, including programs from the federal government.

FHA Loans

The Federal Housing Administration (FHA) is one of the oldest and largest sources of mortgage assistance available to the general public.

What makes FHA financing so attractive? Traditionally, the answer has been low down payments and liberal qualification standards. Simplicity has also been a hallmark, at least until the past few years. Today, the program is increasingly complex and increasingly expensive, qualities not normally associated with good financing for first-time buyers or moderate income purchasers.

FHA financing is not actually a loan program in the usual sense. The government does not lend money under the FHA program. Instead, the federal government acts as a co-signer and guarantees re-payment to lenders. This guarantee is so powerful that FHA borrowers can obtain loans with excellent terms and little down.

By "FHA financing" most people mean loans developed under Section 203(b), the largest of many mortgage insurance programs available through FHA. Let's look at some questions:

How Much Can I Borrow?

The amount you can borrow under the FHA program depends on where you live, the number of units (one to four), and the current FHA loan limit. At least one unit must be owner-occupied. Special funding limits are used for properties in Alaska, Hawaii, Guam, and the Virgin Islands.

FHA loan limits for so-called high-cost areas are equal to 87 percent, and the result is that FHA single-family loan limit in 1999 is as much as $208,800 in high-cost areas. FHA loan limits for high-cost and low-cost areas can be obtained from local brokers and lenders as well as on the Internet at https://entp.hud.gov/cgi-bin/websql/idapp/html/hicostlook.hts.

To find the maximum loan amount, you first look at the sale price and the appraised value. Pick the lower number and then multiply. In states with low closing costs, the calculations look like this:

- For properties where the sale price or appraised value is $50,000 or less, multiply by 98.75 percent.
- For properties where the sale price or appraised value is more than $50,000 but less than $125,000, multiply by 97.65 percent.
- For properties where the sale price or appraised value is more than $125,000, multiply by 97.15 percent.

In states with high closing costs, the numbers change somewhat.

- For properties where the sale price or appraised value is $50,000 or less, multiply by 98.75 percent.
- For properties where the sale price or appraised value is $50,000 or more, multiply by 97.75 percent.

So, if you buy a home for $170,000 and have $5,000 in borrower-paid closing costs, under the formula for high-cost areas you would

FHA **Down Payment Calculations**

	Low-Cost Area	High-Cost Area
Sale Price	$170,000.00	$170,000.00
Buyer-Paid Closing Costs	$3,000.00	$5,000.00
Loan Percentage	97.15 Percent	97.75 Percent
Loan Amount	$165,155.00	$166,175.00
Cash to Close*	$7,845.00*	$8,825.00*

*Does not include various closing costs such as mortgage insurance premiums paid at closing, certain repairs, points paid by a borrower, etc. See lenders for details.

be able to borrow $166,175 ($170,000 × 97.75 percent = $166,175). The minimum down payment would be $8,825 ($175,000 − $166,175).

In addition to the minimum down payment, you might have other closing costs as well. Such additional costs could include prepaid expenses, points, repairs, and improvements that cannot be financed under FHA; rounding down to the nearest $50, mortgage insurance premiums paid in cash; non-realty expenses; and miscellaneous costs. Because each transaction is different, check with real estate brokers and lenders for final cash requirements.

Expect to pay at least 3 percent of the purchase price at closing. To see why, just look at how FHA explains the 3 percent requirement in Mortgagee Letter 98-29:

> The National Housing Act requires the minimum cash investment to be 3 percent of the Secretary's estimate of the cost of acquisition. FHA has determined that the minimum cash investment be based on sales price without considering closing costs to further Congressional objectives of simplifying the FHA maximum mortgage amount calculation without significantly increasing FHA's risk. Closing costs will not be included in calculating the 3 percent cash requirement, but may be included in satisfying the 3 percent requirement.

There. Now, isn't that clear?

What Is the Mortgage Insurance Premium (MIP)?

With FHA financing borrowers are putting down substantially less than 20 percent. Less down equals more risk for lenders, but lenders accept FHA loans because they know that in the event of foreclosure Uncle Sam will pay off the debt.

Uncle Sam, however, is not running a charity. If you want the federal government to be your co-signer you have to pay a Mortgage Insurance Premium, or MIP.

MIP comes in two forms for 30-year financing with less than 10 percent down:

First, there is a single, lump-sum payment due at closing equal to 2.25 percent of the mortgage balance. This insurance premium can be reduced to a flat 1.75 percent if you have not owned a home in the past three years and attend a home ownership class. See lenders for details.

The up-front insurance fee need not change the amount of cash required for this deal because the fee can be added to the amount borrowed. Adding the insurance fee to the loan will increase monthly costs and the amount that must be paid off at closing.

Second, there is a monthly insurance premium. If we are financing 90 percent or more of the property with an FHA loan, we first multiply the outstanding loan balance by .50 percent and then divide by 12.

• **Caution:** In addition to a down payment, borrowers will want additional dollars for closing, moving, reserves, etc. Under current FHA rules, all *allowable* closing costs can be financed and added to the loan. Speak with lenders and real estate brokers for specifics.

FHA **Mortgage Insurance Premiums**

Home Price	$100,000.00
Amount Borrowed	$97,750.00
Up-Front MIP (2 percent)	$1,750.00
Monthly Fee, 1st Month (.5 percent/12)	$40.73

• **Pre-Payment.** Residential FHA loans may be pre-paid in whole or in part without penalty. You can make pre-payments at any time during the loan term; however, if a pre-payment is not made on the monthly due date, it will be credited to the next due date. For complete information on FHA pre-payment planning, consult with your lender.

Are FHA Rates Set by the Federal Government?

No. FHA rates float with the market and parallel the ups and downs of other mortgage products. Because the terms and conditions of one FHA loan are exactly the same as every other FHA loan in the same program, it follows that pricing is a core issue. Look for lenders with the best market rates, and be wary of lenders who offer rates that are significantly below going interest levels.

Can FHA Loans Be Assumed?

In basic terms, current FHA assumption rules look like this:

• Loans made prior to December 14, 1989, are freely assumable.
• FHA loans made after December 15, 1989, may be assumed only by qualified owner-occupants.
• No FHA loans issued after December 15, 1989, may be assumed by investors.

Do I Need to Be an Owner-Occupant to Get New FHA Financing Under the 203(b) Program?

FHA loans can be an attractive financing tool to acquire properties with one to four units—but you must live in one unit.

The ability to finance two-, three-, and four-unit properties with FHA loans is an investing option that should not be overlooked. FHA loans feature little down and liberal qualification standards—values that may not be available with regular investor financing.

How Do I Qualify for FHA Financing?

With conventional loans, borrowers need 28/36 qualifying ratios—that is, as much as 28 percent of your gross monthly income can be

FHA Versus Conventional Loan Standards

	Conventional	FHA
Gross Annual Income	$50,000.00	$50,000.00
Gross Monthly Income	$4,166.67	$4,166.67
Front Ratio	28 Percent	29 Percent
Amount Available for Basic Housing Costs	$1,166.67	$1,208.33
Back Ratio	36 Percent	41 Percent
Amount Available for Basic Housing Costs and Credit Debts	$1,500.00	$1,708.33

used for basic housing costs and up to 36 percent of your income can be used for basic housing costs plus monthly credit costs for items such as credit card bills and auto payments.

FHA qualification standards are vastly more liberal. The 203(b) program uses 29/41 qualifying ratios. To see how much more you can borrow with FHA, just look at this example:

Do I Need an FHA Appraisal?

Yes. To obtain FHA-backed loans properties must be evaluated by an FHA-approved appraiser. If it is found that the FHA appraised value is less than the selling price, then either the sales price must be lowered or the purchaser must be willing to cover the difference in cash. The FHA will not permit the use of a second trust to bridge the difference between the sales price and the appraised value of the property. The FHA will permit the use of second trusts as long as the combined value of the first and second trusts does not top FHA loan limits or required loan-to-value ratios.

Are There Special Rules That Will Help Me Qualify for FHA Financing?

Yes. FHA has a number of underwriting standards that can prove valuable to borrowers.

- **Automated Underwriting.** Lenders may now use artificial intelligence software to process and approve FHA loans. *Loans rejected by automated systems must be reviewed by human underwriters.*

- **Bonus, Part-Time, and Overtime Income.** Income from bonuses, part-time employment, and overtime can be counted when seeking a loan if such income can reasonably be expected to continue.

- **Child Care.** Child care is not regarded as an "expense" for qualification purposes.

- **Debts.** FHA rules say that only obligations that cannot be paid off within 10 months can be counted when computing the back ratio. For example, you have a $200 monthly car payment and seven payments to go. For FHA qualifying purposes, this obligation will not count as a debt.

- **Flexible Ratios.** Although the FHA program retains the 29/41 ratios it has long used, the agency now allows greater flexibility than in the past. FHA guidelines state, "It has always been HUD's intent to allow ratios to be exceeded where significant compensating factors exist. We also do not set an arbitrary percent by which ratios may never be exceeded nor may any local HUD office."

What this statement means is that the front and back ratios used for FHA loans are guidelines and not absolute barriers. There may be instances where borrowers who do not qualify in strict numerical terms can get an "exception" and still obtain financing.

- **Income Stability.** FHA wants lenders to presume that borrowers will have steady income at current levels or better for at least the next three years.

- **MCC Financing.** FHA loans are sometimes combined with state mortgage credit certificate (MCC) programs for first-time buyers. Under the FHA guidelines, underwriters can deduct the MCC tax credit from the borrower's annual housing cost, making it easier for MCC buyers to qualify for financing.

For instance, suppose an MCC borrower pays out $5,000 a year in mortgage interest. Of this amount, $1,000 is a federal tax credit and $4,000 is a regular deduction. The $1,000 tax credit can be used to reduce front ratio housing cost calculations by $85 per month ($1,000 ÷ 12).

• **Mattress Money.** Cash saved and kept at home may be used to purchase property with FHA financing, providing a borrower can explain how such funds were accumulated.

This is important because a Federal Reserve study ("Family Finances in the U.S.: Recent Evidence from the Survey of Consumer Finances," January 1997) shows that 13 percent of all households—perhaps 40 million people nationwide—have no checking or savings accounts. Eighty-five percent of such households have annual incomes of less than $25,000—households that may benefit from FHA loan programs.

• **Private Savings Clubs.** Among many ethnic and national groups it is a common practice to accumulate money in private savings clubs. Although the FHA directive does not list such groups specifically, it is likely to include associations known as "Hoi" (Vietnamese), "Tontines" (various), "Tanamoshi" (Japanese), "Hui" (Chinese), "Kye" or "Keh" (Korean), "Isusus" (Nigerian and Ghanaian), "stokvels" (South African), "Susu" (Indian), "Ekub" (Ethiopian), "Pasanaqu" (Bolivian), etc.

• **VA-Qualified Buyers, National Guard Personnel, and Reservists.** Individuals who are VA-qualified or have served in the National Guard or Reserves may benefit from a 203(b) provision which says that up to $750 normally required for the FHA down payment can be waived for qualified individuals. The FHA includes guardsmen and reservists with at least 90 days of continuous active-duty service—including training periods—among those who qualify for this benefit. (Note: check with lenders regarding VA-qualified, National Guard, and Reserve preferences under the FHA program. As this is written, such preferences are scheduled to expire in October 1999, and although they are likely to be extended, borrowers with an interest in this matter should ask lenders for an update.)

Questions to Ask

What is the current FHA interest rate?

What is the current FHA loan limit for single-family housing under Section 203(b)?

What is the current FHA down payment schedule for Section 203(b) loans?

What is the current FHA insurance premium? Is it due at settlement?

If you do not want to pay the FHA insurance premium in cash at settlement, can you get a larger loan? If you elect to finance the premium, how much will your mortgage increase? What portion of the premium can be financed through a larger mortgage?

How many points, if any, are lenders generally seeking for FHA 203(b) loans today? How many points, if any, are being charged for other FHA programs? Contact several local mortgage loan officers to compare costs.

Can you use a VA appraisal when seeking FHA financing?

If a home now has FHA financing, is it freely assumable? Can it be assumed by a qualified buyer? If the loan can be assumed by a qualified buyer, what are the qualifications and costs?

FHA Refunds

MIP money is placed in *pools* (common accounts) and used to off-set costs when homes financed with FHA loans are foreclosed. If the pool that includes your loan has few defaults, it is possible to obtain a refund when

- your loan was made after September 1, 1983
- you paid an up-front fee
- you have paid off or refinanced your loan

So how do you get a refund?

Plan ahead. At closing or as soon thereafter as possible, write down your FHA case number. If you do not have your FHA case number and settled years ago, contact your lender—they will have the number. Do this now.

Save the case number with your loan documents. You will need it to make a refund claim.

When you sell or refinance, contact your lender for refund information.

If the lender cannot help, contact the FHA at (800) 697-6967 or visit their Web page (http://www.hud.gov/fha/fhahome.html) for current information.

Warning: If you pay off an FHA loan, you may receive a call or letter from a private party claiming that the government owes you— yes *you*—actual cash money minted in this country! And for a "small" fee, say 20 to 30 percent of the amount collected, this party will obtain those funds for you. However, it costs nothing to get a refund. Just call the refund information number or visit the FHA website. You do not need a third party to collect such money as the FHA may owe.

FHA 203(k) Financing

Some of the most attractive properties are those that happen to be in poor physical condition. The cost to acquire and improve such properties is often far below the cost of like properties in good condition.

The financing needed to acquire and repair property is usually a two- or three-step process—get a mortgage to acquire the property, pay for repairs, and then refinance at the new and higher value when all improvements are completed if the property is to be retained.

But not everyone has the dollars to both acquire and fix up a home, a need addressed in many cases by the FHA 203(k) program.

Under 203(k) you can buy or refinance a property and fund repairs with a single mortgage. FHA loan limits and qualification standards used for the 203(b) program generally apply with 203(k) financing.

The way it works is that you buy a property with one to four units. Raw land does not qualify for the program—there must be a foundation in place for at least a year.

Condo units can be financed under the program, providing they are owner-occupied or are being redeveloped by a non-profit organization. No investors are allowed at this writing, though the program has been open to investors in the past. Only internal condo repairs are permitted. "Mortgage proceeds," say the regulations, "are not to be used for the rehabilitation of exteriors or other areas which are the responsibility of the condominium association, except for the installation of firewalls in the attic of the unit." (See HUD Mortgagee Letter 95-0040 regarding "Single Family Loan Production Revisions to the 203(k) Rehabilitation Mortgage Insurance Program," page 10, for details.)

The program can also be used for mixed-use properties where the majority of the square footage is used for residential purposes. No dollars under 203(k) can be used to improve the commercial portion of the property. Up to 25 percent of a one-story building can be used for commercial purposes, up to 49 percent of a two-story building, and up to 33 percent of a three-story structure.

Instead of a loan based on the acquisition cost of the property, financing under 203(k) can be based on as much as 110 percent of the projected value when all repairs are completed. Thus, you could acquire a property for $80,000, plan on spending $20,000 for repairs, but obtain a loan based on the final market value after repairs, say, for $115,000 in this case.

The 203(k) program requires approved repairs of at least $5,000. By "approved" repairs, FHA generally means necessary repairs rather than luxury items.

With a 203(k) loan, the lender's job continues after closing. Funds to acquire the property are disbursed at closing, but additional money for repairs is released only as work is completed. Because of the additional work involved, lenders may charge a 1.5 percent supplemental fee or $250 (whichever is greater) to process this type of mortgage.

The 203(k) program also has a special allowance available for energy-efficient improvements. Under the HUD regulations, a borrower can finance 100 percent of all qualified "energy efficient improvements" even if this means the size of the overall loan is enlarged to the point where the borrower would not normally qualify.

The 203(k) program is fairly complex, and HUD will actually finance an "independent consultant fee" under the program, money used to hire an experienced professional to guide borrowers through the 203(k) plan. Given reams of documentation and requirements, this is not a bad idea, especially for someone who has not used the program previously.

(As an alternative to the 203(k) program, look into the buy and fix-up options associated with Fannie Mae's HomeStyle program as discussed in Chapter 12.)

Questions to Ask

What is the current interest cost for conventional financing?

What is the current cost to borrow under the FHA 203(k) program?

What is the maximum 203(k) loan amount in your community?

What is the 203(k) down payment requirement for owner-occupants?

What repairs will FHA allow under the 203(k) program?

Has the lender done 203(k) loans previously?

Can you obtain references from past 203(k) borrowers? (The lender will need their permission before releasing their names.) It may be helpful to speak with past borrowers to understand the practical issues associated with the program.

Can you do any of the repair work yourself? (This is allowed under the 203(k) program providing the work meets normal construction standards. The 203(k) program will pay for materials, but not borrower labor.)

How much extra can the lender charge to process a 203(k) loan?

What paperwork (estimates, plans, and such) is required by the lender?

Can the lender recommend several consultants to assist with the project?

Are investors allowed to use the program? If yes, how much down is required?

VA Financing

Virtually everyone has heard of VA loans and with good reason: this is one of the best financing programs available.

In 1930 federal bureaus and offices concerned with veterans' issues were consolidated within a new entity, the Veterans Administration. Home mortgages backed by the agency subsequently became known as VA loans. On March 15, 1989, the VA was promoted to Cabinet-level status and renamed the Department of Veterans Affairs, DVA for short. Because loans for veterans have long been known as VA financing, we'll continue to use the term VA generally.

What makes VA financing unique? There are several major factors:

• **Loan Guarantees.** The VA is not a lender. Instead, the VA acts as a co-signer to assist qualified individuals who need home mortgages.

• **No Down Payment.** Unlike conventional loans, which require 20 percent cash down, there is no VA requirement for a down payment unless the purchase price of the property is greater than the VA's estimate of reasonable value or if a lender requires a cash down payment as a condition of the loan. Many VA buyers elect to make a down payment to reduce their debt and monthly payments even when a down payment is not required.

• **Loan Limits.** Mortgage amounts are *not* limited by the VA. Lenders, however, typically restrict the size of VA loans to $203,000 in mid-1999 because of the guarantees in place.

• **Insurance Costs.** Originally the VA mortgage program was seen as a cost-free loan "guarantee" rather than insurance product. Now the VA charges a "funding fee" (read *insurance premium*) to vets based on the amount down. Current funding fees look like this:

- With less than 5 percent down, the fee is 2 percent of the loan value.
- With more than 5 percent down but less than 10 percent down, the fee is 1.50 percent of the amount borrowed.
- With at least 10 percent down, the funding fee drops to 1.25 percent.
- In the case of a veteran refinancing under the program to get a lower interest rate, the funding fee is .50 percent of the loan amount.
- A vet who uses his or her eligibility a second time or more (perhaps to borrow more or to buy a new home) will pay a 3 percent funding fee for new financing.
- National Guard members and reservists with six years of service are now included in the VA program. They pay a .75 percent premium to acquire a new VA loan. For example, a reservist who uses VA financing to buy a home with nothing down would pay a 2.75 percent funding fee.

- **Assumptions.** A major attraction of VA financing has historically been the ability to freely assume such loans regardless of your income or credit. However, VA loans—those made after March 1, 1988, are no longer freely assumable—borrowers must qualify to assume. In addition, a small percentage of VA loans made through state and local housing agencies may be assumed only by individuals otherwise qualified to participate in such programs.

- **Rates.** VA rates float with the marketplace.

- **Amortization.** VA financing is self-amortizing if held for the complete loan term.

- **Pre-Payment.** VA-backed loans may be pre-paid without penalty. However, pre-payments must be made on the loan's due date; otherwise, you may face a penalty of as much as one month's interest. Speak to your lender for details.

- **Qualifications.** New VA loans are generally available to those with military experience. Individuals who served in peacetime prior to September 7, 1980, are generally required to have 181 days of continuous active duty service in peacetime or 90 days of such service in wartime. Those who have served since September 7, 1980, are typically required to have at least 24 months of continuous active-duty service.

Individuals with six years of service in the National Guard or Reserve, officers in the United States Public Health Service, and certain other individuals may also qualify for VA benefits. Speak with lenders for details before entering the housing marketplace.

How the VA Entitlement Works

The VA mortgage program embodies a guarantee on which lenders rely to reduce their risk. The VA promises to repay a maximum today of $36,000, a figure that represents each veteran's "entitlement."

When the VA program was first established during World War II, the initial entitlement was $2,000. By the end of the war, the entitlement figure was raised to $4,000, and it has gradually risen ever since. For VA-qualified buyers, the rise of entitlement means that it is possible to have purchased a home many years ago and still have some entitlement remaining. A purchaser who bought a home for $25,000 in 1960 when the entitlement level was $12,500, for instance, will now have a remaining entitlement balance of $23,500, essentially an unused line of credit from Uncle Sam.

Important: it may be possible for a vet to have his or her entitlement reinstated in certain circumstances. A veteran's entitlement can be restored to the full current level when a previous VA-backed loan has been completely re-paid as part of a sale or when a VA-qualified purchaser assumes a VA mortgage and *substitutes* his or her entitlement for that of the original borrower.

With the $36,000 guarantee, a lender will generally loan $144,000 to a financially qualified buyer. However, the $144,000 figure is not a legal limit, and a lender could—and many do—make far larger loans.

Beyond the $36,000 entitlement, the VA guarantees 25 percent of loan amounts above $144,000, up to a maximum exposure of

$14,750. Ginnie Mae—the big secondary lender—has agreed to buy VA mortgages from local lenders providing individual loan amounts do not exceed $203,000. Between the VA guarantee and the Ginnie Mae loan limitation, most VA lenders will provide loans up to $203,000 at this time.

If VA interest rates decline, an owner-occupant vet can refinance an old GI loan without using any additional entitlement. The size of the new VA mortgage, however, can be no greater than the value of the old loan balance plus any settlement fees required to obtain the new financing.

VA Paperwork Simplified

To qualify for VA financing, a veteran must possess DD Form 214, a form given out when leaving the service, and VA Form 26-1880, a "Request for Certificate of Eligibility." These forms are used to get a "Certificate of Eligibility." For current information, visit VA regional offices, write the VA, call via toll-free phone lines, or visit the VA website: http://www.va.gov.

VA mortgages would seem to be limited to veterans alone, the VA program actually benefits a far broader scope of the population.

Non-veteran purchasers can assume VA mortgages at their original rates and terms, a significant financial advantage in many cases.

Non-veteran sellers can participate in the program by offering their homes to VA-qualified purchasers. To get VA financing, a home must be evaluated by the VA to determine its economic worth. An appraisal, or "Certificate of Reasonable Value" as it is called, may be ordered by contacting regional VA offices.

The VA points out that its "Certificate of Reasonable Value" is for financial purposes only and is *not* intended to be a structural inspection. It is therefore possible to buy a VA-financed house that is in something less than pristine physical condition.

The question of when to order a VA appraisal is an issue that should be of some importance to sellers. Clearly an appraisal will be required to get VA financing, but should an appraisal be sought earlier in the marketing process, before there is a purchaser with whom to deal?

By getting an appraisal before a home is offered for sale, sellers will at least have the VA's view of what their property is worth. This can be a valuable selling tool because property advertising can then be directed toward VA buyers ("VA appraised at $179,990"). But what happens if the appraisal is low? Sellers in such situations have spent money for an appraisal they are not likely to publicize.

Sellers are best served by having the buyer get and pay for an appraisal as part of the loan application process after an offer on the property has been made. An offer is a product of the marketplace and is surely an important benchmark by which the value of the property can be measured, one that cannot be ignored in the appraisal process.

If the VA appraisal is less than the sales value of the property, the VA will guarantee a loan equal only to the estimated worth of the home. When an appraisal is below the sales value, the VA requires that purchasers have the option to withdraw from the deal, in which case their deposit must be returned in full.

In the event of a low appraisal, two other strategies can be employed. First, a buyer can pay the difference between the sales price and the estimated value in cash. Second, the seller can reduce the sales price to the appraised value. As a matter of negotiation, buyer and seller may meet somewhere between these two choices.

VA Loan Release Tips

Borrowers with financing who wish to get a release of liability will need the approval of both the lender who issued the loan and the organization that provided the guarantee, if any. Veteran borrowers can be released from all VA liability, according to that agency, "by having the purchaser assume all of the veteran's liabilities in connection with the loan and having the VA approve the assumption agreement and specifically release the veteran from all further liabilities to VA." Being released from liability is a process distinct from the possible restoration of a VA entitlement. Again quoting VA materials, borrowers may have their entitlements restored when (1) "the loan has been paid in full, or the VA otherwise has been relieved of the obligation under the guaranty and the home has been disposed of" or (2) a VA-qualified buyer has "agreed to assume the outstanding balance of the loan, has consented to substitute his or her entitlement for that of the original veteran-borrower," and meets all other current VA requirements. For more information, contact the nearest VA office and ask for Pamphlet 26-5 and the "ROL/SOE Package."

VA Loans and the COW Committee

In the past, the VA has vigorously sought to recover money lost from defaults, even when a loan was assumed and the original VA borrower was not involved in fraud, material misrepresentation, or bad faith. Because loans made prior to March 1, 1988, were freely assumable, it could happen that a vet would sell a home, the loan was assumed, the vet was not released from liability, and seven years later the vet receives a letter saying the buyer—or the buyer's buyer—had defaulted on the loan, the property was sold at foreclosure, and now the vet owes Uncle Sam for a $12,000 loss.

In an absolute sense the veteran surely does owe the $12,000 because no release was provided. But is it fair or reasonable to pursue a vet who acted in good faith, made his payments, and was not a direct party to the foreclosure?

The VA, with prodding from Congress, has come to the conclusion that there are times when VA loans fail, vets are liable on paper, and yet circumstances are such that it is unfair and unconscionable to pursue all claims against the vet.

The VA has established a Compromise and Waiver Committee (also known as COW) to aid veterans with liability problems stemming from loans issued prior to March 1, 1988. The committee has the authority to reduce or waive claims, depending on the facts and circumstances in each case. More details are available from local VA offices.

The VA policy does not affect more recent mortgages because VA loans issued after March 1, 1988, can only be assumed by financially-qualified individuals. After the assumption is made, the original borrowers no longer have liability.

Questions to Ask

What is the current VA interest rate?

What is the largest VA-backed mortgage offered by most local lenders?

What is the current number of points sought by lenders making VA loans? Check with different lenders, as this figure may vary.

What is the current VA entitlement?

If you have used your VA entitlement in the past, do you have any remaining entitlement? Check with your local VA office.

If you are a seller, do you want to order a VA appraisal? If yes, what is the cost of such an appraisal?

Can you substitute an FHA appraisal for a VA appraisal—a "Certificate of Reasonable Value"? This may be possible in some areas, so contact your local VA office for more information.

If you are a buyer, do you have a "Certificate of Eligibility" in hand? If not, how long will it take to get one?

What are the latest assumption rules? Is there an assumption fee? If so, how much?

Is there a funding fee being charged at the time you apply for VA financing? If so, how much?

What course of action will you take if the VA appraisal is less than the agreed sales price for a property?

Are there new VA rules that impact your ability to get VA financing? Check with your local VA office.

15

PRIVATE MORTGAGE INSURANCE (PMI)

THERE ARE HUNDREDS of thousands of home sales each year that would not occur except for the availability of FHA or VA financing, loan programs that provide mortgages with little or no money down. Yet the FHA and VA programs are not for everyone. Many buyers are not VA qualified, and a large portion of all home sales require more money than can be insured by the FHA.

The FHA and VA programs, however, are not the only sources of third-party mortgage assistance or even the largest. When the success or failure of a sale depends on a small down payment, many buyers turn to a unique financial product called *private mortgage insurance*, or PMI, as it is known in the real estate industry.

PMI is nothing more than the promise of a private insurer to repay a lender in the event a mortgage with little down is in default. Without this promise a lender will not make a low down payment loan because such financing represents an excessive level of risk.

If conventional financing is available at 7.5 percent interest with 20 percent down, then conventional financing with PMI will also be available at the same rate—but borrowers will need only 5, 10, or 15 percent down. It is the combination of conventional financing rates plus reduced down payments that make PMI loans a valuable marketplace option.

PMI is insurance and where there is insurance there are premiums. With PMI, premiums are determined by several factors:

• **Down Payment.** A larger down payment presents less risk to the lender, so there is a correspondingly lesser need for insurance coverage. With 10 percent down, for instance, there is usually 20 percent PMI coverage. With only 5 percent down, there is 25 percent insurance coverage. Thus, if someone puts down 5 percent on an $85,000 property and has PMI coverage, the lender will be insured initially for at least $20,187 ($85,000 − 5 percent = $80,750; $80,750 × 25% = $20,187.50)

• **Loan Type.** Because fixed-rate loans are regarded as less risky than adjustable-rate mortgages, PMI premiums are lower for fixed-rate financing.

• **Payment Plan.** PMI can be paid annually, in which case borrowers will make a small payment at closing as well as payments each month for as long as the lender requires coverage.

PMI can also be paid in a lump sum, what the industry calls a "single premium." Because most borrowers want to hold down closing costs, lump-sum PMI can be added to the loan amount and paid out over time. In general, lump-sum PMI is not available with loans that have 5 percent down or less.

• **Refund Provision.** Lump-sum PMI is available in two varieties: with the possibility of a partial refund and without a refund provision. Lump-sum PMI without a refund clause is cheaper.

Which program is best?

For those borrowers who intend to own their property for a long time, lump-sum PMI without a refund is likely to be the most attractive choice. If you intend to be a short-term owner, then annual premiums are likely to be cheapest.

Under some annual premium programs, borrowers must pay hefty costs up-front—the equivalent of the premium for one-year in advance plus two months in escrow—in effect, 14 monthly payments in advance. This is a big cash cost, but it is now possible to obtain PMI with just a single month's payment at closing. The requirement for a two-month escrow remains, but in total the new programs reduce PMI up-front costs from 14 payments to 3, a big improvement by any standard.

Another way to cut up-front costs is to use the zero initial premium concept. In this case, borrowers trade somewhat higher monthly premiums for cash relief at closing. One could concoct a fairly complex analysis to see if this is a good choice, but, basically, if you have concerns about cash at closing, the zero initial premium option should not be overlooked.

Lenders are willing to accept a lower down payment because with PMI-backed loans they have less risk. If a PMI buyer defaults, the lender faces one of two choices, either of which is far more attractive than an uninsured foreclosure.

A PMI insurer may pay off the entire loan and thus gain title to the property. This happens in 30 to 40 percent of all PMI defaults.

Alternatively, the insurer will pay 20 to 25 percent of the total claim. The *total claim* can include not only the outstanding mortgage balance, but also such items as accrued interest, foreclosure costs, attorney's fees, and property tax payments made after the loan is in default.

It may seem that with only 20 or 25 percent PMI coverage the lender still has considerable financial exposure, but this is not the case.

First, the original size of the loan was less than the sales value of the property. The difference between the loan amount and the selling price is represented by the purchaser's down payment.

Second, over time the buyer will reduce the original loan balance with each monthly payment. If the value of the property rises (or even if it just stays level) as the loan balance drops so does the lender's risk. For example, if a home costs $100,000 to buy and a borrower puts down $5,000, the loan-to-value ratio is 95 percent—very high. If the property is worth $120,000 five years later and the loan balance is down to $90,000, the property now has a loan-to-value ratio of 75 percent—good news for lenders.

Third, there is the possibility that the value of the property will increase over time. Again, as the gap between the loan balance and the market value of the property is enlarged, the lender has less risk.

Fourth, the property has a foreclosure value that may be equal to or greater than the outstanding loan balance plus related costs. If the foreclosure value covers 100 percent of the money due to the lender, then the lender will have no claim against the private mortgage insurer. If the foreclosure value falls short of the amount of money due to the lender, then the lender can make a claim against the insurer up to the value of the policy.

Although a private mortgage insurance premium is paid by the real estate purchaser, the lender is the policy beneficiary. This feature, as well as several others, makes private mortgage insurance and the companies that offer such policies unique. Here's why:

• Although real estate buyers pay the premiums, private mortgage insurance agreements are actually contracts between lenders and insurers. A common provision of such agreements is that lenders must foreclose when monthly payments are four months behind.

• Private mortgage insurance premiums are established at the time a policy is issued and may not be changed.

• Private mortgage insurance may be canceled by the insurer only in the event of fraud or unpaid premiums.

• Private mortgage insurance is not sold through general insurance brokers. Instead, policies are marketed directly to lenders, who then make such policies available to borrowers as a condition of granting a loan. Lenders do not and cannot collect a sales commission for the placement of private mortgage insurance.

• PMI helps lenders re-sell loans in the secondary mortgage market, an important consideration for lenders. Because of the substantial reserves private mortgage insurers are required to maintain, PMI-backed loans are regarded as secure mortgage investments. Secondary lenders such as Fannie Mae, Freddie Mac, and private pension funds have bought millions of conventional loans backed with private mortgage insurance—purchases worth billions of dollars each year.

• Private mortgage insurers benefit from inflation. The reason: inflation reduces the worth of the dollar, so it takes more cash dollars to acquire a given piece of real estate. Because mortgages are valued in terms of cash dollars, it follows that mortgage insurers face fewer claims as property values rise, regardless of whether the increase in value is a product of inflation or real economic appreciation.

• Private mortgage insurance is often mistaken for mortgage life insurance, a different product. *Mortgage life insurance* is designed to protect purchasers if they are unable to pay their mortgage as a result of disability or death.

Mortgage life insurance is available through many lenders as well as general insurance agencies. Policies obtained through lenders often name the lender as the beneficiary, while policies placed through insurance brokers allow the buyer to select the beneficiary. For further information about costs and coverage, speak with knowledgeable loan officers and insurance brokers.

Questions to Ask

How much cash down is required?

What is the current premium for the first year of a private mortgage insurance policy and for each renewal year thereafter for loans with 5 percent down, 10 percent down, and 15 percent down?

If buying a multi-year policy, how many years of coverage will the lender require? What is the one-time cost of a multi-year PMI policy? Can you add this expense to the mortgage amount you are seeking?

As a condition of obtaining a mortgage, does the lender require the purchaser to place any money in an escrow account to assure that PMI premiums are paid? If so, how much?

Ending PMI Coverage

The usual deal in lending works like this: if you put down 20 percent there is no PMI requirement—and no PMI premiums. But if you put down less than 20 percent, then PMI is required.

So far this makes sense because lenders want to reduce their risk and borrowers want to buy with less than 20 percent down. By any standard, private mortgage insurance is a legitimate, useful, valued form of coverage, a product that has allowed millions of people to buy homes with little down.

What makes less sense is the fate that awaits many borrowers who use PMI. They don't have 20 percent up front, but over time the difference between the remaining loan value and the market value of the property is 20 percent or more.

Federal rules require lenders to end PMI coverage for loans made after 1988 under certain conditions. The major requirements include:

1. Borrowers with good credit have the right to *ask* for an end to PMI coverage once their loan balance has declined 20 percent, providing the value of the property has not dropped. For example, you borrow $100,000 and the loan balance falls to $80,000.

2. Lenders *must* end PMI coverage once the loan balance has been reduced 22 percent, except if the loan is a so-called "high-cost" loan. With high-cost mortgages, lenders can maintain PMI coverage for 15 years, regardless of loan balance reductions. For example, you borrow $100,000 and the loan balance falls to $78,000 or less. The lender must cancel PMI unless you have a high-cost loan.

In truth, the federal rules will impact few borrowers. They end required PMI coverage when *initial loan amounts* are reduced by 22 percent. But the federal rules say nothing about equity. Declining loan balances coupled with rising home prices can create 20 or 22 percent equity long before loan balances are reduced to required levels.

Depending on the interest rate, the type of loan, and several other factors, it may well take eight years or more before loan balances are reduced 22 percent. The catch is that many loans are refinanced or homes sold in less time than it takes to reduce initial loan balances to the required percentages. In effect, many and perhaps most borrowers will get no relief under the federal cancellation rules.

But there is a piece of good news. If you have solid credit and the value of the property has been maintained or has risen (as shown by an appraisal—see your lender for details), many lenders will allow you to cancel PMI coverage when you have 20 percent equity. After all, the federal guidelines do not prevent lenders from acting sensibly; they merely impact those lenders who would never agree to cancel PMI premiums.

Using Piggyback Loans to Avoid PMI

There is little doubt that private mortgage insurance is among the most useful and accepted insurance products around. Mortgage insurance has made home ownership possible and plausible for millions of people who do not have the 20 percent down required for conventional loans.

But despite its utility and value, PMI comes at a cost. It is insurance, there are premiums, and not every insurance application is accepted. No less important, there are ways to avoid PMI.

We know that lenders require mortgage insurance in situations where buyers do not have enough cash for a 20 percent down payment. Seen another way, what lenders really want are first loans that represent 80 percent or less of the purchase price.

Once you have financing that represents 80 percent or less of the purchase price, lenders no longer require mortgage insurance because they believe the 20 percent gap between the purchase price and the loan will protect them in the event of default. Thus, to avoid PMI the trick is to have a first loan that represents 80 percent or less of the purchase price.

One way to get that 80 percent financing is to put up 20 percent in cash. Another approach works just as well for many borrowers: use so-called piggyback financing.

For instance, suppose McDowell has enough cash for a 10 percent down payment. To finance a $150,000 home, she will need 90 percent financing, not enough to avoid private mortgage insurance.

But suppose McDowell takes a different approach: a $120,000 first trust at 8 percent interest, a $15,000 second trust at 10 percent interest, and $15,000 in cash—what lenders call 80-10-10 financing.

To a lender this arrangement includes 80 percent financing (the $120,000 first trust), and thus there is no requirement for private mortgage insurance. There are no private mortgage insurance premiums or fees because PMI is not necessary.

Are there negatives in this deal? Several come to mind.

If McDowell borrowed 90 percent of the purchase price with a single loan, she would have to qualify for such financing. In the same manner, if she borrows 90 percent of the purchase price with two loans she will again need the income and credit necessary to borrow such money.

A second concern is the term of the second trust. The last financing most borrowers want is a short-term balloon note. Thus, it is important to ensure that the second loan continues for a long period, say at least 10 to 15 years—enough time to reduce the loan amount, refinance, or pay off the second loan.

A third issue with 80-10-10 financing and similar loans is that like all financing with little down, there is minimal equity in the property—a big problem if real estate values fall or an owner wants to obtain a home equity loan.

Another approach to the piggyback concept is the 75-15-10 loan—75 percent financing from a lender, a 15 percent second loan, and 10 percent down in cash.

Caution: As this is written, some loan sources have begun to insist on private mortgage insurance even when homes are financed on an 80-10-10 basis. Check with loan officers for details.

PMI Versus Piggyback Financing			
	Conventional	**80-10-10**	**75-15-10**
Loan Amount	$150,000.00	$150,000.00	$150,000.00
Down Payment	$30,000.00	$15,000.00	$22,500.00
First Loan	$120,000.00	$120,000.00	$112,500.00
Second Loan	$0.00	$15,000.00	$15,000.00
PMI Required	Yes	No	No

Questions to Ask

What is the prevailing interest rate for conventional financing?

Does the lender offer 80-10-10 financing or similar programs?

What are the rates and points for first and second loans under the lender's 80-10-10 program?

What is the term of the second loan? Longer is better.

Given your income, credit, debts, and down payment, would you qualify for piggyback financing?

Will the lender who supplies the first loan also supply the second? Many will.

16

No Money Down Versus All Cash

Buying real estate would certainly be much easier if no cash was required. Not only are such deals possible, they are commonplace—millions of veterans have bought property with 100 percent financing, and similar deals by non-vets are made daily.

No Money Down

Properties can be bought without cash in a number of ways. A short list of alternative approaches might include the following purchases:

1. The seller or a third party takes back a self-amortizing mortgage for the property's entire value, plus all closing costs.
2. The purchaser assumes a first trust and the seller or a third party finances the balance with a second trust; at the end of the loan term a balloon payment is due.
3. The purchaser gets a new mortgage and the owner or a third party takes back a second trust with a balloon payment.

4. The buyer assumes or gets a new first mortgage, a second trust from the seller, and a third trust from still another source.

5. The purchaser assumes a first trust or gets a new loan and trades a 1947 Rolls Royce in mint condition for the balance due.

6. The purchaser is a veteran and gets 100 percent financing with a VA-backed mortgage.

7. A rich aunt pays for the property.

8. The buyer trades a house in Tampa for the seller's home in Iowa.

9. A property is bought and—before settlement—re-sold to another buyer at a profit.

10. A property is bought and, coincidentally with settlement, a portion is sold to pay all costs above the financing.

No Money Down

Money Down	None
Loan-to-Value	100 percent
Monthly Cost	Largest possible for property
Balloon Notes	None with VA, but balloon notes are common with many no-money-down deals.
Loan Term	30 years with VA, but often far shorter with other loan formats
Pros	No-money-down deals allow borrowers to acquire property with no initial capital. Large loans mean large tax deductions for interest payments.
Cons	No-money-down deals mean high monthly mortgage bills and the possibility of huge balloon payments. Also, closing costs may be high because a large loan is being recorded.

In every case, the term *no money down* means the buyer owes money in the future, paid money in the past (for the purchase of the Rolls, the house in Tampa, the public service to earn VA benefits, or the psychological cost of an aunt's goodwill), or devalued the property by selling off a portion.

Deals with no money down make great sense in those cases where enormous balloon payments can be avoided and purchasers can afford monthly carrying costs—the precise arrangement used by the VA. The problem is that some borrowers equate the idea of "no cash" with "no responsibility." They forget that not everyone can afford high monthly mortgage payments or raise enough cash to pay off balloon notes.

No-cash financing is often used by investors, but in such cases monthly mortgage payments often exceed rentals, a situation known as *negative cash flow*. This polite term means that each and every month the investor must make cash payments to keep the property. Negative cash flow is not a serious problem for investors who can readily make up the lost money from their general income or who find that the tax and appreciation benefits of ownership offset monthly cash losses.

For example, suppose Harding buys a four-unit apartment building that produces a rental income worth $2,000 a month. Harding's costs for first and second mortgages, property taxes, repairs, maintenance, etc., total $2,250 per month. Harding thus has cash losses of $250 per month, or $3,000 a year, a sum Harding can readily pay from other income.

Where Harding benefits in this deal is that his income tax deductions for mortgage interest, property taxes, electricity, depreciation, and other items total $15,000 annually. In his tax bracket, these deductions reduce Harding's tax bill by $4,200. In addition, each month the mortgage is being paid down and so the equity in the property rises even if market values remain stagnant.

Moreover, Harding takes steps to reduce his losses. He paints the hallway and plants new shrubs to make his property more attractive. Rather than raising rents directly at first, he invests $4,000 and installs individual utility meters so that electric bills are paid directly by tenants. With the new meters in place, Harding air-conditions each unit. A year after he bought the property, Harding raises monthly rentals by $35 per unit but the tenants stay. Why? Because the property is a better place to live.

The problem is that not every Harding—or Smith or Brown—can afford $250 in cash each month. Not everyone can invest several thousand dollars in a rental property or is in an income bracket that will produce the same tax savings as Harding's.

To be successful, investment deals with no money down must be affordable in case property income does not rise, vacancies occur, or major repairs are required. Buyers must also have a clear, reasonable plan to both carry and re-pay all debt, particularly short-term balloon payments, which are a frequent feature of no-money-down investing. Without such planning, no-cash deals are a sure prescription for financial disaster.

Questions to Ask

What is the interest rate for conventional financing?

What is the interest rate for the first loan? Second loan? Third loan? Etc.

Does the no-cash deal include financing to cover the cost of closing?

Are balloon payments part of the deal? If so, when are they due and exactly how will they be re-paid?

Are you making a no-cash investment with the expectation of raising rents? If so, why is it that you will be able to raise rents, but the present owner has not? How will a rent increase affect vacancy rates?

Do you have sufficient income to cover negative cash flow?

Do you have enough capital to make repairs and cover vacancies?

Is it possible to subdivide the property? Because the property is security for at least one loan, will the lender(s) allow you to subdivide?

How will a no-cash deal affect your tax position? Speak with a tax adviser for specifics.

Is your financing assumable?

Can your financing be re-paid in whole or in part without penalty at any time?

"No-Cost" Loans Strain Belief

A down payment is not all the cash one needs to buy a home. Settlement expenses have evolved into a big-ticket item with corpulent closing costs, steep transfer taxes, and hefty reserve requirements. The result is that it's not enough to merely save for a down payment.

A number of strategies have emerged to hold down closing expenses. The state of Maryland, for example, now defers the collection of certain taxes due at closing for several months. Lenders increasingly require substantially less than the 14 months of prepaid private mortgage insurance (PMI) premiums they once sought. And in areas where values are stagnant or falling, buyers routinely seek "seller contributions" to offset closing expenses.

Now some lenders have stepped in with so-called "no-cost" and "zero-cost" financing. Get financing from a no-cost lender and closing expenses are not an issue—the lender will pay some or all of them.

This outbreak of no-cost financing is hardly evidence of lender generosity. Like unicorns and mermaids, there is no such thing as no-cost financing. No-cost financing is merely a loan arrangement where borrowing costs are moved from one place to another. Such costs must be re-paid somehow, re-payment that often takes the form of higher interest rates or bigger loan amounts.

To see how this works, consider that 30-year fixed-rate financing is available at 8 percent interest with 0 points—so-called par pricing. A borrower can also get financing at 7.75 percent with 1 point, 7.50 percent with 2 points, and 7.25 percent with 3 points.

Seen another way, if a buyer seeks $100,000 at 7.50 percent he or she will have to pay 2 points—$2,000 at closing.

No-Cost Financing			
Loan Amount	$100,000.00	$100,000.00	$100,000.00
Rate	7.5 Percent	8 Percent	8.5 Percent
Points	2 Points	0 Points	0 Points
Closing Credit from Lender	$0.00	$0.00	$2,000.00
Additional Annual Cost	$0.00	$0.00	$500.00*

*Annual interest cost declines each year as principal is reduced.

Now suppose that closing costs are $2,000. We know in this example that rate reduction of 0.5 percent is worth $2,000. Therefore if we *add* 0.5 percent to the interest rate, we can increase the value of the loan by $2,000. The lender has three ways to recapture this sum:

1. a loan with a higher interest rate—say 8.5 percent rather than 8 percent, which equals roughly $500 a year in extra interest
2. a loan that can be re-sold at a higher value (because the 8.5 percent interest rate is more attractive to mortgage buyers than a loan paying 8 percent)
3. a bigger loan, one increased by the size of the closing advance

The no-cost loan, despite its name, is not cost free. At least one state, California, reportedly bars lenders from using such terms as *no-cost* and *zero-cost* because these expressions are inherently misleading. Other states, if they have any sense, will follow suit.

If we can get past the identification issue, there is nothing inherently wrong with a loan that includes lender contributions in exchange for a higher interest rate or loan amount. We already trade less down for mortgage insurance coverage, so why not trade lower closing costs for higher rates or bigger loans?

There are three situations where loans with lender-paid closing costs make sense.

First, if you expect to be a short-term owner, then no-cost financing can be attractive. Closing fees are lost forever once paid, but higher monthly charges end once a property is sold. It should be said, however, that in the general case short-term real estate ownership is not likely to produce resale profits.

Second, if you lack cash for closing, then a no-cost loan surely has advantages.

Third, no-cost loans can be enticing when refinancing. The borrower who can go from a $200,000 mortgage at 8 percent to the same loan at 7.5 percent with no up-front costs will save roughly $1,000 per year. However, if you take out a no-cost loan where up-front costs are buried in a higher interest rate and then quickly refinance with another loan from a second lender, the first lender may have big losses. To prevent quick refinancing, some lenders now offer *no-cost financing* that just happens to include a pre-payment penalty.

A clearly explained mortgage with a *closing relief provision* (still another term for *no-cost financing*) would surely sell many homes and open home ownership to large numbers of individuals who otherwise might not be able to buy. But although more sales help everyone, let us also consider a possible downside: Loans with higher rates and less money down represent more risk for both borrowers and lenders, particularly if home values fall. Such financing must be re-paid at some point, and if a borrower sells and does not have enough equity at closing to pay the loan, additional cash will be required. If the additional cash is not available, then a borrower may well face foreclosure and bankruptcy.

Questions to Ask

What is the cost for a conventional loan?

What is the interest rate for a no-cost loan?

How much credit will you receive at closing?

How long do you intend to own the property? (The less time you own the property, the more attractive no-cost loans may become.)

Farm and Rural Loans

Although much of the United States is defined by huge cities and endless suburbs, a trip to the Cheyenne, Wyoming, rodeo shows another side of the domestic realty market: there is vacant land as far as the eye can see, as well as future home sites for a growing number of urban refugees.

Cheyenne, the capital of Wyoming, is an immaculate microcity (population 50,000) that symbolizes a different way of life—a place without subways, two-hour commutes, or soaring office towers. And the rodeo—the biggest outdoor event of its kind in the world— reminds everyone that in a high-tech society there is still no substitute for ranches, fields, and the people who work them.

In the not-too-distant future, we may well find that a steady stream of city folks (and suburban ones) will be heading to places like Cheyenne in search of a quieter lifestyle. This migration can occur today in large part because jobs are no longer localized—a growing army of people can live on the prairie, in the mountains, or by the sea and still connect with employment centers via faxes, modems, and e-mail.

In addition to a new lifestyle, rural immigrants may also discover a new world of mortgage financing. Although such common financing choices as FHA, VA, and conventional mortgages are available, there are restrictions in country settings that may be unfamiliar to city dwellers.

Many lenders, for example, will not finance property that is not habitable year-round. There must be road access 12 months a year— even if the roads are unpaved. Barns, silos, and stables are okay, but the property must be a residence rather than a working farm, ranch, or orchard.

Low- to moderate-income buyers with an interest in rural property should get in touch with the local Rural Economic and Community Development office (RECD), a part of the Agriculture Department.

The 502 Direct Lending Program—which is available only through RECD offices—allows buyers to purchase homes with no money down. However, a qualifying property cannot have more than 1,050 square feet of interior space nor can it be located in communities with more than 25,000 people. Interestingly enough, under this program, a direct loan for less than $2,500 need not be secured with a mortgage. Instead, it can be a personal loan.

The 502 Guaranteed Rural Housing Loan Program is more liberal. It allows purchasers to buy with 100 percent financing and with qualification standards that match those used for FHA loans—as much as 29 percent of gross monthly income can be used for principal, interest, taxes, and insurance (PITI). In addition, as much as 41 percent of gross monthly income can be used for all monthly debt such as credit cards, student loans, and PITI. Loan limits parallel local FHA maximums, depending on location. A one-time mortgage insurance fee of .9 percent is required, but the insurance fee may be financed over the life of the loan.

For those who want not just a residence but a working farm, ranch, or orchard, the deal is different. Although such properties may seem like real estate, they are regarded (not unreasonably) as businesses and require business financing.

RECD-guaranteed financing for as much as $300,000 is available for those who want to buy farms, are U.S. citizens or legal resident aliens, and are unable to obtain financing from commercial mortgage sources. In addition, up to $400,000 is available for *production* financing; that is, money to operate the property.

When you finance a home, no one asks if you know how to adjust the furnace or seed the yard. With a farm, the situation is different. Loan applicants first meet with a local eligibility committee, three area residents familiar with farming and credit, to discuss the loan. After passing muster, one then meets with the local RECD county supervisor.

RECD also operates a "limited-resource" farm-loan program. This program makes available as much as $200,000 to beginning farmers with agricultural training and skills but limited capital. An interesting aspect of this program is that before a loan is granted, the borrower and local RECD officers work out a "farm and home" plan, essentially a budget and management feasibility study that is required before the first seed is planted.

All-Cash Purchases

The least cumbersome way to buy real estate is to pay cash. If you've got the money, paying cash will save dollars by eliminating loan discount fees (points), mortgage application charges, and origination fees (generally 1 percent of a mortgage). Settlement costs will also be reduced, because there is no need to set aside escrow funds for the payment of taxes; FHA, VA, or private mortgage insurance (PMI); or other expenses.

But if buying a home with cash has attractive aspects, there are also problems. The most basic difficulty is that few people have the dollars needed to buy a home without financing. But even when the dollars are available, buying for cash is not always a sound financial choice. A home without a mortgage is a home without a major tax deduction. A home without a fixed-rate mortgage is a home that cannot fully profit from inflation.

Given the balance of benefits and problems, when should real estate be bought for cash? The answer depends on alternative investments and your personal preferences.

First, are you making high-interest credit payments for credit cards, cars, or furniture? If so, paying cash for property is not likely to be your best financial choice.

Second, are you about to retire? Selling a large home may generate enough dollars to buy a retirement property for cash. Buying for cash, in turn, will cut monthly living costs. If you pay cash, will you have enough income from other sources to live in the style to which you are accustomed?

Third, what is your tax situation? Check with a CPA, enrolled agent, fee-only financial planner, or tax attorney for specifics.

Fourth, what about liquidity? Traditionally it has been difficult to get cash out of a house without selling or refinancing. This tradition has changed with the ready availability of home-equity loans. Still, real estate is not a liquid investment in the sense of a savings account or mutual fund. After all, you can apply for a home-equity loan and be rejected.

Fifth, how does "investing" in a mortgage compare with such alternatives as stocks, bonds, mutual funds, and retirement plans in terms of both return and risk? Because no one knows what will happen in the future, such comparisons should be seen only as estimates (guesses?) based on what is hopefully the best evidence available today.

One attraction of paying cash for a prime residence is that you can finance the property at a later date, perhaps when rates have come down or you have a specific need for capital. However, paying cash requires some element of crystal-ball gazing. What if you pay cash today and interest rates rise? Will you qualify for all the new financing you need or want at a later date?

In considering the possibility of buying for cash now and refinancing later, be aware that there may be unhappy tax consequences arising from such an approach. In general terms, only the interest from "acquisition" financing with residential real estate is deductible, plus as much as $100,000 in a second loan. Thus, if Harris buys a $200,000 home for cash and 10 months later obtains a $150,000 mortgage, it may well be that only interest on the first $100,000 in debt is deductible. See a tax pro for details.

Paying cash for real estate is a strategy that insures control over real estate dollars. Some people who never pay cash for investment property have homes free and clear of any debt. Why? Because home ownership—as distinct from investment real estate—implies certain psychological values. It may be that buying for cash is not a sound financial choice in many cases, but it is an alternative that some people find more comforting than high rates of return.

Questions to Ask

What is the prevailing interest rate for conventional mortgages in your community?

What is the current return you can expect from the conservative investment of your funds?

What are the tax implications of an all-cash purchase?

What are the tax implications if you buy for cash and later finance?

Do you anticipate reduced income as a result of retirement in the next decade?

Do you expect to move to smaller housing within the next 10 years?

Do you believe that home mortgage rates will generally rise or fall from current levels over the next several years?

As a matter of personal preference, would you want to own a home that is free and clear of all mortgage debt? Although this may not be the best choice in terms of dollars and percentages, it is a choice that comforts many people.

17

SECOND LOANS

WE USUALLY THINK of a real estate transaction this way: one deal, one loan. However, some transactions involve two loans, a first trust or mortgage and a second trust or mortgage.

The use of two loans can create both important financial advantages and more than a few complications. For instance, if there is more than one loan and a buyer defaults, which lender gets paid first?

An order of re-payment among private lenders is established in the loan papers created between property owners and lenders. Claims will be fully settled in the order recorded; that is, the claims of the first-mortgage holder will be completely repaid before any claims by a second-loan holder are addressed. In turn, the claims of the second-loan holder must be fully satisfied before the debt of a third lender can be addressed, and so on.

The catch for *junior loan holders* is that there may not be any cash remaining once prior claims have been satisfied. Second loans and mortgages thus represent more risk than first loans and therefore command higher interest rates. Here's an example:

A home is bought for $150,000, and Cleveland, the buyer, knows he can get a conventional, 30-year loan for $125,000 at 7 percent interest. The rest of the money will come from Cleveland, who has

Cleveland's Loans	
Purchase Price	$150,000.00
Cash Down	$10,000.00
First Loan	$125,000.00 at 7 Percent Interest
First Loan Term	30 Years
First Loan Payment	$831.63
Second Loan	$15,000.00 at 9 Percent
Second Loan Term	5 Years
Second Loan Payment	$311.37
Total Monthly Payment	$1,143.00
Balloon Payment	None in This Example

$10,000 in cash, and a $15,000 loan at 9 percent from Uncle Bob. It's agreed that Uncle Bob's loan will be in the form of a five-year second mortgage secured by the property.

Cleveland, with Uncle Bob's money in hand, gets a first mortgage for $125,000 from a lender. After two years, Cleveland defaults and the property is sold at foreclosure for $120,000. The first-mortgage holder takes the $120,000 and sues Cleveland for the unpaid balance and foreclosure costs. As for Uncle Bob, he gets nothing and seems grumpy at family affairs.

In this example, the first-loan holder has no incentive to sell the property for more than $125,000 plus foreclosure costs. And although a second-loan lender may foreclose in the event of default, triggering a foreclosure may result in no re-payment—one reason second lenders charge high rates.

It is possible that a junior loan can resemble a first mortgage in all particulars, but this is not likely. In a typical situation, several distinctions are common:

• **Loan Term.** Although conventional loans last 30 years, second mortgages and trusts are generally for a shorter term, say 2 to 10 years, with many being 5 years or less. If you are a borrower, you want the longest possible term because long terms mean lower monthly payments for self-amortizing loans and more time to refinance if a balloon payment is due when the loan ends. A *balloon note* features a huge final payment due at the end of the loan term.

• **Amortization and Monthly Payments.** Because second loans have a short term, they can only be self-amortizing if they have large payments. For example, a 30-year $85,000 loan at 7 percent interest requires monthly principal and interest payments of $575.59. A 10-year, 7 percent self-amortizing loan for this amount requires monthly payments of $1,057.96, and a five-year note will call for payments of $1,854.85 per month.

Instead of being self-amortizing, however, second financing is likely to feature relatively small monthly payments. Such payments have two effects: they make the loan affordable to a borrower, and they likely create a balloon note. Indeed, if the interest rate is sufficiently high and the monthly payments are sufficiently low, the balloon payment can be larger than the original debt.

• **Coverage.** With conventional loans, the purchaser typically makes a 20 percent down payment in cash, while a lender puts up the rest of the sale value in the form of a mortgage. With a second loan, the buyer usually needs less cash to close. For example, if a buyer puts down 10 percent of the purchase price in cash and gets a second loan for 15 percent, then the balance of the purchase price, 75 percent, can be financed with a conventional loan. The attraction of this arrangement, sometimes called a *piggyback loan*, is that no PMI is required.

In those situations where a seller or other party takes back a second loan, lenders will often accept such arrangements as long as the buyer is financially qualified to make both first and second loan payments. Some lenders, however, will not make loans where second loans are involved. Others will make loans, but only if buyers put down at least 5 to 10 percent of the purchase price with their own money.

Questions to Ask

What is the interest rate for conventional financing?

What is the interest rate for second loans?

Can you get a lengthy second loan, say 10 or 15 years? (If you're a buyer, the longer the better.)

Will second loan financing involve a balloon payment? If so, how large a balloon?

If you are getting a new first mortgage will the lender allow second loan financing? This is a question that must be answered *before* making a purchase offer.

How to Cut Housing Costs with Second Loans

Second loans can be regarded as a kind of financial ball of putty, loans that can be stretched, compressed, pulled, and flattened into any shape acceptable to both borrower and lender. In those cases where the seller becomes a lender by taking back a second loan, second loans can be molded to favor either buyer or seller.

Imagine a situation where the prevailing rate of interest for a conventional loan is 7 percent while second loans are available for 9 percent interest. In a particular sale, a property is sold for $200,000. By adjusting the cost, size, and terms of a second loan, different results—and advantages—can be produced from a single core transaction.

• **Case One.** The property is sold for $200,000, and a lender puts up $160,000 at 7 percent for a first loan. The seller takes back a $16,000 second loan at 9 percent interest, and the buyer puts up the balance ($24,000) in cash. In this illustration there is market financing for both the first and second loans, and 80 percent of the deal is financed so there is no PMI. This is an essentially neutral deal for the buyer or seller, assuming the property has a market value of $200,000.

• **Case Two.** The property is sold for $200,000, and a lender puts up $160,000 at 7 percent interest for a first loan. The seller takes back a $16,000 second loan at 7 percent and the buyer pays the $24,000 balance in cash. Here the buyer has an advantage because the interest charge on the second loan is less than the pre-vailing market rate for such financing.

• **Case Three.** The property is sold for $200,000, and a lender puts up $160,000 at 7 percent for a first loan. The seller provides a $40,000 second loan at 12 percent. In this example, the buyer is trading costlier financing for the opportunity to purchase property with no money down. This scenario works for buyers with enough income to support large monthly loan payments and who are in the upper tax brackets, a factor that partially offsets higher mortgage costs. The seller here is getting $160,000 in cash from the first mortgage plus a note with an above-market interest rate, a good deal for owners who don't immediately need cash from the second loan, $40,000 in this illustration.

Second loans can be manipulated in terms of size as well as interest. It often happens that a buyer or seller has an intense ego commitment to a particular dollar figure. For example, a seller may want $200,000 for a given property, not because the home is worth that much but because the owner feels the $200,000 figure conveys a certain social status. Similarly, a buyer may not want to purchase real estate for more than a particular dollar value, say $195,000.

• **Case Four.** A property is sold for $200,000, and a lender finances $160,000 with a mortgage. The buyer is willing to pay the $200,000 price, which he feels is excessive, but only if the deal can be negotiated further. In this instance the buyer asks for, and gets, a $30,000 second loan from the seller at 6 percent interest and pays $10,000 in cash at settlement. The true economic value of this transaction is less than the recorded price of $200,000 indicates because the interest rate on the second loan has been discounted.

• **Case Five.** A home is marketed for $200,000, but a buyer will only offer $195,000, his "limit." The seller agrees to a deal with a $140,000 first loan from a local lender, $10,000 in cash from the buyer, and a $45,000 second loan at 16 percent interest held by the seller. The buyer has not exceeded his paper limit, but the value of this package is worth more to the seller than a cash deal for $195,000 because the second loan has an inflated interest rate.

• **Case Six.** A home is sold for $200,000 and financed with $20,000 in cash from the purchaser, $160,000 from a local lender, and a 3-year $20,000 second loan from the seller at 12 percent interest. The catch: the buyer must re-pay or refinance the second loan in three years or else face foreclosure. The buyer has enough equity in this deal (the $20,000) to make foreclosure attractive.

To negotiate second loan alternatives it is necessary to calculate the costs, benefits, and disadvantages for each loan arrangement. One useful way to make such comparisons is to create a chart showing monthly payments, the length of the loan, the loan's total cost (the number of payments times the monthly expense less the principal amount), any balloon payment, etc. Using such a chart will allow you to compare second loan alternatives to see which is best for you.

Sellers as Take-Back Lenders

The concept of real estate financing usually implies that an institution such as a savings and loan association, mortgage banker, mortgage broker, credit union, or bank will somehow be involved in the mortgage process. However, sometimes second mortgages are seller *take-backs*, direct arrangements between buyers and sellers in which sellers make loans to purchasers and thus assume a new role, that of lender.

The rules governing second loans are established in the jurisdiction where the property is located. Different jurisdictions have vastly different approaches to second loans, and both buyers and sellers should investigate such financing with care *before ratifying a real estate sales agreement* where the obligation to create a seller takeback can be found. Here are the major areas to consider:

• **Interest.** What is the proposed rate of interest? Many states have usury laws that establish maximum rates of interest for various kinds of financing. If the interest rate exceeds the usury level, the lender may suffer severe penalties. In some cases, a distinction is made between the rates permitted for residential second loans and for loans that are part of an investment purchase, so the loan's purpose may influence the rate allowed. See an attorney for details.

• **Payment.** Second loans are usually designed so that borrowers can make relatively small monthly payments. These payments, plus the short term that second loans generally feature, mean that a balloon payment is required when the loan ends. Buyers and sellers should ask several questions to avoid problems: how large is the monthly payment? How large is the balloon payment? Where, specifically, will the borrower get the money to re-pay the balloon payment? By refinancing? Savings?

• **Format.** Standardized real estate contracts commonly call for loan agreements to be "in the lender's usual form." This means lenders get to make the rules. If you are a seller/lender, then surely you should insist on the same right and have your attorney draw up or approve all loan documents.

• **Servicing.** Commercial loan payments can be made at the institution where the loan originated, by mail, or electronically from one commercial lender to another. But what about loans made by property owners? In many cases, borrowers simply mail monthly payments to second-loan holders, a system that may be disrupted

Sellers as Second Lenders			
	Deal 1	Deal 2	Deal 3
Sales Price	_____	_____	_____
Cash Down	_____	_____	_____
First Loan	_____	_____	_____
Interest Rate	_____	_____	_____
Term in Years	_____	_____	_____
Monthly Payments	_____	_____	_____
Second Loan	_____	_____	_____
Interest Rate	_____	_____	_____
Term in Years	_____	_____	_____
Monthly Payments	_____	_____	_____
Total Monthly Payments for Both Loans	_____	_____	_____
Balloon Payment	_____	_____	_____
Points	_____	_____	_____

if payments are delayed or lost in the mail. To assure that payments are received in a timely manner, it may be best to make payments to a local lender who can date and verify the payment and then forward the money to the second-loan holder. For more information about establishing such accounts, speak to officers at local savings and loan associations or banks.

• **Insurance.** Sellers making second loans should be concerned with two insurance issues:

1. Commercial lenders insist on title insurance, of which they are the beneficiary, to at least the value of their loan so they will be protected in the event title to the property is faulty. Junior note holders often require similar protection so they can be re-paid in the event of a title dispute.

2. Commercial lenders routinely require property owners to maintain adequate fire, theft, and liability insurance. Seller/lenders should also get copies of the original policy (at settlement) as well as updates showing that the policy remains in force during the loan term and that timely premium payments are being made.

• **Continuation.** If a situation develops where a borrower cannot re-pay a balloon note, serious questions arise for both the buyer and seller/lender. Should the property be foreclosed? Is there a way the note can be refinanced or extended? Sometimes the government steps into such situations. For instance, in Maryland, certain borrowers who made balloon notes after July 1, 1982, may unilaterally extend the term of their notes for up to two years, a situation that means that monthly payments will continue but the balloon payment is postponed.

• **Default of the First Trust.** Because first and second mortgage holders are often paid separately, the maker of one note may not know if payments on the other loan have been missed. Many second loans contain a provision so that they are automatically in default if the first mortgage is not properly paid.

• **Exceptions.** The rules that generally apply to lenders may not apply to self-sellers. For instance, is a seller take-back a loan? It sure seems like a loan, but *some lawyers argue that there is no loan because no cash was provided to the borrower*, and, therefore, usury limitations and other rules don't apply.

- **Taxes.** Seller/lenders will certainly want to know that property taxes are being paid in a full and timely manner, and loan documents may require borrowers to present proof of payment.

- **Trustees.** If the junior note is a "loan" and not a "mortgage," then the seller/lender should have the right to name the trustee or trustees. If the trustees change, then certain notices may be required for the borrower.

- **Credit.** The willingness of an owner to hold a second loan should be contingent on a review, satisfactory to the seller/lender, of the borrower's finances and credit. A seller/lender should have the right to see a borrower's credit report and two or three past tax returns as well. It may be wise to have all credit information evaluated by a CPA.

The areas above clearly suggest that second loans contain a host of potential traps for the unwary. To avoid needless difficulties, it is essential for seller/lenders—and borrowers—to consult with an attorney familiar with such financing in the jurisdiction where the property is located *before* agreeing to any sale arrangement that includes a seller take-back.

Questions to Ask

What is the rate of interest for conventional financing?

What is the interest rate on savings accounts and money market funds?

What interest rate is available if you make a second loan?

What is the usury rate in the jurisdiction where the property is located?

Will the second loan be a self-amortizing loan, or will it require a balloon payment?

What portion of the purchase price is in the form of cash from the buyer?

Are there restrictions that limit the use of a second loan in your transaction? Speak to an attorney for complete advice.

Can you as a seller/lender meet your financial needs in the event your borrower fails to make timely payments?

Can you as a seller/lender meet your financial needs in the event your borrower stops making all payments?

Can you as a seller/lender meet your financial needs if you must spend several thousand dollars in a foreclosure procedure?

Can you as a seller/lender meet future obligations, perhaps a balloon payment of your own, if your borrower fails to make his or her balloon payment to you?

Does the buyer have a unilateral right to continue the note and delay a balloon payment? Does this type of regulation govern balloon notes in your area? If you are a seller, how will the deferral of a balloon payment affect your personal finances? Would such a regulation make a second loan unworkable?

What will a local lender charge to service your loan?

What are the tax implications of deferred payments? Speak to a CPA, enrolled agent, or tax attorney for complete information.

How to Save $100,000 with Second Loans

Second loans can be used effectively both to acquire real estate and refinance property. When compared with 30-year conventional loans, second loans are often a cost bargain even when they have higher interest rates.

Second loans can be surprisingly cheap in terms of actual interest costs because they have short terms. Combined with an assumable first loan in a sale, or added to an existing loan when refinancing, second loans can save borrowers thousands of dollars in many cases. The catch is that such savings may not be affordable.

Suppose Hansen has an assumable 7 percent mortgage. He needs $45,000 to pay his daughter's college tuition, and so he looks at refinancing alternatives. The Hansen home is worth $200,000; the present mortgage balance is $100,000 and has 15 remaining years. The original loan amount was $135,525, and the monthly payment is $901.65.

Hansen can go out and refinance the entire property by getting a $145,000 loan at the current rate, also 7 percent in this example. That loan will require 360 payments of $964.69 each. Or, Hansen can get a $45,000 second loan at 9 percent interest. If this is a 10-year second loan, 120 monthly payments of $570.04 will be needed for a self-amortizing loan—on top of the $901.65 for the existing first loan.

Hansen's Loan Refinancing Options		
	New Loan	**Old Loan and Second Trust**
Original Loan Amount	$0.00	$135,525.00
Current Loan Balance	$0.00	$100,000.00
Current Payment	$0.00	$901.65
New Financing	$145,000.00	$45,000.00
Interest Rate	7 Percent	9 Percent
New Monthly Payment	$964.69	$570.04
Remaining Old Monthly Payment	$0.00	$901.65
Total New Monthly Payment	$964.69	$1,471.69 for 10 Years, $901.65 for 5 Years
Remaining Interest on the Original Loan	$0.00	$61,984.15
New Financing Interest	$202,288.00	$23,405.09
Total Interest	$202,288.00	$85,389.24
Savings	$0.00	$116,838.76

If Hansen refinances totally, he trades the 15 years remaining on his current loan for 30-year financing. The longer term means borrowed money is outstanding longer and so interest costs are higher.

If he keeps the current loan, he has 15 years remaining. He will also have a 10-year second loan. The result of the old loan–second loan combo is that Hansen can save more than $116,000 when compared with new financing—but he will pay an additional $507 a month for 10 years, something not everyone can afford.

Could Hansen make more money by taking the longer, bigger loan and then using his monthly savings for investments or to pay down high-cost bills? There's no certain answer, but no doubt a lot of people will look at that monthly payment represented by the old mortgage–second loan combo and prefer to keep nearly $507 a month in their pocket—and ultimately pay more than $116,000 in excess interest.

18

ASSUMPTIONS

THE LARGEST SINGLE source of below-market financing is the multi-billion-dollar pool of existing mortgages, loans where payments may be continued by new owners. Known broadly as *assumable* mortgages, such financing is available in every community and represents a source of significant dollar savings for many purchasers. An assumable loan situation can look like this:

Mr. Pace likes a $100,000 house in the country and offers to buy the property with $5,000 down. The sale also includes assuming a first trust with a $70,000 balance and getting a $25,000 second trust from the seller.

The reason Pace wants to assume the first trust is that it has a 6 percent interest rate. His payments on the note will total only $532.10 per month, and the loan has a little more than 18 years to go. (The original loan was for $88,750.)

The second trust, a 10-year, self-amortizing note at 9 percent interest, costs $316.69 per month.

As an alternative, Pace can get a 30-year $95,000 first trust at 7 percent interest with monthly payments of $632.04. Although the assumption–second trust arrangement costs $216.75 extra per month when compared to new financing, Pace will save $74,777.15 by using the combined financing package.

Pace's Loan Options

	New Loan	Assumption
Sale Price	$100,000.00	$100,000.00
Down Payment	$5,000.00	$5,000.00
New Loan	$95,000.00	$0.00
Second Loan	$0.00	$25,000.00
Assumable Loan	$0.00	$70,000.00
Monthly Payment	$632.04	$848.79
Excess Monthly Payment	$0.00	$216.75
Interest Savings	$0.00	$74,777.15

Assumable mortgages offer three major advantages to borrowers like Pace.

First, assumable mortgages offer the possibility of below-market financing. When you can take over a loan with 6 percent interest in a 7 percent market, you're ahead.

Second, buyers who might otherwise be frozen out of the real estate market by high interest rates can often find affordable housing when they locate property with assumable financing. Sometimes rates 1, 2, and even 3 percent below prevailing interest levels are available.

Third, assumable mortgages produce faster equity growth. In their first years, monthly mortgage payments are heavily tilted toward interest costs and only a limited number of dollars remain to reduce the principal balance of a loan. Over time, the balance between interest payments and principal reductions changes, with more and more money going to pay down the debt.

Because loans are typically assumed several years after they originate, buyers who assume benefit from larger equity reductions each month. For example, a 30-year $70,000 mortgage at 8 percent interest will require monthly payments of $513.64. Of this amount, only $46.97 will be used to reduce the principal balance in the first month. If such a loan were assumed after 60 payments, the monthly cost would be the same but the principal reduction would rise to $69.52.

As loans age they have smaller remaining principal balances, so buyers will need more cash or secondary financing to obtain such loans. A $100,000 home may well have an assumable loan at 6 percent interest but the principal balance may be just $20,000. To buy this property a purchaser will have to come up with $80,000 in cash, loans, or both—financing that is not available to everyone.

Although low interest assumptions are clearly something for which buyers should search, the benefits of assumable financing are not always certain.

Consider a situation where a property is available for $100,000. There is a $50,000 assumable first trust at 8 percent. The buyer has $20,000 in cash and asks the seller to take back a $30,000 second trust. The seller will do this, but only if the buyer pays 11 percent interest.

If accepted, the result of this arrangement will be a blended overall interest rate of 9.13 percent. The question is whether the combined rate and high monthly payment required for the two loans is a better deal than simply refinancing on a conventional basis.

In addition to comparing interest rates and monthly payments, financing costs must also be weighed. Is there a modest assumption fee or is a large payment required? How does the expense of an assumption compare with the expense of new financing, including loan application fees, points, and origination costs?

The element of time must be considered when comparing assumptions with alternative financing arrangements. An assumed mortgage plus a second trust may have higher monthly costs than a new conventional loan, but the combination package may have a term that is considerably shorter. If you intend to hold property for many years, the higher payments (if affordable) may actually be a bargain if there are fewer of them.

Questions to Ask

What is the assumable loan's remaining mortgage balance?

What is the assumable loan's interest rate?

What is the assumable loan's remaining term?

How much cash is required to take over an assumption?

What is the prevailing interest rate for conventional financing?

What is the prevailing interest rate for a second trust?

How large is the assumption fee?

In comparison, what is the cost of new financing in terms of a loan origination fee, points, title insurance, legal fees, etc.?

Is lender approval required for an assumption?

Where to Find Assumable Loans

For many years home loans were "freely-assumable"—anyone could assume a loan regardless of their income or credit. But in the late 1970s lenders began to restrict the assumability of new loans. New mortgages made in the "lender's usual form" began to commonly include a due-on-sale clause (also known as an *alienation clause*). Such clauses said either the entire loan would be immediately payable if the property was sold, or the mortgage could be assumed by a new borrower—but only with the lender's consent.

And what must one do to get the lender's consent? In many cases lenders will not agree to assumptions under any conditions, although in other situations lenders will approve assumptions when interest rates are raised, new fees are charged, or both.

In addition to the lender's consent, there is also a related issue: is the original borrower released from the debt? In other words, when loans were freely-assumable the original borrower was responsible for re-paying the entire debt. Today, if a new borrower is approved by the lender, then the original borrower should be *released* from the debt. This means if the loan is defaulted, the original borrower is not responsible for the debt. Original borrowers should always require in writing from lenders, that as a condition of a qualified assumption they are released from liability. Speak with your attorney for details.

Although new mortgages routinely contain due-on-sale clauses, the pool of loans that are assumable encompasses millions of mortgages. Here, in general terms, is a catalog of loans that are commonly assumable:

• FHA **Mortgages.** Traditionally one of the most important sources of assumable financing, most FHA loans made prior to December 14, 1989, are freely-assumable. FHA loans made after December 15, 1989, can only be assumed by qualified owner-occupants. Investors need not apply.

• VA **Mortgages.** VA loans issued before March 1, 1988, are freely-assumable. Loans made after March 1, 1988, are qualified assumptions, and would-be purchasers must pass muster with both the lender and the VA before such financing can be assumed. Although only veterans can originate loans under the VA program, both vets and non-vets can assume VA financing.

• **Silent Loans.** Conventional loans not containing due-on-sale clauses should be freely-assumable at their original rates and terms.

• **Due-on-Sale Loans.** In some circumstances a lender may elect not to enforce a due-on-sale clause. For instance, if the loan has a 9 percent interest rate and the prevailing interest level is 7 percent, then the lender will logically want the loan to continue. When a loan has a due-on-sale clause that the lender elects to ignore, be certain to obtain a clear, written statement from the lender noting that the loan can be assumed and detailing all conditions.

• ARMs. Adjustable-rate mortgages (ARMs) are commonly assumable at current rates by qualified buyers.

• **Estates.** When a borrower dies and the property is willed to a relative who lives on the property, the heir may assume the loan at the original rates and terms.

• **Divorce.** In divorces, if the property has five or few dwelling units, lenders cannot use a due-on-sale clause to prevent one spouse from giving title to the other. However, the lender cannot be required to release a loan co-signer.

• **State Bans.** In some jurisdictions, due-on-sale clauses may be prohibited under certain conditions. For specific information, contact a knowledgeable real estate attorney in the jurisdiction where the property is located.

• **Consent Loans.** In those instances when a loan assumption requires the lender's consent, such consent may be given in exchange for an interest increase, fees, and new paperwork.

The question with assumed loans is whether they make sense for new borrowers when compared with new mortgages. Borrowers need to look at such issues as interest rates, cash required to close the transaction, points, closing costs, and application fees.

Questions to Ask

Is the loan freely-assumable?

If the loan is assumable, is there an assumption fee? (As a matter of negotiation, try to get the other party to pay this cost or at least share this expense.)

If there is a due-on-sale clause, will it be enforced? If no, get a letter from the lender confirming this arrangement.

What actions will be required to satisfy a lender whose "consent" is needed for an assumption? Will interest levels rise? Are new mortgage papers required?

If a loan is assumed with the lender's consent, is the original borrower released in writing from liability?

Assumptions Versus *Subject to* Financing

Although the term *assumption* is used generally to describe mortgages passed from seller to buyer, more specific definitions are required to resolve an important issue: Who is responsible to the lender if loan payments are missed?

To determine the precise obligations of buyer and seller one must see if a property has been purchased subject to the mortgage or if the loan has been assumed.

In those cases where property is purchased *subject to* the mortgage, it is understood that the new owner is *not* responsible to the lender for the loan's repayment. If payments are not made by the new borrower, the lender will seek compensation from the original borrower. Although the buyer may have little direct responsibility to re-pay the loan, it would take a truly irrational person not to recognize that default means foreclosure, the loss of any equity invested in the property, and the total improbability of new mortgage borrowing in the near future. These are powerful financing considerations that no purchaser can reasonably overlook.

When mortgages are assumed, the buyer agrees to be responsible for the entire debt and the lender can pursue *both* the original borrower and the purchaser in case of default.

Lenders may not be able to prevent the take-over of freely-assumable mortgages, but they are also not required to release original borrowers from their obligation to re-pay loans. After all, if sellers could merely pass on the responsibility to re-pay mortgage debts, it would be a simple matter to hurt the lender. Here's what can happen in the worst case.

Wainwright bought a property 10 years ago for $100,000 that was financed with $20,000 in cash and a freely-assumable $80,000 mortgage. Because of flooding—and a lack of flood insurance—the value of Wainwright's property has dropped substantially, and to reduce his loss, Wainwright sells his home to a vagrant who agrees to assume the original loan. The vagrant makes no payments, and the lender soon forecloses. The mortgage balance is $75,000, the foreclosure value is only $40,000, and so the lender suffers a loss of $35,000 plus foreclosure expenses. Because the loan was freely assumable, the lender is stuck.

How much liability, in real terms, do original borrowers have when a loan is assumed or payments are continued "subject to"? The overwhelming majority of all mortgages are never in default, so there is only the most limited possibility that a lender will need to pursue an original borrower for compensation. Even when a loan is defaulted, original borrowers still benefit from several practical considerations.

First, the property's innate value is generally far greater than the balance of assumed financing.

Second, in sales where buyers make strong down payments, the probability of default is limited because purchasers have a big stake in the property. *With assumptions, seller take-backs, and no-money down deals, it is sellers who have big risks.*

Third, there are some who argue that it is a good strategy to remain liable for a mortgage. If the buyer defaults, it is suggested, it may be possible to get the property back at discount by repurchasing it from a buyer faced with foreclosure.

Whether or not it will be possible for original borrowers to get a release depends on the lender's policies. Lenders have little incentive to release original borrowers except in those cases where mortgage terms can be structured more favorably in their behalf. Several incentives may encourage lenders to release original borrowers:

• **Higher Interest.** A lender may authorize a release for the original borrower if the interest rate on the loan can be raised.

• **Buyer Qualification.** Lenders have a clear and understandable desire to ensure that new borrowers will be credit-worthy individuals. Raising interest rates is a useless exercise if the new borrower cannot afford monthly mortgage payments.

• **New Papers.** In some instances, lenders will release original borrowers if they can issue a new mortgage, called *new papers*, with the exact same terms as the first loan. A new mortgage, rather than a mere continuation of the old loan, will generate additional fees to the lender.

In certain cases, new papers may be profoundly important. When a loan is used to acquire real estate, such financing is known as a *purchase money mortgage*. If that loan is replaced with new papers, we have a refinancing and something other than a purchase money mortgage.

In California, for example, if a borrower defaults on a purchase money mortgage for a principal residence, the lender cannot seek a "deficiency judgment" for the unpaid balance. Without a deficiency judgment, the lender cannot go after other assets and income the borrower may hold. However, if the loan is refinanced, there is no longer a purchase money mortgage, and the lender can seek a deficiency judgment.

For details, please consult a local attorney. And be aware that even if a lender cannot obtain a deficiency judgment, a borrower's credit can be ruined for many years by a foreclosure action.

• **Fees.** Assumption fees are charges made by lenders to cover the cost of processing new paperwork. However, some lenders undoubtedly see such charges as profit centers and exact substantial payments to permit an assumption.

When considering an assumption, be certain to get all details and requirements in writing from the lender.

Questions to Ask

If you are a buyer, are you assuming old financing or purchasing property subject to an existing loan?

Is a release from the lender necessary to have an assumption?

If you are a seller and your loan is assumable, can you get a release? Get release information in writing from the lender.

What are the lender's release policies?

19

ADJUSTABLE RATE
MORTGAGES (ARMS)

WE KNOW THAT a conventional fixed-rate loan is a form of debt with few surprises. Such mortgages have a single interest rate and a monthly payment established when the loan is first signed. When the loan term is finished, nothing is owed to the lender.

But suppose we say that because interest rates rise and fall, why shouldn't loan rates? Why must rates be fixed? And if rates move up and down, then why shouldn't monthly payments be equally flexible?

Welcome to the adjustable-rate mortgage (ARM), a form of financing that offers more risk for borrowers (because rates and costs can climb in the future) in exchange for easier qualification standards and lower initial interest costs than might be available with stodgy fixed-rate loans.

How do ARMs really work? Here are the factors to consider.

• **Start Rate.** The initial rate of interest is generally below conventional financing levels. Lower initial interest rates allow buyers to qualify more easily for ARM financing, a major advantage. The initial interest rate—known in the lending industry as the *teaser rate*—can be in effect for as long as several years or as little time as a few months.

- **Interest Rate.** Once the initial rate lapses, interest is then computed with a two-part formula that includes both an *index* and a *margin*. Common indexes include:

  - Treasury securities such as those with 6-month, 1-year, 3-year, and 5-year terms. Lenders use a floating average to obtain rates, an approach that tends to moderate interest levels.
  - The London Interbank Offer Rate (LIBOR) is used as an index for some ARMS. The LIBOR reflects Eurodollar borrowing costs for five British lenders.
  - The Federal Home Loan Bank of San Francisco publishes the 11th District Cost of Funds Index, or the 11th District COFI (pronounced "coffee"). This index reflects the borrowing costs of approximately 200 savings and loan associations in California, Nevada, and Arizona. Used nationwide, this index is widely regarded as the most stable index, the one least likely to rise rapidly but also the one least likely to fall quickly.

The interest rate, as mentioned earlier, includes both an *index* and a *margin*. We can see how the index changes up or down, but that is not the case with a margin. A margin, perhaps 2 or 3 percent,

---

Indexes Move, Margins Stay Put

Here's how an ARM with a 2.5 percent margin can move from 8.5 percent interest to 7.5 percent interest.

Index Level, Year One	6.0 Percent
Margin	2.5 Percent
Total Rate	8.5 Percent
Index Level, Year Two	5.0 Percent
Margin	2.5 Percent
Total Rate	7.5 Percent

stays the same throughout the life of the loan. Let's look at how the combination of the index and margin result in the interest rate.

Suppose we have an index at 6 percent and a 2.5 percent margin. The interest rate will be equal to 8.5 percent (6 percent plus 2.5 percent). If the index falls to 5 percent, the interest rate will drop to 7.5 percent (5 percent plus 2.5 percent).

• **Qualifying Rate.** When borrowers apply for fixed-rate financing, they're qualified according to the loan's interest rate. With an ARM, lenders have different policies for different loans. Many qualify borrowers on the basis of the interest rate for the loan's second year. Still other lenders add 1 percent to the start rate to determine a qualifying rate.

• **Rate Changes.** Depending how the loan is written, a lender may have the right to change the interest rate as often as every month. Most ARM contracts, however, allow the lender to change the rate once every six months or once a year. *The fact that the interest rate changes does not necessarily mean that monthly payments will rise or fall, because payment changes may be restricted to once a year or once every six months.*

• **Rate Caps.** An ARM may provide for an absolute cap on the maximum interest rate that can be charged, say 5 or 6 percentage points above the start rate. Conversely, there is likely to be an interest rate minimum.

• **Monthly Payment Caps.** Many ARMs have payment caps that limit monthly cost increases or decreases. For example, if a loan has a 7.5 percent annual payment cap and the monthly cost is $500, then if interest rates go up, monthly payments can only rise to $537.50 ($500 plus 7.5 percent of $500 equals $537.50).

• **Negative Amortization.** Some ARMs allow negative amortization, a concept that works this way: Suppose monthly payments are set at $500, but suppose also that interest rates rise to a point where paying off the loan requires monthly payments of $575. With a 7.5 percent payment cap, a borrower would only need to pay $537.50. What about the missing $37.50? ($575 less $537.50 = $37.50)

If negative amortization is allowed, the additional $37.50 will be added to the borrower's debt.

• **Negative Amortization Prohibited.** Most ARMs do not permit negative amortization. If rising interest rates mean that a borrower "should" pay $575 a month but the payment cap limits the monthly payment to $537.50, then any amount above $537.50 is simply uncollectible if "neg am" loans, as they are called, are not allowed.

• **Principal Cap.** In loans with negative amortization, it is possible to increase the debt. How much can it increase? Neg am loans often have a principal cap that limits debt increases to 125 percent of the original loan amount. For example, if the original loan amount was $90,000 and the balance rises to $112,500 over many years because of negative amortization, the borrower will have to make a lump-sum payment to keep below the cap, refinance the property with another loan, or sell.

• **Loan Term.** Because it is possible that the size of the loan balance may increase when negative amortization is allowed, many neg am ARM loans have a built-in extension provision. With the lender's approval, it is usually possible to extend the loan term from 30 to 40 years. The advantage of a loan extension is that it may eliminate the need to refinance the property.

• **Pre-Payment.** Because ARM loans reflect current interest costs, a lender will not lose money if a loan is re-paid early. For this reason, ARMs can usually be re-paid in whole or in part without penalty.

• **Assumptions.** ARMs are generally assumable by qualified buyers.

With all its specialized provisions and clauses, an ARM may seem unusually complex. In practice, however, such loans are not hard to follow. Here's an example:

Willoughby is looking for a $100,000 mortgage. A local lender offers either an 8 percent, fixed-rate, conventional mortgage (a good rate at the time) or an ARM with the following terms:

• The loan will have an initial interest level of 5 percent for six months, the so-called teaser rate.

Willoughby's ARM Versus 8 Percent Financing

	ARM	Conventional
Loan Amount	$100,000.00	$100,000.00
Loan Term	30 to 40 Years	30 Years
Initial Interest Rate	5 Percent	8 Percent
Initial Monthly Payment	$536.82	$733.76
Term of Initial Payment	6 Months	360 Months
Frequency of Payment Changes	Annual	None
Maximum Interest Rate	11 Percent	8 Percent
Minimum Interest Rate	4 Percent	8 Percent
Possible Negative Amortization	No	No

- The loan will use an index based on the average weekly yield for one-year U.S. Treasury bills, an index published in most major newspapers.
- The margin will be 2.5 points above the index.
- The lender can change the interest rate and monthly payment schedule once a year. The maximum payment increase after the teaser period is limited to 7.5 percent per year. In other words if the monthly payment is $600 today, it cannot rise to more than $645 ($600 × 7.5 percent) when the payments are changed next year.
- The loan does not permit negative amortization.
- The maximum yearly interest increase is 2 percentage points annually. The maximum *lifetime* interest rate is 11 percent, and the minimum is 4 percent.

What happens with this loan? In the first six months Willoughby has regular mortgage payments for principal and interest of $536.82. Once the teaser period is finished, the loan balance is $99,271.53 and the interest rate goes to 7 percent. Payments rise to $663.77 per month.

The next year inflation raises the index to 5 percent, which means Willoughby must pay 7.5 percent interest (5 percent plus the 2.5 percent margin). Her monthly payments on the new loan balance of $98,222.03 go up to $696.60. Under the 7.5 percent cap the payment could have been as high as $713.55 ($663.77 + 7.5 percent).

A year later the world is a better place, inflation has been conquered (at least for the moment), Willoughby's debt is down to $97,149.65, and the index plummets to 4 percent. That rate, plus the 2.5 percent margin, means that Willoughby's ARM has a 6.5 percent interest rate and regular payments drop to "just" $632.63 per month.

Willoughby may want to make larger payments at this point (more than $632.63 per month) to reduce her mortgage balance and effectively invest in her own mortgage. This should be fairly painless because she has been making higher payments for the past year.

In the same way that the cobra and the mongoose are natural enemies, so too are inflation and fixed-rate loans. Adjustable-rate mortgages effectively shift the burden of inflation from the lender to the borrower. With an ARM, the loan's interest rate will rise with inflation, thus preserving the *lender's* buying power.

If ARMs are good for lenders, are they also good for borrowers? ARMs are generally enticing to borrowers because they feature low initial interest rates: say 5 percent at a time when conventional loans are available at 7 percent. In particular, during periods when interest rates are high, ARMs may well be the best available financing for two reasons: first, with a low initial interest rate, an ARM can represent below-market financing at a time when most buyers may not qualify for conventional loans. Second, ARM borrowers are not eternally committed to the high interest rates in place at the time they make their loans. ARM costs can fall once high market rates pass.

Consider the example of an astute buyer who gets 7.5 percent ARM financing for an $85,000 loan when 30-year conventional loans are not available for less than 10 percent. The 7.5 percent rate is guaranteed for one year, and, after that, interest levels can rise only 2 percent per year. There is a 12.5 percent interest cap on the ARM loan and a 6 percent interest minimum.

One year later conventional loans are still at 10 percent, and the ARM rate has risen to 9.5 percent. Even though the cost of the loan has increased, the ARM borrower is still ahead of the buyer with a fixed-rate loan. Despite the increased monthly expense, here's where the buyer benefited:

- At 7.5 percent interest computed on a 30-year basis, the ARM borrower pays $594.33 per month in the first year, or a total of $7,131.96. In the second year, with the interest cost at 9.5 percent, the borrower pays $714.73 per month, or $8,576.71. In comparison, a 10 percent fixed-rate loan costs $745.94 per month, or a total of $17,902.46 over two years. The ARM buyer pays a total of $15,708.67 ($7,131.96 + $8,576.71). The difference: a savings of $2,193.79.

- The purchaser acquired property in a high-interest buyer's market—a time when few people qualify for financing because mortgage rates are steep. This means the buyer had a substantial negotiating advantage that potentially translated into a lower purchase price and thus a smaller mortgage than might otherwise have been possible.

- Only when ARM rates go above 10 percent does the ARM purchaser suffer when compared to others who bought with fixed-rate loans at the same time.

- The ARM borrower had far lower initial monthly mortgage costs and thus qualified for a larger loan than his income might otherwise have allowed.

- If ARM rates drop, ARM borrowers may actually see a decrease in monthly costs. Not so for fixed-rate debtors. To pay less interest, fixed-rate borrowers will have to refinance their property—an expensive proposition with new settlement costs, title fees, and so on.

In looking at how the buyer benefits with ARMS, it's also fair to say where there is a risk. If rates rise, ARM costs follow. If rates rise high enough, many buyers could be financially strapped—or worse.

Combo ARMs

Although many people like the low introductory rate and liberal qualification standards associated with ARMS, they are leery of frequently changing payments. Combo loans, such as the Fannie Mae "two-step" program, strike a useful middle ground.

With a combo loan, the buyer has a set rate and payment for 3, 5, 7, or 10 years. Because this rate adjusts after the initial loan period, it is typically lower than conventional interest levels, say .25 to .375 percent less. This may not sound like a big deal, but suppose a $100,000 mortgage is available at 7.5 percent interest and a seven-year combo loan starts at 7.125 percent. The monthly payment for the conventional loan would be $699.21 and the interest cost for the first seven years of the loan term would be $50,568.23. In contrast, the combo would require monthly payments of $673.72 and the interest cost for the first seven years would be $47,915.53—a savings of $2,652.70.

Once the initial period is completed, the combo loan then adjusts. The new rate for the remainder of the loan term is determined by a formula such as the 10-year Treasury bond index plus a margin. There is typically a maximum interest level, say not more than 6 percentage points above the initial interest rate. And, because interest rates rise and fall, it is possible that the rate for the loan's second stage could be lower than the initial interest level.

In considering combo loans, think about how long you expect to own the property. If you think you will live in a home for 7 years and can get a combo loan where the initial period runs 10 years, then with a two-part mortgage you are essentially getting a discounted, fixed-rate loan, one that likely offers easier qualification standards.

Combo Financing Versus Fixed-Rate Loans

	Combo	Conventional
Loan Amount	$100,000.00	$100,000.00
Loan Term	30 Years	30 Years
Initial Interest Rate	7.125 Percent	7.5 Percent
Initial Monthly Cost, Years 1–7	$673.72	$699.21
Higher Possible Rate, Years 8–30	Yes	No
Lower Possible Rate, Years 8–30	Yes	No

Fixed and Mixed ARMs

The combo loan features a single rate adjustment, but we could also structure loans somewhat differently. Instead of two interest levels over the life of the loan, why not a fixed rate up front and then conversion to a one-year ARM? Here are how several typical products work.

- **The 10 and 1 Loan.** An ARM with an initial rate that lasts 10 years and then adjusts annually.
- **The 7 and 1 Loan.** An ARM with an initial rate that lasts seven years and then adjusts annually.
- **The 5 and 1 Loan.** An ARM with an initial rate that lasts five years and then adjusts annually.
- **The 3 and 1 Loan.** An ARM with an initial rate that lasts three years and then changes annually.
- **The 3/3 Loan.** An ARM where there is a three-year rate initially, and then rates are re-set every three years thereafter.
- **The 5/5 Loan.** An ARM that has an initial rate for five years and then a new rate every five years thereafter.
- **The 5/25 Loan.** A loan with rates that float the first five years and then evolve into fixed-rate financing for the last 25 years of the loan term.
- **The 10/10/10 Loan.** ARM financing with rates and payments that can change every 10 years.

ARM Consumer Issues

With the two-step loan backed by Fannie Mae, regardless of how much interest rates rise or your finances change, you have a 30-year commitment as long as you make full and timely payments. What other loan programs sometimes say is this: if interest rates rise a certain amount, say 5 percentage points, then the lender is not obligated to continue the mortgage.

Imagine that you have a 5/25 loan with an initial rate of 7.5 percent. Imagine also that five years later the time has come to adjust the interest level for the loan's remaining life and that rates are pegged at 13.5 percent. At this point a lender with a bail-out clause set at 5 percentage points can say, "Look, the loan contract provides that if the interest rate rises 5 percent or more, we are simply not obligated to continue the loan. Either refinance with someone else within 30 days or we will foreclose." Lenders worry that at higher rates, borrowers may not re-pay and the home may not be saleable at a price sufficient to cover the debt and foreclosure costs.

Another not-so-cute trick is to have a combo mortgage where the borrower must qualify to continue the loan after the first five or seven years. In this case, the catch is that to "qualify" a borrower must meet standards established by the lender, regardless of whether those standards are appropriate, fair, or reasonable. The lender, of course, is not a neutral party, but rather an entity with a great interest in the outcome of such qualification procedures.

ARMs with bail-out clauses should be seen for what they are: potential time bombs that can ruin a borrower. In the situation above, where interest rates have risen to 13.5 percent, a combo borrower with a weasel clause can be forced to refinance in a poor market or at a time when personal finances are weak. At best the result will be the loss of time, fees, and energy; a great increase in monthly mortgage costs; and a vast amount of aggravation.

Although one can construct situations in which ARMs represent favorable financing, there are times when ARMs are simply inappropriate. For example, if ARM and fixed-rate financing are available at the same rates, the fixed-rate mortgage is the better deal because it places the burden of inflation on the lender. ARMs that permit *monthly payment changes* should be avoided, because they can play havoc with personal budgets.

In addition, although ARMs clearly have a place in the mortgage market—especially when rates are steep—they raise serious issues that should concern both borrowers and lenders.

First, ARM borrowers cannot anticipate mortgage costs over the life of their loans. Not only are payments subject to change, but if negative amortization is allowed, it is entirely possible that the loan will not be paid off in 30 years. ARMs thus make personal financial planning more difficult than financing with fixed-rate loans. With some ARMs, one cannot count on having the mortgage paid off by the time Junior goes to college.

Second, ARMs do not guarantee lender profits. What ARMs do, at best, is shield lenders from the worst effects of inflation and limit losses.

Third, because the whole ARM structure is based on an index, it is important to determine which measure is used to set interest rates. In general terms, the longer the span of events being measured, the less volatile the index. Thus borrowers should greatly prefer an index based on the weekly average of five-year U.S. Treasury securities adjusted to a constant yield rather than daily stock averages.

Fourth, lenders may have less security with ARM financing than is now believed. If indexes rise substantially, it is possible that many ARM borrowers will be unable to meet monthly payments and wholesale foreclosures will ensue. The ability to foreclose in such times may be of limited value because few people will be able to buy housing. Lenders who do foreclose—in addition to having a considerable public relations problem—may find they control properties that can be sold only at steep discounts.

Fifth, the opportunity to own a home is one of the most sensitive political matters existent. If ARMs result, or are perceived to result, in an excessive number of foreclosures, one would expect to see immediate regulatory and statutory restrictions. Iowa, for example, enacted a 1985 law that gave farmers a one-year grace period during which time lenders could not foreclose.

Sixth, ARMs supplement but do not replace fixed-rate, conventional financing. Fixed-rate financing is important to pension fund managers who need investments with predictable returns. Each year pensions buy mortgages worth billions of dollars through secondary lenders, so there is a continuing demand for fixed-rate loan products. That demand, in turn, means that fixed-rate financing will remain available in local communities.

Convertible ARMs

To make ARMs more attractive, such loans often come with a fixed-rate conversion feature: during the first three to five years the loan is outstanding, borrowers may convert to a fixed interest rate. The conversion cost is typically modest—say $250 to $500—but the fixed interest rate is likely to be .625 percent to .750 percent above then-prevailing interest levels for fixed-rate financing. For borrowers who intend to own their property for many years, it may actually be cheaper to get new financing, even with all the closing costs involved, than to pay high rates over a long period of time.

No-Risk ARMs

We know that ARM rates and payments can move up and down, but suppose we changed the rules and created an ARM where rates only moved south. Such loan products have begun to appear and they merit serious consideration by ARM borrowers.

ARMs traditionally have lifetime cap rates so that, over the term of the loan, the interest level can rise no more than 5 or 6 percent above the start rate. But if inflation soars and rates zoom upward for several years, a loan that starts at 6 percent could well evolve into 12 percent financing. For a borrower with a $100,000 loan balance, the difference is significant: $599.55 per month for a 30-year mortgage versus $1,028.61.

It's the upside risk that scares borrowers, one reason fixed-rate loans are often preferred. But suppose we had a no-risk ARM? The way it works is that you get your loan and the initial rate is the highest rate. While the rate can go no higher, it can be lowered if rates fall.

What we really have here is not an ARM so much as a loan, which can be modified under certain conditions. Because the loan is modified and not refinanced, there is no need for a new closing, appraisal, credit check, survey, or title exam.

Questions to Ask

Is the start rate higher or lower than the rate for conventional financing? It may be higher, a trade-off for the possibility of future rate reductions.

Under what conditions can the rate be lowered? Plainly the lender will not want to revise the loan every time rates fall by an eighth of a percent.

Is there a minimum loan rate regardless of what happens to interest costs generally?

Can you ask for a new and lower rate if you've missed payments in the past year or had payments at least 30 days late?

Are there any reasons a lower rate can be denied, such as poor credit or the addition of a second loan?

Can the loan be assumed by a qualified buyer? If so, under what terms and with what costs?

Can the loan be pre-paid, in whole or in part, without penalty?

The FHA ARM

Perhaps the least known yet most interesting ARM has been the one developed by the FHA.

- Interest costs can rise or fall 1 percent yearly. This compares with the 2 percent changes allowed by many private ARMS.
- The maximum interest rate cannot rise or fall more than 5 percentage points over the initial rate. This compares with a 6-percentage-point increase allowed by many ARM programs.
- FHA ARM loan rates are based on an index selected by the government, most likely a floating weekly average for one-year Treasury securities.
- Maximum loan limits are the same as those established under the basic 203(b) program.
- Negative amortization is not permitted.
- The loans can be prepaid in whole or in part without penalty.
- FHA ARMS are assumable under the same guidelines that cover other FHA financing. In other words, today's FHA ARMS can be assumed by qualified owner-occupants.

The VA ARM

Although the VA program once included both fixed-rate and adjustable-rate mortgages, as this book went to publication ARM loans are no longer available under the VA program. The reason is that the ARM program was "experimental" and not renewed when the VA program was reauthorized in Washington. Some VA ARMs are still out there, however, and can be assumed by qualified borrowers. If VA qualified, please speak with lenders regarding VA ARMs to see if this program has been revived. The VA program had features similar to the FHA ARM but with attractive VA down payment and qualification standards.

Questions to Ask

Because there are so many potential ARM formats, borrowers should carefully compare lender programs. With ARMs, it is not enough to know interest rates, down payment terms, or initial monthly payment costs.

What is the current interest level for fixed-rate, conventional financing?

How much cash down is required?

What is the initial teaser rate for an ARM?

What is the initial monthly payment?

How long does the initial interest rate last?

Is your qualifying rate the same as your ARM start rate? If not, what is your qualifying rate?

What ratios are used when qualifying loan applicants?

How frequently can the lender change the monthly payment?

How often can the lender adjust the interest rate?

Is there a cap that limits the size of each payment change?

What index is used to adjust the interest level?

What is the margin above the index rate?

Is there a cap on the amount by which the interest charge can be raised or lowered at each change?

Is there a lifetime cap on the loan's maximum interest? Is there an interest minimum?

If the monthly mortgage payment is insufficient to reduce the mortgage principal balance, is negative amortization permitted?

Relative to the original mortgage principal, how much negative amortization is allowed? That is, can the mortgage balance grow to 105 percent of the original balance, 110 percent, 125 percent, etc.?

If you have negative amortization, can the loan term be extended? If so, by how many years?

Is a request to grant an extension given automatically or is the extension at the lender's option?

Are there extension fees that must be paid to the lender? If so, how much?

Is the lender obligated to continue the loan regardless of how high interest levels rise?

Will the lender refinance the property if you reach the negative amortization limit? If so, are any terms, such as maximum interest levels, guaranteed in advance?

Do you have the right to pre-pay the loan in whole or in part at any time without penalty?

Is the loan assumable by a qualified buyer? Is there an assumption fee? How much?

Does the lender offer FHA ARMs? What are the precise terms associated with this program currently, including such items as maximum loan amounts, payment caps, margins, and indexes? What ratios are used to qualify borrowers?

Are VA ARMs now available?

20

ALTERNATIVE
LOAN OPTIONS

HARDLY A DAY passes without the introduction of a "new" loan format, yet the reality is that very few loan ideas represent a quantum leap beyond the current frontiers of finance. Instead, most "new" loans are variations of older, core ideas.

Although it is not practical to examine all possible mortgage options, it is feasible to review central loan concepts. For instance, there may be 500 slightly different ARM variations, but they are each built around a single financing concept. Understand the core concept, and most variations can be quickly evaluated.

The loans that follow are included in this guide because they discuss home financing ideas that arise from time to time. As a group these mortgage programs raise an important point: there are numerous loan options available today, a fact that can translate into big dollar savings for informed borrowers.

15-Year Financing

If there is a single word to describe today's mortgage world, it's *complexity*. We have loans with variable interest rates, and mortgages where you can wind up owing more than you borrow. But instead of all this confusion, what about something simple? Why not a self-amortizing loan with level monthly payments, one interest rate (preferably something low), and sensible overall interest costs?

At first it might seem that cutting a loan term in half will double monthly payments, but this is not the case. For a $90,000 mortgage paid out over 30 years at 7.5 percent interest, the monthly cost will be $629.29. If the loan term is only 15 years, the monthly payment will rise to $834.31, a difference of $205.02 per month.

The very fact that a loan has a term of 15 years rather than 30 years means monthly payments must be higher because there are fewer of them. However, because the loan term is shorter, less principal is outstanding over time and so interest costs are greatly reduced. The potential interest bill for the 30-year loan is $136,548.60, but the greatest possible cost for the 15-year mortgage is only $60,176.23—a savings of $76,372.37.

So now we have an example where the loan term is cut in half, monthly payments rise by $205, and we can save more than $76,000 in potential interest costs. Sounds OK, but there is one slight problem: this example is unrealistic.

The reason this illustration does not work goes back to the concept of risk. The longer the loan term, the greater the risk to the lender. Conversely, the shorter the loan term, the smaller the risk. Less risk, in turn, means lenders can accept lower interest rates.

30-Year and 15-Year Financing Compared

Loan Amount	$90,000.00	$90,000.00	$90,000.00
Loan Term	30 Years	15 Years	15 Years
Interest Rate	7.5 Percent	7.5 Percent	7.25 Percent
Monthly Payment	$629.29	$838.31	$821.58
Additional Monthly Cost	None	$205.02	$192.29
Potential Interest Cost	$136,548.00	$60,176.00	$57,883.00
Potential Interest Savings	None	$76,372.00	$78,665.00

In our example, we see that it is possible to have both 15- and 30-year loans with equal rates. Although some lenders will gladly charge equal rates, smart borrowers should be able to do better. How much better depends on local market conditions, but interest savings of one-quarter percent or so should be readily available.

If we cut the interest rate on the 15-year loan to 7.25 percent, we will have monthly payments of just $821.58 and the total potential interest cost will drop to $57,883.27. Monthly costs will go from $629.29 to $821.58—an increase of $192.29, but we will save as much as $78,665.33 when compared to our model 30-year mortgage at 7.5 percent interest.

The use of 15-year financing clearly results in significant interest savings. It is also clear that such mortgages are becoming increasingly common. But are 15-year mortgages appropriate for everyone? Should it be the new "conventional" mortgage, the loan by which other mortgage formats are measured?

Even though 15-year loans have obvious economic benefits, the marketplace reality is that many people will not be able to select such financing. With the loan above, an additional $195 may not be feasible for first-time home buyers, purchasers with limited means, or those buying on the brink of affordability. Fifteen-year mortgages can be extremely attractive, however, and they seem to make the most sense for three groups of borrowers:

1. Second-time buyers who have accumulated cash from the sale of house number one. Such individuals typically can make larger down payments than first-time buyers and have larger incomes to support monthly payments.

2. Those seeking an enforced savings program—people with additional money to spend each month but who will otherwise fritter the money away if not obligated to spend it for mortgage payments

3. Borrowers who look at potential interest costs and recognize that huge savings are possible with minimal additional payments

As attractive as 15-year loans may appear, many buyers will not qualify for such financing because monthly costs are higher than payments for 30-year loans. The solution to this dilemma is to create a "back-door" 15-year mortgage. It works this way:

1. Find a 30-year loan, either a fixed-rate or adjustable product.
2. Make certain the loan documents state that the mortgage can be prepaid in whole or in part, at any time, and without penalty.

Borrowers now need only to qualify for a 30-year loan. As income grows over time, larger monthly payments can be made voluntarily. If monthly payments grow enough, the loan can be re-paid in 25, 20, or 15 years, as the borrower elects.

A major advantage to back-door 15-year loans is that borrowers do not have a contractual obligation to make large monthly payments. If a period arises when money is tight, just send in the amount required for a 30-year payoff. That's all the lender can expect.

Whatever the economics of 15-year mortgages, these loans at least have the advantage of being understandable to consumers. With a 15-year mortgage no one worries about obscure indexes or negative amortization—the loan and its terms are clear. Lenders also like the 15-year concept because it offers less risk and fewer administrative problems than long-term mortgages or loans with changing payments and interest levels.

As for the interest "lost" by lenders under a 15-year re-payment schedule, don't worry. The faster a loan is paid off, the faster lenders get cash to issue new loans that generate not only interest, but also additional fees, charges, and points. All together, not a bad deal for everyone.

Questions to Ask

What is the interest rate for conventional financing?

What is the best local interest rate for a 15-year mortgage?

What is the cost per month for conventional financing?

What is the cost per month for a 15-year loan?

What is the additional monthly cost for 15-year financing?

What is the total potential interest cost for a 30-year mortgage?

What is the total potential interest cost for a 15-year mortgage?

What are the potential savings from the use of a 15-year mortgage?

What is the difference in terms of interest and monthly payments between your current mortgage and a 15-year loan?

How much will it cost to refinance your property?

If you refinance your property, based on monthly savings alone, how long should you remain in the house to recapture refinancing costs?

Blend Loans

Many borrowers believe they are at the lender's mercy when it comes time to negotiate loan rates. Although this may be true with marginal borrowers, it is surely not accurate in all cases.

If you've got a loan with a low interest rate, you've got leverage. Lenders want to dump old financing, particularly low-rate mortgages that can be assumed, and that means they want your old loan off the books. In many instances, lenders will encourage you to trade in your old, low-interest, low-balance mortgage for a new loan with higher interest and more principal. However, although the interest rate on the new financing may be higher than your current rate, it can be less than the going market rate.

What if Mr. Rivera has an ancient mortgage with a 6 percent interest rate and a $70,000 principal balance? The loan has 10 years to go. Current interest rates are 7.5 percent.

Rivera wants to build a $25,000 addition to his house, and he can get the extra money with a new mortgage for $95,000 ($70,000 plus $25,000) or a $25,000 second trust. Another approach would be a $95,000 wraparound loan, a subject discussed later in the book.

However, what Mr. Rivera would really like is a 30-year loan but at something less than 7.5 percent interest. So he makes the following agreement with the lender: Rivera will give up his old assumable loan if the lender will give him new, 30-year financing worth $95,000 at 7.25 percent interest—a "blended" rate below market interest levels but above the old rate on Rivera's current financing. Because the lender wants to purge his books of Rivera's loan, he agrees to the deal.

A blend loan and a wraparound mortgage are essentially the same concept. The major difference is that with blend financing, the original loan is wiped off the books; but with a wraparound agreement, the old mortgage is retained—usually to the discomfort of the original lender.

Negotiating a blend loan is a contest between borrowers and lenders, and whoever has the better position wins. Sometimes the "better position" is a matter of perception rather than reality. Here are three advantages borrowers need to get the best refinancing deals:

First, the interest rate on old financing must be well below current mortgage levels.

Second, the original loan may or may not be assumable, but you will have a much stronger position if the loan can be assumed.

Third, you cannot be dependent on the lender for financing. If you "need" money, the lender will have little incentive to offer a bargain rate. You must have alternatives that do not require the cur-

Rivera's Blend Loan

Original Loan Balance	$70,000
Original Interest Rate	6 Percent
Current Interest Rate	7.5 Percent
Blend Loan	$95,000
Blend Rate	7.25 Percent
Savings	.25 Percent

rent loan's re-payment such as cash on hand, home-equity loans, or the ability to borrow against security accounts.

In those cases where borrowers want a blended rate to buy rather than refinance, the situation is somewhat different.

To start, the current financing must be freely-assumable at its original rate and terms. If the existing loan is not freely-assumable, the lender has little incentive to bargain. Look for older FHA and VA loans to meet this requirement.

The purchaser must show the lender that it is possible to acquire the property without disturbing the original mortgage. This can occur if the seller or third party is willing to take back a second loan or the buyer can pay cash above the current financing.

Questions to Ask

What is the remaining loan balance?

What is the interest rate on present financing?

Is the current loan freely-assumable?

What are the current monthly payments?

How much additional cash do you need?

What is the current interest rate for conventional financing?

Are local lenders making wraparound mortgages and second trusts? If so, how does a blend loan arrangement compare with a wraparound deal or a combination of the old financing plus a new second loan?

What fees and points will the lender charge in a blend deal? These costs, like interest, are negotiable.

Bi-Weekly Mortgages

In the eternal search for better mortgages, lenders and borrowers have tried every possible financial concoction. Today we have a tremendous number of loan alternatives, including what may be the most publicized and least-used home financing idea in recent history, the bi-weekly mortgage.

The bi-weekly mortgage is distinguished by the fact that instead of 12 mortgage payments per year, borrowers make 26 payments. Each payment, however, is only half the size of regular monthly payments, and so the results are lower costs per payment, higher costs per year, faster loan amortization, shorter loan terms, and reduced interest costs.

If we borrow $100,000 on a conventional 30-year basis at 7.5 percent interest, we will have monthly payments of $699.21. The interest bill over 30 years will total $151,771.98.

Here's what happens if we borrow $100,000 at the same interest rate but on a bi-weekly basis:

First, we just about divide the conventional payment in half, paying out in this case $349.60 every two weeks.

Second, we make 26 bi-weekly payments per year. This gets us to the "secret" of bi-weekly financing. Twenty-six bi-monthly payments are equal to 13 monthly payments, not the 12 payments usually made by borrowers. The interest savings from bi-weekly mortgages come from larger annual payments. In effect, bi-weekly loans are nothing but a complicated way to pre-pay a mortgage.

Third, the loan is paid off in 23.28 years (605.3 payments divided by 26 per year).

Fourth, the interest bill totals just $116,612.88, a savings of $35,102.72 over the conventional loan.

So we have a loan that does indeed result in huge interest savings. But although the bi-weekly loan produces significant interest economies, it does so in a needlessly complex manner.

The basic question about the bi-weekly loan is this: why bother? There are other ways to accomplish the same goal with far less hassle. For instance, why not just make 280 monthly payments of $757.32? The loan will be re-paid in the same number of years (23.3) and the potential interest bill will total $112,049.60—again a huge savings when compared with conventional financing.

Just as important, the *annual* cost of mortgage payments will remain essentially equal, going from $9,089.60 with the bi-monthly

Conventional Versus Bi-Weekly Mortgage Options

Loan Amount	$100,000.00	$100,000.00	$100,000.00
Interest Rate	7.5 Percent	7.5 Percent	7.5 Percent
Loan Term	30 Years	23.3 Years	23.3 Years
Payments per Year	12	26	12
Monthly Payment	$699.21	$349.60	$757.32
Additional Cost per Year	None	$699.08	$697.32
Potential Interest Cost	$151,715.60	$116,612.88	$112,049.60
Potential Interest Savings	None	$35,102.72	$39,666.00

program to $9,087.84 when monthly payments are simply increased—a difference of about $2 a year.

From the lender's point of view, the bi-weekly mortgage poses bothersome administrative headaches. There are 26 payments to record each year and 26 chances to enter the wrong information on a computer. At a time when lenders have their hands full trying to account for ARM variables, why would any lender joyously suggest a loan that is difficult and costly to administer?

One answer is probably related to lender competition rather than the economics of the bi-weekly loan. Lenders vigorously compete for business, and lenders who can get an extra bit of notice are likely to attract more borrowers than those lenders who are virtually anonymous. The bi-weekly mortgage is something to talk about; it draws publicity. Whether it makes sense as a practical mortgage option for either lenders or consumers can be debated.

Another possible attraction of bi-weekly financing is that payments can be tied to automatic deposit plans, which means borrowers must maintain accounts with the lender. Rather than sending in a check every two weeks, payments are deducted directly from an account with the lender. The lender benefits by opening additional accounts (which he hopes will allow him to generate extra loans and interest) and by the possibility of offering additional services to the borrower, such as auto loans and checking accounts.

Not only are bi-weekly mortgages needlessly complex and undistinguished in terms of the benefits they offer consumers, they have also spawned a mini-industry of advisers, helpers, and consultants who will gladly take your money in exchange for their assistance.

In essence, for $400 or so plus charges per bi-weekly payment, a "consultant" will collect your money for you on a bi-weekly basis and then ensure that your lender receives full and timely payments. Why anyone needs such a "service" is beyond comprehension, because lenders can calculate bi-weekly payments, you can send in payments by yourself, and if you otherwise feel compelled to spend $400, the money can be donated to a worthy cause such as a community group or your retirement account.

Bi-weekly consultants appear to be largely or totally unregulated. How do you know that the payments sent to a third party will actually be delivered to your lender? Some bi-weekly programs mention that they are "insured" and "bonded" but they do not say how much insurance is available, the size of their bond, or whether such protections will cover all potential claims.

Another important question concerns where the borrower mortgage money is held. Is it "co-mingled" and kept in the same account as the consultant's business or personal funds? Or is the money kept in a separate "escrow" account? Consumers will want their money in an escrow account.

Worse yet, it is not clear that all bi-weekly programs offer true bi-weekly benefits.

To see how this works, imagine that you send $500 to a bi-weekly agency every two weeks. Imagine as well that your regular mortgage payment is $1,000. In this situation you would normally pay $12,000 a year to the mortgage lender, but the bi-weekly collection agency is receiving $13,000 (26 × $500).

But suppose your lender does not accept bi-weekly payments. If the bi-weekly agency makes a $1,000 payment to your lender for 11 months and then a single $2,000 payment, your loan will be pre-paid because an extra $1,000 has been deposited with your lender. The catch is that by not making payments every two weeks, the bi-weekly intermediary pockets the interest on the money not immediately paid to the lender, and you do not get the full benefit of bi-weekly deposits.

Although one expects lower interest rates as loan terms become shorter, this is not necessarily true with bi-weekly mortgages. Even though there is a shorter pay-back period, which should mean less risk and therefore lower interest rates, the high administrative costs associated with bi-weekly financing may limit or disallow interest discounts.

Are bi-weekly mortgages a plausible financial option? They certainly save money when compared with 30-year loans, but one has to compare such programs with loans that just use bigger payments.

Questions to Ask

What is the interest rate for conventional financing?

What is the interest rate for bi-weekly financing?

What is the monthly payment for a conventional loan?

What is the payment cost for each bi-weekly installment?

What is the total annual cost of a bi-weekly mortgage?

Can you repay the loan in whole or in part without penalty?

If you obtain a 15-year or 18-year loan with monthly payments, how much will you pay per month? How much will you pay per year?

If you have a bi-weekly mortgage, must you open a savings or checking account with the lender? If so, what interest will your funds earn?

Bridge Loans Close Financing Gap

Although first-time buyers play an important role in the real estate marketplace, most buyers are seasoned vets who have bought before and own a home even as they look for a replacement residence.

Many owners—if they sell their current property—will have more than enough capital to buy a new house. But what if house number one does not sell *and* settle at the same time as house number two?

Although most move-up buyers sell and settle before buying home number two, sometimes home number one does not sell on time. This situation is usually temporary but may mean that seller/buyers need bridge financing.

Bridge financing is nothing more than a loan secured by the unsold property. The loan can last a few days, a few months, or longer, and it is instantly re-paid as soon as the property sells.

Although bridge financing can provide the cash needed to buy a new home, it is a form of financing that has a number of curiosities.

Some seller/buyers, for example, effectively create their own bridge loans by taking money from an *existing* home equity loan and using that cash to buy a second house. This is generally okay with lenders, provided the borrowers are living in the house that secures the home-equity loan.

Rather than use home-equity financing, another choice is to obtain a true bridge loan, new financing that remains in place until house number one sells or for a given time period, say six months.

Many lenders offer bridge financing, but to get the best deal borrowers should ask several questions.

• **How much can you borrow?** Generally lenders will not exceed a certain proportion of the property's value. If a home is worth $200,000 and there is an existing $110,000 mortgage, that means the owners have equity worth $90,000 before marketing costs. But if a lender will only provide bridge financing that does not exceed 75 percent of the property's value, then the largest possible bridge loan will be $40,000 ($110,000 + $40,000 = $150,000, or 75 percent of $200,000).

• **What happens if the property does not sell by the end of the loan term?** Lenders, perhaps for an additional fee, may extend the loan term. But what if they don't?

• **How are monthly payments handled?** With some bridge loans, there are no monthly payments, and others require the payment of interest only.

• **What are the fees and charges?** Lenders will generally require a full-blown closing for a bridge loan. Relative to the amount borrowed, and relative to the amount of time the loan is expected to remain outstanding, such fees can be expensive.

• **Are there points to pay?** In general, borrowers are best off not paying bridge loan points. Here's why.

Suppose you have a $50,000 bridge loan and pay 10 percent interest at a time when first mortgages are available for 7.5 percent. You are paying a premium rate because the bridge loan is typically a second trust or second mortgage, and thus more risky than a first trust.

If you pay 1 point, $500 in this case, look what happens to the interest rate.

If the loan is outstanding three months, and if no payments are made until the home is sold, interest will amount to $1,250. Add $500 for a nonrefundable point and the total interest cost jumps to $1,750. That's an effective interest rate of 14 percent annually.

If the loan lasts a year, then the interest cost is $5,000. The interest cost, plus $500 for a point, gives an effective interest rate of 11 percent.

And if the bridge loan only lasts a week? That would cost $96.15 for interest and $500 for a point, or a total of $596.15 — that's an annualized rate of 62 percent.

The bottom line: higher interest is likely to be cheaper than a somewhat lower rate and a nonrefundable point paid up front.

Another choice seller/buyers should consider are bridge loans offered by new-home builders and brokers. In this situation both builders and brokers are motived to complete the transaction, so terms are likely to be especially favorable.

Buy-Downs and Buy-Ups

When interest rates soar, owners are often stuck with unsalable properties. Even though properties are not moving, interest costs accrue, taxes continue, and owners want to sell as quickly as possible to preserve their profits and lower their costs.

Buy-Down Comparison Chart

	Buy-Down Loan	Discounted Sale	Conventional Loan
Sale Price	$106,250.00	$102,650.00	$106,250.00
Loan Size	$85,000.00	$82,120.00	$85,000.00
Down Payment	$21,250.00	$20,530.00	$21,250.00
Effective Interest Rate			
Years 1–3	10 Percent	12 Percent	12 Percent
Years 4–30	12 Percent	12 Percent	12 Percent
Monthly Principal and Interest			
Years 1–3	$745.94	$844.70	$874.32
Years 4–30	$868.87	$844.70	$874.32
Projected Interest	$223,361.00	$221,972.00	$229,755.00
Potential Interest Savings	$6,394.00	$7,783.00	None
Interest and Price Savings	$6,394.00	$11,383.00	None
Qualifying Income	$39,397.00	$42,630.00	$42,742.00

With a buy-down, someone other than the borrower pays a portion of the mortgage, thus making properties more affordable. In effect, buy-downs are a subsidy. When times are tough and properties don't move, it's usually the seller who pays the buy-down.

Suppose prevailing interest rates are 12 percent and builder Thompson has unsold houses priced at $106,250. With interest rates so high, payments for a 30-year $85,000 loan total $874.32 monthly. To qualify for such financing, assuming that insurance and taxes cost $150 per month, a buyer must earn at least $42,742 a year if a lender will allocate no more than 28 percent of the purchaser's income for principal, interest, taxes, and insurance.

Thompson is paying interest on his construction loans, prime plus 2 points, 14 percent in this case. He figures it's better to sell the properties at discount than hold on and pay construction loan interest, so he offers this deal: he will pay about $100 a month for the first 36 months of ownership to any buyer. (Alternatively, Thompson can pay points to a lender to bring monthly costs down. Whether he pays the buyer or lender directly is not important—the significant idea for borrowers is that their loan costs are subsidized.)

With monthly payments for principal and interest down to $745.92, an income of $38,397 is now required for financing worth $85,000. The effective initial interest rate, at least to the buyer, is 10 percent. The lender is being paid the full amount due for a 12 percent loan, $874.32 in this case ($775.92 from the buyer and the rest from builder/seller Thompson).

With lower monthly costs, Thompson soon sells one of the remaining units, but he must pay out $3,600 (36 × $100) for the buy-down, although his actual cost is somewhat less. The reason: he doesn't pay all the money up front. Instead he deposits or invests the money, collects interest, and pays out only $100 a month.

The second house is sold differently. The buyers, Mr. and Mrs. Poppin, want Thompson to apply the $3,600 buy-down as a credit against the purchase price, bringing the cost down to $102,650. The 20 percent down payment will drop from $21,250 to $20,530—a $720 saving. The mortgage will also drop, from $85,000 to $82,120. A 30-year $82,120 mortgage at 12 percent interest will require monthly payments of $844.70 for principal and interest. If we estimate that taxes and insurance will cost $150 per month, a borrower will need a $42,630 income to qualify for this loan if 28 percent of the purchaser's income can be allocated to housing costs.

Buy-downs are not restricted to any term—one can have a buy-down for the entire length of the loan. However, if the numbers are right, even a short-term buy-down can be a good deal. For example, if you had a 10-year buy-down but only intend to own the property seven years because of a planned retirement relocation, then a buy-down represents an interest reduction for what is presumably the entire ownership period.

3-2-1 Buy-Downs

Another approach to buy-downs is the "3-2-1 buy-down," a loan that works like this in a market where conventional financing is now available at 7.5 percent interest.

1. In the first year, the interest rate is 3 percent lower than the base rate, or 5.5 percent.
2. In the second year, the interest rate is 2 percent lower than the base rate, or 6.5 percent.
3. In the third year, the interest rate is 1 percent lower than the base rate, or 7.5 percent.
4. In the fourth year and each year thereafter, the interest rate is set at 8.5 percent.

There are two catches to this loan. First, the base rate is likely to be set at 8.5 percent rather than the lower 7.5 percent rate that is otherwise available. Second, to get the buy-down, borrowers must pay additional points up front.

Why would anyone want a 3-2-1 buy-down? With a lower start rate, it will be easier to qualify for financing. But although qualifying may be easier, paying additional points up front is hard, if not impossible, for most borrowers—unless the points are paid by a seller.

With a 3-2-1 buy-down, borrowers will reach the prevailing interest rate (7.5 percent in our example) in just three years. In the fourth year, the loan rate will be a full 1 percent higher than conventional loans. This is not the world's best deal—but it may be the best available and it may get you into a house. The reason is that the lower interest up front creates reduced monthly payments, and lower monthly payments for the first two years of a loan make qualifying easier. Seen the other way, without lower payments up front, it may not be possible to buy the property.

We saw with buy-downs that borrowers were able to get lower rates when money was paid to the lender up front. But what happens when buyers can afford monthly payments but not closing costs?

Buy-Ups

If we have a situation where loans are available at 7.5 percent interest, then a lender might trade a 1 percent interest hike for a closing credit equal to 3 percent of the sale price, or a 2 percent hike in exchange for a 6 percent credit. Such trades are sometimes called *buy-ups* and use the same logic and finances as so-called no-cash financing.

Suppose a home sells for $175,000, and a buyer puts down $17,500. The lender will finance the deal with a $157,500 loan at 7.5 percent. Or the lender will finance the deal at 8.5 percent and make a $4,725 contribution at closing (3 percent × $157,500). If the borrower will pay 9.5 percent interest, the lender will pay $9,450 at settlement.

Is this a good deal?

To answer the question, borrowers must consider that they are exchanging higher monthly costs for lower closing expenses.

In our example, if there is a $157,500 loan at 7.5 percent interest, then over a 30-year term the monthly payments will be set at $1,101.26. If we borrow at 8.5 percent interest, the monthly cost for principal and interest will be $1,211.04.

The difference between the two loans is $109.78 per month. If we divide $109.78 into the money contributed up front, $4,725, it will take 43 months before the lender's credit is eaten up in higher monthly costs.

The deal with 9.5 percent interest works the same way. Monthly payments rise from $1,101.26 to $1,324.34, and the payment difference is $223.08 per month. Because $9,450 was credited up front in exchange for a 2 percent interest rate increase, it will take 42 months ($9,450 divided by $223.08) before the borrower loses ground.

Buy-ups can be attractive for those borrowers who need additional cash to close a deal, have stable incomes, and live in a community where property values are generally rising. However, because higher rates mean higher monthly costs, borrowers with limited incomes will not qualify for buy-up programs.

Questions to Ask

What is the current rate of interest for conventional financing?

What is the effective rate of a loan with a buy-down provision?

How much cash down is required?

How long will the buy-down remain in effect?

What is the buy-down total value?

If the buy-down is to be a monthly mortgage supplement, what happens if the builder or owner goes bankrupt? Is there any requirement to set aside buy-down funds in an escrow account?

If buy-down funds are to be held in escrow, who gets the interest? If you are the purchaser you should certainly argue that it belongs to you.

If the buy-down's value is applied to the sales price of the property, how will down payment, mortgage size, and monthly payments change?

How long do you expect to own the property?

Is the loan assumable by a qualified buyer at the buy-down rate?

Can the loan be prepaid in whole or in part without penalty?

Does the lender offer buy-up financing? If so, what credit is available up front? How much will interest rates rise?

Construction Financing

Financing and refinancing real estate usually means the purchase of an existing home or buying from a builder. But what if we want to build a dream home from scratch? How do we pay for our new home?

From a financing perspective, the process has three stages: property acquisition, home construction, and permanent financing.

When it comes to raw land, lenders tend to be very cautious. Raw land may be scenic, well-located, sizable, and greatly valued by the owner, but it can be enormously difficult to re-sell in the event of default. Thus, lenders tend to stay away from raw land financing if possible, but when they do make loans, they look for a large down payment—20 percent with high interest (think credit cards) or 50 percent down and 1 to 3 percent over prime.

Buying raw land for construction has become an absurdly complex process. If an endangered species nests on your property, construction may be prohibited. If the land has been polluted by past owners, in certain circumstances the new owners may be liable for clean-up costs. And if you need to clear the property of a dilapidated shell that someone else regards as "historic," that too can be a battle. Other issues include—but are not limited to—zoning, percolation tests (to determine drainage characteristics), and deed restrictions.

The result of so many tests and hurdles is that buying land is not a casual event; you'll need help from experienced buyer brokers or attorneys or both, and you'll need to wade through a lengthy list of concerns to identify the right property. Once you find the right ground, you must then find a helpful lender unless you're willing to pay cash.

Paying cash may well be possible because money from savings or funds extracted from a home-equity loan can be used to acquire property. The catch is that raw land may not be the world's most salable commodity in rural areas (because there may be a lot of inventory) or during periods when realty markets are weak. As well, it's tough to get cash out of raw land once it is acquired.

Once you have title to the property, the next stage is to obtain construction financing. Lenders will want you to have plans and specs, a licensed and bonded builder, and appropriate permits in hand or pending.

With construction financing, however, you will not merely get a check at closing. Instead, what happens is that a lender will release loan money in stages (*draws*) as the project evolves. To insure that each stage of construction is properly completed, the lender will send someone to physically inspect the property. As a result, construction financing is more expensive than routine mortgages because it involves more work for reviews, inspections, and draws.

Construction financing, naturally, should end when the building process is over, which means that the loan must be paid off. This is typically accomplished by refinancing with a permanent loan in the same way that any property is refinanced.

Hidden within the three-phase process above is a major problem: if we have three loans we also have three closings, and three closings can be very expensive with lots of taxes, settlement costs, legal fees, and loan charges.

So rather than three loans we would prefer to have two or one. And the good news is that such financing is out there.

One approach is to acquire land and then to use the equity in the land as the down payment for construction and permanent financing—a mortgage that is first used to build the house and then automatically converts to a 30-year loan. In this situation there are two closings, one for property acquisition and one for financing.

But the best approach is simply to have one loan and one closing, a combo loan. In this scenario, the lender looks at the land, the builder, and all the other elements needed to complete the project and then grants a loan with a down payment based on the final cost, usually 10 to 20 percent down. Another advantage to combo financing is that the interest rate reflects residential mortgage costs rather than high-cost construction financing interest.

The whole process of buying and developing raw land raises a number of questions not seen in other forms of financing.

I want to build a small home on a very large piece of property. Can this be a problem?

Yes. Many loan programs limit the value of the land to one-third of the final pricing of the property with completed improvements.

My lender will provide a 90-day construction loan. Is this enough time to complete a home?

Maybe, but what if it isn't? Small stick-built homes can go from foundation to closing in less than two weeks, but this is rare. Before accepting this loan, speak with builders to see what's reasonable. Be aware that bad weather, permit delays, inspection waits, and other problems can seriously delay work schedules.

I can get a construction loan with a lower rate if I pay points up front. Is this a good deal?

Probably not—but at least run the numbers. Construction loans are short-term financing, so points paid up front are expensive. For example, a six-month loan for $100,000 at 8 percent with 1 point will have an interest cost of roughly $4,000 plus $1,000 at closing—that's a total of $5,000, or 10 percent. In this situation, a 9 percent loan would be a better deal than 8 percent plus a point.

What if I want to do some of the work myself?

Lenders are wary of owner-builders, particularly those without prior construction experience. In the usual case, home-building is not a do-it-yourself activity.

Do I need insurance?

What if a worker is hurt or the builder goes bankrupt? See the lender for details. Ask about completion bonds, workmen's compensation, liability coverage, etc.

I bought a lot last year for cash. Can I use my equity in the lot as a down payment credit?

Yes, but with a caution. Under many programs, if a lot has been held for less than two years, the lender will determine its value on the basis of the acquisition price or a current appraisal, whichever is less.

What if there are defects in workmanship?

Items not up to code will be caught, or should be caught, by local building inspectors. A good approach is to engage a private home inspector to monitor progress. Inspectors can check once the foundation is in place, when the framing is up but the drywall is not yet installed, and a third time when the home is completed.

Aren't three inspections a little pricey?

What's really pricey is a deficient home that creates headaches and costs for years to come.

What is the tax impact of construction financing?

In general, interest on a construction loan is not deductible. Instead, it is a capital cost added to the property's cost basis. See a tax pro for details.

Ecology Loans

It was Jimmy Carter who said that the use of oil pricing and the withholding of energy to further political aims were the "moral equivalent of war," a comment we ignore at our peril.

With America dependent on foreign oil (but not coal, natural gas, or nuclear power), and with a growing interest in conservation and ecology, the mortgage industry offers loan programs to encourage the construction of energy-efficient housing and the use of appliances that hold down energy consumption. Such loans, known as energy-efficiency mortgages (EEMs), can save more than kilowatts.

Although the programs vary somewhat, EEMs are available with conventional financing as well as FHA and VA backing. Here's how they work.

Suppose the Shermans can afford to borrow $100,000 at 7 percent interest. With a typical conventional loan, and with conventional loan standards, the Shermans will pay $665.30 per month for principal and interest.

The Shermans can make a conventional loan because lenders will allow up to 28 percent of their income to be used for principal, interest, taxes, and insurance. With an EEM, however, up to 30 percent of a borrower's income can be used for home expenses.

The addition of a 2 percent qualification allowance may not seem important, but with an EEM it represents three significant values.

First, a family such as the Shermans can borrow more. In this case, $107,142 rather than $100,000.

Second, several EEM programs allow buyers to purchase properties and to then make the homes more energy-efficient with improvements made after closing. For example, the Shermans might borrow $107,000 plus some additional amount to make approved, energy-related improvements. The money for improvements will be held in an escrow account by the lender and disbursed as the repairs are completed.

The amount available for repairs will depend on how the property is financed. With FHA as much as $3,500 in additional funds can be borrowed, and the VA program allows up to $5,000 in extra funding for energy improvements. For conventional loans, the situation is somewhat more complex: there is no formal limit on the financing of approved upgrades; however, at the time a lender sells a mortgage in the secondary market, the rules change somewhat.

Freddie Mac and Fannie Mae—the two big secondary lenders—will buy energy-efficient mortgages but only if the escrow fund does not exceed 10 (Freddie Mac) to 15 (Fannie Mae) percent of the amount borrowed. Because lenders may look for a quick sale in the secondary market, it is possible that some will simply limit the funds available for improvements to 10 or 15 percent of the basic mortgage amount so that the loan can be sold immediately.

Third, to qualify for an EEM, the Shermans must buy an energy-efficient house. Such a home will consume less energy per month and cost less to operate. Not only will the borrowers benefit, but so will everyone in town.

To see how the Shermans help themselves and the rest of us, look at the way we fund generating stations, gas lines, and other big energy projects.

To insure there are no shortages, utilities must always have excess capacity to account for energy surges (such as peak use on the hottest days) and future growth. But if energy consumption declines, there is less need to fund generating stations and other fixed-cost facilities. The result is that the utilities borrow less, pay less interest, buy less fuel, and have less idle equipment. The benefit for consumers is that utility rates need not go up so quickly.

Questions to Ask

Does the lender handle EEM financing? If so, are there any additional charges? More points? (With an EEM loan where an escrow account is established for improvements and upgrades, the lender has additional work when compared to a traditional loan arrangement.)

What, specifically, will qualify a property for energy-efficient financing?

What improvements can you make with EEM loans? How much time is available to make improvements? (Figure 120 days after closing, unless a lender says otherwise.)

How much additional money can you borrow with an EEM mortgage? What improvements and upgrades can be funded with additional EEM funds?

How much will you save each year on fuel when you buy an energy-efficient home?

Graduated-Payment Mortgages (GPMs)

Most of us enter the workforce with the thought that our incomes will rise over time. Unfortunately, we often buy real estate long before we enter our peak earning years, a situation that creates two problems:

First, because our incomes are limited, we can only afford smaller mortgages and perhaps less house than we really want.

Second, what mortgage payments we do make are difficult to afford because we are also buying furniture, cars, and first trying to support households.

Graduated-payment mortages (GPMs) are designed for people with rising incomes. They feature fixed interest rates plus low initial monthly payments that rise annually during the loan's first years. Here's how a GPM works:

The Hunts were married last July and are now looking for their first home. They have a combined income of $42,000. If 28 percent of their income can be devoted to the payment of baseline home ownership expenses, they can pay $980 a month for principal, interest, taxes, and insurance (PITI). If taxes and insurance in the Hunts's price range cost $150 per month, then the Hunts have $830 available each month for principal and interest. At 7.75 percent interest, a monthly payment of $830 will support a 30-year mortgage worth $115,855.

But suppose the Hunts consider a GPM mortgage where monthly costs rise 7.5 percent per year for five years and then plateau. Assuming that the Hunts are qualified on the basis of first-year payments, they can borrow $154,513.

Because payments in the first five years of the Hunts's loan are not high enough to produce a self-amortizing loan, negative amortization occurs. This problem can be resolved by making an extra-large down payment at settlement, monthly pre-payments, or higher payments in the loan's last 25 years. Because the Hunts do not have the dollars to make a big down payment and monthly income is tight, they opt for larger monthly costs in future years. They make this decision because they assume they will have a future income sufficient to easily carry such costs.

GPM **Versus Conventional Financing for the Hunts**

	GPM	Conventional
Loan Size	$154,513.00	$115,855.00
Loan Term	30 Years	30 Years
Interest Rate	Varies	7.75 Percent
Monthly Payment		
Year 1	$830.00	$830.00
Year 2	$904.30	$830.00
Year 3	$980.20	$830.00
Year 4	$1,057.03	$830.00
Year 5	$1,133.44	$830.00
Year 6–30	$1,207.67	$830.00
Year-End Loan Balance		
Year 1	$156,600.69	$114,838.15
Year 2	$157,932.50	$113,739.64
Year 3	$158,427.20	$112,552.91
Year 4	$158,006.20	$111,270.86
Year 5	$156,601.19	$109,885.85
Year 6	$154,160.25	$108,389.60
Year 30	$0.00	$0.00
Negative	**Amortization**	
Year 1	$2,087.69	
Year 2	$3,419.50	
Year 3	$3,914.20	
Year 4	$3,493.20	
Year 5	$2,088.19	
Year 6	−$352.75 (Positive Amortization)	
Total Interest Cost	$245,186.91	$182,945.00
Extra Loan Amount	$38,658.00	None

There are lenders who will qualify GPM borrowers on the basis of low initial payments. However, borrowers considering GPMs should be aware of several potential hurdles.

- Some lenders who qualify borrowers on the basis of initial GPM payments also charge a lock-in fee so that the rate they've quoted will actually be available at settlement.
- Some lenders who offer very attractive GPM rates also require borrowers to pay an up-front "subsidy" account. In effect, the money paid up front offsets low initial payments.
- Some lenders offer GPMs with a 15-year payment schedule, a schedule that produces higher monthly costs than 30-year GPM loans. Higher monthly costs translate into less ability to qualify for financing.
- GPMs commonly produce negative amortization in their early years. This means if a borrower has to refinance or sell after just a few years, the loan balance is likely to be greater than the amount originally borrowed.
- Although a GPM may allow individuals to increase their borrowing ability, the cost of such borrowing is not extravagantly more expensive on an overall basis. A $115,855 loan at 7.75 percent interest would have a potential interest cost of $182,945 over 30 years. A GPM for $154,513 has a potential interest cost of $245,187. That's a difference of $62,242 over 30 years—but then the GPM borrower has a loan which is $38,658 bigger.
- A GPM is a woefully bad idea for those with declining incomes. Conversely, a GPM may be attractive for individuals with growing salaries.

In addition to conventional GPM mortgages, such financing is also available under FHA Sec. 245(a) for owner-occupied, single-family homes and condos. This program features low down payments—usually less than 5 percent—plus the value of deferred interest (negative amortization). The program has five repayment plans:

1. Monthly payments increase 2.5 percent each year during the loan's first five years.
2. Monthly payments increase 5 percent each year during the loan's first five years.
3. Monthly payments increase 7.5 percent each year during the loan's first five years.
4. Monthly payments increase 2 percent each year during the loan's first 10 years.
5. Monthly payments increase 3 percent each year during the loan's first 10 years.

The GPM concept can be combined with an adjustable rate to produce a GPARM, or graduated-payment adjustable-rate mortgage. With a GPARM, there will be set—but rising—monthly payments in the loan's first few years. Because payments are set but the interest rate is not, it is possible that negative interest will occur in the first years of the loan. After the initial period when monthly payments are set, a GPARM will behave just like a regular ARM with payments and interest rates that can vary throughout the loan's life.

A GPARM is probably a better financing choice than an ARM, especially for young property buyers. Individuals first entering the workforce are the people least able to cope with rapidly rising housing costs because they have relatively little disposable income. By fixing initial costs, a GPARM gives buyers the below-market interest levels that ARMs often feature at first plus some time in which incomes can rise.

GPM loans in general represent one of the best forms of first-time financing, because they are fixed-rate mortgages attuned to the needs of entry-level purchasers. Be aware, however, that buyers may find that they owe more with GPM financing than they borrowed if they move in less than five years. And, of course, this is not a form of financing that should be considered by anyone who expects a steady or falling income.

Questions to Ask

What is the GPM interest rate?

How many points, if any, are being charged for conventional financing and for GPM loans?

When points are considered, what is the true annual percentage rate (APR) for a GPM loan?

What GPM formats are available from local lenders?

How much money down will you need for a conventional GPM? How much for an FHA-backed GPM?

How is negative amortization handled? By an enlarged down payment? By higher monthly payments through most of the loan term? By a balloon payment? By extending the loan term?

If you are selling a home with a GPM where you have paid additional money up front to account for negative amortization, have you received any credit from the purchaser?

If you are assuming a GPM loan, is a balloon payment scheduled?

Home-Equity Loans

Real estate has traditionally been considered a nonliquid asset, property that can be converted to cash only by selling or refinancing—two very expensive and time-consuming ways to raise capital. But the old image of real estate is now changing. Today property can be converted to cash immediately through the use of home-equity loans secured by real estate.

Credit is the great wonder of American society. You can be born on credit, live on credit, and probably die on credit. Like gravity, credit is silent, invisible, and with us every moment.

Although credit is all around us, all forms of credit are not identical. Consumer credit differs from traditional real estate financing, another form of credit, in three ways.

First, the credit represented by hundreds of millions of flat plastic cards is unsecured debt. When you make a credit purchase, the card company advances money to a gas station or department store on the theory that you will re-pay. Real estate debt, in contrast, is secured by the value of your property. If you don't pay, the property will be sold to cover what you owe.

Second, real estate debt traditionally has been advanced at one time. Consumer debt is usually a revolving line of credit. You may have the right to borrow $5,000 from a single credit card company but can borrow just some of the available money. If you borrow only $150, you pay interest only on the outstanding debt. Moreover, once you pay back the $150 you can again borrow up to $5,000. With most real estate loans, it's understood that once you pay back any portion of the principal, the lender is not obligated to loan to you again.

Third, there are few if any charges to get consumer credit. Companies will gladly send you credit cards with the fervent hope you really do buy now and pay later. Real estate lenders will not only charge a fee to apply for financing, they are also likely to have a variety of closing costs that the borrower must pay.

Home-equity mortgages are hybrid loan products that take features both from traditional mortgages and consumer credit practices. A real estate loan with a line of credit can work like this:

The Taylor house is worth $125,000 in today's market and has a $40,000 mortgage balance. The Taylors feel they may need some ready cash in the next two years to start a small business and send Junior to college, so their lender suggests a credit line arrangement.

The lender says the Taylors can borrow up to 70 percent of the equity in their home and values their equity like this: 70 percent of $125,000 equals $87,500 less the remaining mortgage balance, $40,000, equals $47,500. (Some lenders today will allow home-equity loans equal to 95 percent, 100 percent, and even more.)

The lender tells the Taylors that the minimum home-equity loan is $5,000 and the minimum loan advance is $1,000. Because they have equity worth $47,500, the Taylors elect to get a $25,000 line of credit.

To get this loan, the Taylors pay for a credit report, title search, and other closing expenses. Their application costs are figured on the basis of a $25,000 loan, but they do not pay any points. Although interest rates for second trusts at the time of their application average 8 percent, the Taylors pay 1.5 percent over the prime rate charged by a major bank, or 7.5 percent in this case. The lender has the right to change the rate of interest every three months. In contrast the cost of consumer credit ranges from 16 to 24 percent.

The lender explains that the Taylors may select any loan term they choose, from 1 to 30 years. They select 15 years and make their first draw, $12,000, 18 months after their application is approved, so they have a maximum of 13.5 years to repay the $12,000 debt. The Taylors can repay the loan in advance, however, without penalty.

How do the Taylors withdraw their money? The lender offers four choices: a check mailed to their home or business; a deposit in a savings or checking account maintained with the lender or at another financial institution; a telephone transfer; or most interestingly, a book of blank drafts that the Taylors can use up to their credit limit.

After six years the Taylors have paid down their debt to $7,000. Because of the revolving nature of the credit line system, the Taylors can still borrow $18,000 ($25,000 less $7,000). In effect, by making their monthly payments, they have raised their available credit line from a low of $13,000 ($25,000 less $12,000) at the time they made their first draw.

Taylors' Home-Equity Loan	
Home Value	$125,000
70 Percent	$87,500
Existing Loan	$40,000
Available Home Equity	$47,500

Home-equity loans are attractive to lenders because they can collect processing fees up front even though actual monies may not be advanced for months or years—or at all. Also, such loans are commonly in the form of adjustable-rate mortgages, so lenders are largely protected against inflation.

Borrowers like credit lines because they have the ability to instantly convert bricks and pipes to cash with relatively little cost up front and far lower interest than they would normally pay for unsecured consumer credit. The access to such credit may prove extremely valuable. For instance, when they wish to buy a new home the Taylors need not wait to sell their house before placing a down payment on a new property. Instead they can just advance the money from their credit line as long as they are able to make the proper payments. As soon as the property is sold the debt will be paid in full from the sale proceeds.

Home-equity loans also have several features that should concern potential borrowers.

Because home-equity debts are second loans, a borrower who defaults can be foreclosed. The difficult issue here is this: suppose a homeowner has a $10,000 credit line, becomes unemployed, and for some reason borrows $500 on a credit line mortgage, which is not re-paid.

Can a lender foreclose if only $500 is outstanding? Absolutely.

Will a lender necessarily foreclose? The answer depends on the facts and circumstances in each case and the lender's policies. As a matter of good public relations, it seems likely that most lenders would try to work out some arrangement before seeking foreclosure.

Another potential problem may seem somewhat contradictory. Home-equity loans may be too accessible for certain borrowers. Many otherwise responsible people overextend themselves with unsecured credit card loans, and it is probable that some homeowners will do the same with credit lines secured by real estate.

At the time of publication, for example, lenders often permit the withdrawal of relatively small sums, say, $300, $400, or $500. To prevent frivolous expenditures that can result in foreclosure, some lenders set higher minimum draws, say $1,000, to prevent creeping credit debt.

Home-Equity Loans and Special Rules

Home-equity lending includes a number of rules and concepts that can be important to borrowers.

One rule that clearly benefits borrowers is that so-called "call clauses" are no longer permitted. With a call clause, a lender has the unilateral right at any time to seek full and immediate re-payment of the entire loan—even if loan payments are up-to-date and the borrower has fully honored all terms.

A second pro-borrower rule eliminates the use of internal indexes. For instance, it was once possible for lenders to raise their prime rates, thereby causing home-equity costs to go up—even if interest rates generally were falling.

A third provision says lenders cannot reserve the right to change fixed rates. It may seem as though a fixed rate should be, well, *fixed*, but in the wonderful world of lending some institutions created home-equity loans with a fixed rate but then reserved the right to change that rate later.

Along with three pro-borrower rules, there are also a few clunkers.

1. If the value of a principal residence used to secure a loan is "significantly less than the original appraisal value of the dwelling," then lenders can freeze withdrawals. In areas where home values have dropped, this rule can cover large numbers of homeowners.

2. If the lender has "any reason to believe that the consumer will be unable to comply with the repayment requirements of the account due to a material change in the consumer's financial circumstances" lenders can stop further home-equity withdrawals. Surely if someone has filed for bankruptcy this rule makes sense, but what happens if borrower Langston is hit by a bus, the accident is reported in the local paper, and a lender stops home-equity withdrawals because one can "reasonably believe" that Langston's financial circumstances have changed. This scenario seems possible under the rules, though not fair or equitable.

The "financial circumstances" regulation raises an important question: how can a lender know when a borrower has financial problems? The answer is that many home-equity agreements now permit lenders to make regular credit checks.

Not only can lenders make credit checks, but other lending regulations virtually ensure that such checks will be made. The rules require lenders to reserve relatively large amounts of capital for home-equity loans, but reserve requirements drop substantially if lenders have the right to limit withdrawals and if they make annual credit checks.

3. If a home-equity interest cap is less than prevailing interest rates, then lenders can freeze withdrawals. Because home-equity loans often have caps set at state usury rates—more than 20 percent in many cases—the possibility of hitting this cap is remote. Conversely, if a cap is hit, not too many people will want to make withdrawals anyway.

In addition to federal legislation, individual state regulations may also apply to home-equity financing. Matters such as interest rate limitations, pre-payment regulations, and rights in the event of foreclosure are generally covered by state rules.

A growing economy, low interest rates, and generally higher local real estate values have limited the impact of the three clunker rules. But if the economy declines such rules could become important for many borrowers.

Lastly, there is the subject of taxes. In general, interest on home-equity loans with principal amounts of $100,000 or less is typically deductible. For details, speak with your tax professional.

Questions to Ask

What is the interest rate for conventional financing?

What is the interest rate for unsecured consumer credit?

What is the market value of your home?

What portion of your equity can be used to calculate a maximum credit line? Various lenders are likely to have different standards, so speak to several loan officers in your community.

Is the home-equity loan structured as an adjustable rate mortgage? If so, how often can payments be adjusted? Is there an interest cap? Is there a payment cap? Can there be negative amortization?

What is the lender's policy regarding late or missed payments?

What are the minimum and maximum credit line?

What are the minimum and maximum draw?

How long is the loan term?

What is the full, up-front cost of establishing a home-equity mortgage?

Do you have the right to repay in whole or in part without penalty?

Listing Improvement Loans (LILs)

At first glance it sounds like a very simple idea: you want to sell your home, the home is likely to sell more quickly and for a better price if it is in tip-top condition, so a lender offers $20,000 to finance home improvements.

With a listing improvement loan (LIL), you'll pay second-loan, high-risk interest levels as long as the money is outstanding. As to points, with a LIL you may pay two or three points, or maybe you won't pay anything. To keep your business, a lender may waive all points for a LIL providing your next home is financed through the LIL lender.

What are the costs and risks of a LIL?

The interest level is not an issue, or much of an issue, because a LIL is likely to be a second trust or mortgage and therefore it should carry a higher rate than a first loan.

Computing a LIL Interest Rate

Loan Amount	$20,000
Annual Rate	10 Percent
Loan Term	3 Months
Interest Cost	$500
Points	$600
Annual Interest Rate	22 Percent

And because the debt is relatively small, it doesn't sound as though points are particularly expensive. After all, 1 percent of $20,000 is just $200, not much in the context of a real estate deal.

However, the points associated with a LIL can be very costly. If the LIL interest rate is set at 10 percent and the loan is re-paid within three months, then a borrower who pays three points has an effective annual interest rate of 22 percent.

How is this possible? If there is a $20,000 loan at 10 percent interest, the cost is $2,000 per year or $500 for three months. Add $600 for points, and costs total $1,100 to "rent" $20,000 for three months. Over a one-year period that works out to $4,400, or an effective three-month rate of 22 percent.

What happens if the home doesn't sell? Then the LIL either continues as a second trust to be paid off when the home closes, or it becomes a balloon note that is due and payable whether the home sells or not.

As an alternative to a LIL, plan ahead and have a home-equity loan in place before you sell. Then, if you need repairs, you can just write a check.

Questions to Ask

What is the cost of conventional financing?

What is the LIL interest level?

How many points will you pay for a LIL?

Can the points be waived if you finance a property with the lender? If so, at what rates and terms?

What happens if the property does not sell within a given period?

If the LIL converts into a second trust, what are the rates and terms?

If the LIL converts into a balloon note, when must it be re-paid and under what conditions?

What is the cost of a home-equity loan?

Low-Cash Closing Loans

It takes cash to close a home sale, a difficult reality for many buyers. But suppose we could take the cash needs of closing and finance them, just like a car or boat? The need for cash would be reduced and the pool of potential buyers would increase—along with real estate demand and home prices.

If Preston wants $100,000 to refinance his home, a traditional deal might look like this: say, 7 percent interest with 2 points ($2,000), a 1 percent origination fee ($1,000), plus closing costs in Preston's community, worth $2,000—a total of $5,000.

Preston's Low-Cash Mortgage				
	Benchmark	Par Pricing	Buy-Up	Combined
Loan Amount	$100,000.00	$100,000.00	$100,000.00	$100,000.00
Interest Rate	7 Percent	7.375 Percent	7.75 Percent	8.125 Percent
Points	2 Points	0 Points	2 Points	None
Origination Fee	1 Percent	1 Percent	$1,000.00	$1,000.00
Other Costs	$2,000.00	$2,000.00	$2,000.00	$2,000.00
Lender Credit	$0.00	$0.00	$3,000.00	$3,000.00
Cash for Closing	$5,000.00	$3,000.00	$2,000.00	None
Monthly PITI	$665.30	$690.67	$716.41	$742.50
Extra Monthly Payment	None	$25.37	$51.11	$77.20

Preston wants to refinance, but $5,000 is a lot of cash. What can he do to reduce cash costs? Several strategies stand out:

• **Par Pricing.** Preston was quoted 7 percent plus 2 points, so he can probably get financing at 7.375 percent and no points. The par-pricing strategy saves 2 points, or $2,000 in this example. His monthly cost increases from $665.30 to $690.67.

• **Buy-Up.** In this case Preston trades a .75 percent interest increase in exchange for a $3,000 lender contribution at closing. Preston "saves" $3,000 at closing with a buy-up, but his interest costs rise to 7.75 percent. His monthly loan payment increases from $665.30 a month for principal and interest to $716.41, a hike of $51.11 per month.

• **Combined.** If Preston combines par pricing with a buy-up, he pays *nothing* at settlement, but now his rate rises to 8.125 percent—.75 percent for the buy-up to cover $3,000 in closing costs, and .375 to offset the cost of 2 points, or a total of 1.125 percent over the original interest quote. His monthly payment rises from $665.30 to $742.50, but saves $5,000 in cash outlays.

Which of the choices above is best? If the goal is to save cash at closing, then the analysis works like this:

The 7 percent loan where Preston pays $5,000 is the benchmark arrangement. If Preston goes to par pricing, he saves $2,000 in cash, his interest rises by .375 percent, and his cost for principal and interest rises from $665.30 per month to $690.67. Over the life of the loan, the total potential interest cost rises from $139,508 to $148,641, an increase of $9,133 or an average of $304.43 over 30 years. To save $2,000 at closing, Preston pays an additional $304.43 per year, or 15.2 percent on his "savings," an interest rate higher than some credit cards.

With the buy-up, Preston cuts up-front costs by $3,000, but interest costs increase by .75 percent. Over 30 years, potential interest costs rise from $139,508 to $157,908. That's an increase of $18,400 over 30 years, or an annual cost of $613.33 to reduce up-front costs by $3,000. The effective interest rate to save $3,000 is 20.4 percent.

With the combined arrangement, lifetime interest costs go from $139,508 to $27,792—an increase of $27,792, or $926.40 a year. In this case, to save $5,000 up front, Preston has an effective cost of 18.5 percent.

Can Preston do better? You bet.

Suppose Preston can extract a $2,000 "seller contribution" from the owner. Preston's cash needs decline by $2,000 and he is able to obtain 7 percent financing. Effectively, Preston not only pays zero points, he gets a lower rate. His monthly costs drop from $690.67 to $665.30.

In considering ways to cut closing costs, borrowers should sit down and look at the costs represented by each choice, speak with many lenders—and then try to get the biggest concessions possible from the seller.

Pledged Asset Mortgages (PAMs)

We usually think of a down payment as money that goes directly from a buyer to a seller. The fact that a purchaser has made a down payment greatly soothes lenders, but perhaps that up-front money can be used more effectively with an arrangement called a *pledged asset mortgage* (PAM).

With a PAM, Mrs. Tilton, the borrower, gets 100 percent financing under the best available rates and terms. Rather than making a down payment, money is instead deposited by Tilton—*or a seller*—with a lender in a pledged, interest-bearing account.

The lender then takes a certain sum from the account, say $150 a month, to offset Tilton's regular mortgage payments until the account is drawn down. If Tilton defaults, the lender can claim the entire account immediately and foreclose on the property. In effect, the pledged account money offsets the lender's risk just like a down payment.

As an illustration, if Tilton buys property for $100,000, a seller can set up a $6,000 pledged account with a lender. Tilton will get a $100,000 mortgage but her monthly payment will be reduced by $150. The $150 comes from the interest-bearing pledged account.

PAMs and Conventional Loans

	PAM	Conventional
Down Payment	None	20 Percent
Account Size	5 Percent	None
Monthly Withdrawal	Regular Sum	None
Term Held	Until Paid Out	None
Can Account Be Taken in Foreclosure?	Yes	Not Appropriate

Once the money in the pledged account is used up, Tilton will then have to make the entire monthly payment.

In most instances PAM accounts are established by sellers as a form of buy-down financing. The idea is to aid purchasers with limited incomes and little capital. Because they are not getting their money out of the property in cash, however, it follows that sellers will want higher prices when they sell. If higher prices are not possible because of depressed market conditions, PAMs may represent a genuine discount.

Pledged accounts can be set up by anyone, not just sellers. A friend or relative might want to help a buyer, and rather than giving cash or being a co-signer or a co-owner, the donor instead sets up a pledged account. In this arrangement, money from the account is transferred to the lender each month to reduce the buyer's payments.

Questions to Ask

What is the prevailing interest rate for conventional financing?

How much money is required to set up a PAM account?

How much is withdrawn monthly from a PAM account?

If you set up a reserve account for a friend or relative who defaults on the mortgage, do you have any recourse to get your money back? In other words, if a reserve account is not intended to be a gift, is it a lien against the property?

With PAM financing, does the donor have a choice of accounts in which the money can be deposited, such as certificates of deposit, money market accounts, and so forth?

With PAM financing, does the donor have any liability beyond the money originally placed in an account with the lender?

In the case of a PAM loan set up by a seller, would the buyer be better off with a direct price reduction instead— or a seller credit at closing?

Reverse Mortgages

Like the Edsel and "New Coke," the reverse mortgage is the subject of enormous public attention and few sales, a situation that raises the magical question: why are reverse loans a marketplace flop?

Having worked hard for decades to own homes free and clear, most owners have no desire to once again have debt and monthly payments. From 1987 through March, 1998, HUD figures show that 9,688,042 loans were insured by FHA—but of this number only 23,067 FHA reverse mortgages were originated.

As they get older, many people would like to remain in their homes but also face declining incomes. With a reverse mortgage, an owner with substantial equity can receive a monthly check and stay in their community. Although the theory is attractive, program costs have plainly dulled public enthusiasm. Here's why:

If you obtain a $100,000 regular mortgage, it means a lender advances $100,000 at closing, which you pay back over time and with interest.

With a reverse mortgage you receive a check (usually monthly, but other options are available), and interest is added to your debt. You typically receive checks until payments *and* interest costs equal the "loan amount," in this case a total of $100,000. In other words, you get less than $100,000 for groceries and auto repairs—maybe a lot less. The good news, at least, is that the lender does not actually collect interest or principal until you move, enter a nursing home, die, or sell the property.

Not all reverse mortgages limit payments to a set amount. Some—called "lifetime annuity" reverse mortgage loans—continue to make payments as long as the borrower lives. "Lifetime tenure" reverse mortgages continue payments as long as the borrower lives *in the house.*

So-called lifetime reverse mortgages with unlimited payments work this way: your home is security for a loan. The loan is used to buy an annuity. The annuity generates payments for as long as you live.

To see if this is a good deal you need to ask some questions:

- Can you get an annuity directly, perhaps by purchasing a contract with savings or other holdings?
- What are the costs of a reverse mortgage–annuity combination? How do such costs compare with a plain reverse mortgage? How does such financing compare with selling the property and living in a less-expensive location?
- What happens if you die in a year, two years, or five years? Who gets the value of the annuity?
- What are the tax consequences of annuity payments?
- What are the social security and Medicaid impacts of an annuity?

Reverse mortgages are touted as a device that allows the elderly to remain in their homes. But some things are not said:

- Reverse mortgage closing costs can be enormously steep. Origination fees equal to 2 percent of the appraised value—not the loan amount—are common.
- Reverse mortgage interest rates are higher than rates for other loans—sometimes much higher. Depending on up-front costs and the length of the loan at the time of death, effective rates in excess of 50 percent are possible.

Controlling Reverse Mortgage Costs

Mr. and Mrs. Nelson are each 65 years old and about to retire. Their house, worth $150,000, is mortgage free. They want more cash once they retire, and so they speak to a lender who suggests reverse financing.

"A reverse mortgage," says the lender, "works like this: each month we give you $500. That money earns 9 percent interest for us." The Nelsons are told that with their projected income they can get a $100,000 reverse mortgage.

Unlike other mortgage formats where the sum of $100,000 represents only principal, with a reverse mortgage $100,000 is equal to the combined total of all principal and interest. The final term of this loan is 10 years and 3 months, and at the end the borrower actually owes $100,461.82. Of this total, $61,500 represents principal and the balance of $38,961.82 is interest.

To control interest costs, it's often best to have a reverse mortgage with set monthly payments rather than payments designed to last a given number of years. For example, if the loan was structured so that the total obligation was simply $100,000 paid out over 15 years, a borrower will receive only $265 per month. The principal payoff will be $47,700, and interest totals $52,577.53. (To be precise, the final principal balance of this loan will be $100,277.53.)

A second way to control interest costs is to have larger payments. If the $100,000 loan illustrated here was arranged so that the borrowers received $600 a month, the loan will run nine years and one month. However, interest payments will roughly total $34,600, and principal will amount to $65,400.

- For instance, if Smith pays $4,000 in fees up front for a reverse mortgage loan, gets $600 a month for 12 months, and pays 12 percent interest, at the end of one year his account will show payments to him of $7,200 and an interest cost of $561.60—a total debt of $7,761.60. If he then drops dead, to receive $7,200 he has paid out $4,561.60 ($4,000 in fees plus $561.60 in interest). In effect, the cost of such financing is 63.36 percent.

- Because of high rates and up-front fees, reverse mortgages are a costly choice for short-term borrowers, say those who have loans outstanding less than 7 to 10 years.

Most lenders do not offer reverse mortgages, and one result is arguably less competition and choice than can be found with other loan formats. Here's why most lenders do not offer reverse mortgage programs:

First, interest from the loan accumulates until the entire mortgage is due. Rather than cash, lenders are getting a credit for income not actually received but that may be subject to taxation. Lenders may charge more points or higher interest to offset this problem.

Second, security for the loan—the house—can be tied up in probate, thus delaying re-payment to the lender.

Reverse Mortgage Payments at a Glance

$100,000 at 9 Percent Interest

Month	Principal	Deferred Cost	Balance
1	$500.00	$500.00	$500.00
2	$500.00	$503.75	$1,003.75
3	$500.00	$507.63	$1,511.38
4	$500.00	$511.33	$2,022.71
5	$500.00	$515.17	$2,537.88
etc.			

Third, the value of the property may decline, thus increasing lender risk.

Fourth, if a reverse mortgage sours, a lender can have an unseemly public relations problem. One can just picture the headline: "Local Lender Forecloses on 94-Year-Old Widow of Town Minister."

The government has tried to make reverse mortgage costs clearer but has been no match for clever lenders.

The current rules require that lenders estimate reverse loan interest costs for a two-year period, the borrower's projected life expectancy (based on the owner's age at the time of application), and the borrower's remaining life expectancy plus 40 percent. In general, the longer the term being described the lower the rate.

Reverse Mortgages and Taxes

With reverse mortgages, borrowers receive cash from lenders. Interest is charged on the cash received, but borrowers do not pay that interest until the loan is paid off or the borrowers die and their estates pay. According to IRS spokesman Roy Young, if borrowers use a cash-based system of accounting, they are not entitled to a reverse mortgage interest deduction until payments have been made. If they have an accrual-based system, a form of accounting often used by businesses, then deductions may be possible. When the loan is paid off by borrowers or their estate, it is then that payments have actually been made and a deduction may be in order.

Monthly payments from a reverse mortgage are generally not seen as "income" and therefore are not taxed. The logic is that the money received is actually principal—debt—which must be repaid. However, if reverse mortgage "income" flows from an annuity, then payments may be taxable.

For specific advice speak to a tax attorney, enrolled agent, or CPA.

The catch is that many reverse mortgage programs—but not all—have an equity participation clause. This clause says that in addition to high closing costs and high interest rates, the lender also gets a piece of the home's equity when it's sold.

And when does the equity participation (*bubble*) clause kick in?

Why, two years and one day after the loan begins—just in time to avoid inclusion in the two-year interest cost disclosure.

Reverse mortgages raise harsh issues. Yes, people would like to stay in their houses and communities—but at what cost? Yes, an increased income for the elderly would be nice—but at what cost? Yes, in many families it is important to provide children with an inheritance, but perhaps everyone would be better off if adult children provided a monthly stipend to aging parents rather than giving much of their birthright to lenders.

There may be instances where reverse mortgages, in limited circumstances and without equity participation, are worthy of consideration. But homeowners should not contemplate such financing on the basis of lender representations alone. Instead—before signing anything—take these steps:

- Contact a fee-only financial planner, an attorney who specializes in elder law, or a CPA to evaluate reverse mortgage options. Ask the professional if he or she is affiliated with any reverse mortgage lender; if he or she will receive any fee, consideration, or business from anyone but you as a result of his or her recommendations; and if you are his or her "client."
- Make certain you have both a will and a living will. Speak with an attorney for details.
- Look into selling the property and moving to a smaller home in the same area.
- Look into refinancing.
- Avoid reverse mortgages to underwrite home repairs— especially if the contractor offers cash on the side. ("Hey, we'll fix your roof plus give you $5,000 . . .")
- Don't rush. Take your time and do your research.

- Never pay for reverse mortgage information from so-called estate planning companies—such information is free from the lenders who make reverse loans.

For detailed information, stop by the website operated by the non-profit National Center for Home Equity Conversion (NCHEC) at http://www.reverse.org. This site is packed with reverse mortgage news and data.

Questions to Ask

Are local lenders making reverse loans?

What is the value of your property? A lender will want an appraisal.

What reverse mortgage terms are best for you? Have a lender provide you with amortization statements to show which alternative monthly payments and terms will work best.

How will a reverse mortgage impact your income tax obligations? Speak to a tax consultant.

How will a reverse mortgage affect your pension, social security, and Medicaid benefits, if at all? Speak to appropriate professionals and administrators.

Does the loan include a written guarantee to refinance the property at then-current rates in the event you reach the reverse loan limit?

Do you have a will and living will? Speak with an attorney or legal clinic for more information.

Would a life insurance policy equal to the value of the reverse mortgage be a good purchase? In the event of death, the policy's proceeds can be used to retire the reverse mortgage debt.

Does the reverse mortgage create any claim against the equity of your home? If so, when does such a claim begin and how does it impact loan costs?

Second Home Financing

If you've reached that point in life and finance where a vacation home looks more and more interesting, congratulations. But before venturing into the wondrous world of ski chalets and beach-front cottages, consider some of the issues represented by second homes.

The first question is whether you're buying a "second home," an "investment property," or a little bit of both. In the eyes of Uncle Sam, a second home is still a residence if you rent it 14 days or less per year, or less than 10 percent of the days the unit is in use. The good news here is that if the property is a "residence" that also produces rental income within the guidelines, then the rental income need not be declared. Because of details involving "fair market" rental rates and other issues, be certain to consult with a tax professional for the latest rules.

If you have a second "residence," then you may deduct mortgage interest and property taxes. The amount of deductible mortgage interest, however, is limited—but only if you are among the landed gentry. Interest on first and second home loans totaling up to $1 million ($500,000 if married and filing separately) is generally deductible, as is the interest on home-equity debt of up to $100,000.

If the second property is rented 15 days a year, or more than 10 percent of the time the property is in use, you then have an *investment property*, which means that mortgage interest, property taxes, repairs, management fees, and depreciation may be deductible. Deductions may be limited or deferred if your adjusted gross income exceeds $100,000, and, again, contact a tax pro for specifics.

Whether the second home is something you use in addition to your principal residence or as an outright investment makes a big difference to lenders. It will be easier to get financing for a second home than for something that falls into the investment category.

There are several interesting concepts buyers should consider for a second home that will be used for personal purposes.

1. A two-, three-, or four-unit property cannot be classified as a second residence under conventional mortgage guidelines. That is, you can get residential financing for a

single-family second home or a vacation condo but not for a vacation four-plex or timeshare.

2. Rental income from a second residence cannot be used to boost buyer qualifications. The logic is that such income is likely to be spotty and inconsistent.

3. Do not expect a big check at closing if you refinance a vacation home. Cash-out conventional refinancing is not available. Refinancing to obtain better rates and terms is allowed.

4. Conventional second mortgages are not available on vacation homes.

Those buying second homes should certainly consider both conventional financing, with 20 percent down (or less, with private mortgage insurance), as well as non-conventional financing, which is likely to have more liberal qualification standards.

Alternatively, if you have a large amount of equity in your current home, it may make sense to refinance your principal residence and pay cash for a second home.

Because lenders are most liberal with loans secured by personal residences, you are likely to encounter the fewest hassles by refinancing your home. As well, interest on as much as $100,000 in new financing may be deductible. See a tax professional before considering this approach.

Whether a second home can be both a personal retreat and a good investment is a complex question. Clearly, where you buy and what you buy makes a difference. If it happens that rent covers expenses and you can still get some personal use out of the property, so much the better.

Moreover, one cannot overlook the fact that what may well have been a remote retreat 10 or 20 years ago is now "nearer" to metro living. With the Internet, fax machines, e-mail, and modems, physical proximity is no longer required to maintain a given income level. What may have been a second-home location in the past may emerge as a prime residence for those with the skills, training, and transferable talents to make location irrelevant. Indeed, it may well make sense to have a second home and to gradually move from an urban location to something more scenic and calm.

If your intent is to buy now and retire later, then purchasing a second home can be a good strategy. If, in the pre-retirement years, the property produces income to offset ownership costs then such income can be seen as a retirement subsidy—sort of an IRA contribution without the paperwork. And if values rise, then the property will effectively have been bought at discount.

Title I: Is This the Best Home-Equity Loan in Town?

There are many people who simply don't like the idea of refinancing their homes. When they need extra dollars, they use checking account overdraft credit, credit cards, and signature loans—anything but the equity in their homes. For these people, and for many others, the FHA has devised a unique form of financing that straddles both real estate and personal finance.

If you need $25,000 or less for home improvement purposes, it may pay to look at the FHA Title I program. If the amount sought is less than $7,500, the loan is regarded as a personal debt and not recorded as a lien against property. From $7,500 to $25,000, the loan is recorded as a lien but one subordinate to other loans, so you can get Title I financing even with other loans on your property. Because 90 percent of the loan is guaranteed by FHA, the risk to your lender is minimal, and there should be little resistance to giving a loan that can be regarded as a personal loan or as a first, second, or even third trust, depending on such other loans as may be in place on the property and the size of the debt.

The FHA loan program provides for a maximum term of 20 years and an interest rate usually not much higher than conventional loans and lower than credit card financing.

Not all lenders handle FHA Title I home improvement financing, so you may have to call your local FHA office (it's part of the U.S. Department of Housing and Urban Development—HUD) to get the names of area lenders who are active in the program.

The rules now in place look like this:

1. Lenders can obtain as much as a 5 percent origination fee.
   This is an unusually high cost when compared with first
   mortgages; however, because the amount borrowed under
   Title I is generally small, a lower origination fee limit
   makes loan processing unprofitable, and therefore lenders
   will not offer such financing.
2. Borrowers will be able to finance the origination fee,
   providing the total loan amount does not exceed the Title
   I limit.
3. Lenders are forbidden from charging excess "discount
   points." In the past, lenders raised their fees by
   increasing the number of discount points associated with
   Title I financing because they were only allowed to
   charge a 1 percent origination fee. In other words,
   because lenders could not charge more than a 1 percent
   origination fee, they simply increased the number of
   discount points to make the loans more profitable.

The catch is that the combination of high interest rates and steep
up-front costs meant that many borrowers could not qualify for Title
I financing. Now, says HUD, the practice of inflated point requirements will no longer be tolerated.

The bottom line is that HUD requirements and marketplace real-
ities are now in synch—lenders need more income to make Title I
loans, and HUD has found a way to create such revenue. At the same
time, borrowers can now finance such costs with fewer dollars at
closing.

Because personal interest is not deductible, borrowers will have
to weigh their Title I options. It's comforting to borrow money without placing a lien on your property—you can save money if there is
no need for a formal closing. Conversely, if you borrow more than
$7,500 under the Title I program, a lien is created, and therefore the
interest should be deductible.

If your need for cash is at or about $7,500, it can make sense to
check with your lender to see what additional costs you might face
if you breach the $7,500 plateau. It will also make sense to speak

with a CPA, tax attorney, or enrolled agent to ensure that if the loan is recorded, your interest payments will be fully deductible.

Questions to Ask

What is the Title I interest rate?

What is the maximum Title I loan?

How much Title I money can you borrow as a personal loan?

Is Title I interest deductible?

Wraparound Loans

One of the most innovative forms of creative financing is the *wraparound mortgage*, a type of loan that in the best circumstances provides below-market financing for purchasers and above-market yields for lenders. Although high yields and low rates sound like the definition of the ideal loan, there are potential complications that make wraparound financing difficult, if not unacceptable, to large numbers of borrowers and lenders.

A wraparound loan—also called an All-Inclusive Trust Deed (AITD)—consists of two parts: first, there is the original financing on the property. This loan remains in place at its original rate and terms. Second, there is the wraparound loan, financing in addition to the original mortgage.

Imagine that a home is sold for $150,000. There is a freely-assumable loan on the property with a remaining balance of $50,000. The assumable loan has a 7 percent interest rate and 20 years left on a 30-year term. This loan requires a monthly payment of $387.65.

To buy this property, a purchaser, Mr. Morton, knows that with $100,000 in cash he can merely assume the original loan. Few people—including Morton—have $100,000 in ready cash, so Morton looks into assuming the original loan and having a lender or the seller take back a second trust.

Wraparound Loans Versus Conventional Financing

	Conventional Loan	Wraparound Loan
Cash Down	$30,000.00	$30,000.00
Assumable Financing	None	$50,000.00
		($387.65 per Month)
Interest Rate	9 Percent	8 Percent
		(Rate to New Borrower)
New Financing	$120,000.00	$70,000.00
		($585.51 per Month)
Term	30 Years	20 Years
Monthly Payment	$965.55	$973.16
		(Combined Monthly Costs)
Potential Interest Cost	$227,598.00	$157,939.00
Interest Savings	$0.00	$69,658.00
First Loan Liability of		
Wraparound Lender	None	$50,000.00
Net Buyer Liability	$120,000.00	$120,000.00

As good as it sounds, this approach has problems too. Second trusts tend to have short terms, high rates, and balloon payments. Add up the first and second trust payments, and the monthly mortgage bill is far more than Morton can afford.

As an alternative, Morton can put $30,000 down and qualify for conventional financing at the market interest rate, perhaps 9 percent in this case. The problem is that 9 percent interest will leave Morton with few dollars for anything other than mortgage payments.

To get a better rate—and reduce monthly payments—Morton suggests a wraparound deal under which the seller will take back a $120,000 mortgage at 8 percent interest from the purchaser. The loan term will be the remaining length of the assumable loan, 20 years in this case. The *seller* will be responsible for re-paying the original $50,000 first loan.

The effect of this deal is to provide Morton with 8 percent financing in a 9 percent market. Not only does Morton get a good rate, but he saves extra interest payments worth $69,658. In addition, if it is the seller who takes back the loan, points and many mortgage application expenses can be avoided.

For the seller or wraparound lender, the deal looks like this: the loan appears to generate 8 percent interest. However, the original 7 percent loan must be re-paid, and thus the seller receives 8 percent interest on $70,000 ($120,000 less $50,000) and 1 percent on $50,000 (8 percent interest from the buyer less 7 percent that must be paid on the assumable loan).

If *yield* is defined as the return on money actually loaned, the seller is taking in far more than 8 percent interest. Because the seller is not actually lending the first $50,000, the yield in this illustration is 8.71 percent.

The interest earned by a wraparound note will be taxed as regular income, and the principal payments are likely to be treated as installment payments if a seller is providing the wraparound loan. For borrowers, the interest paid is deductible in the same sense as any mortgage interest payment.

As good as this deal looks, and in practice properly structured wraparounds can work well, it does raise a number of concerns that need to be carefully reviewed. There are several issues that both borrowers and seller/lenders should discuss with a knowledgeable attorney and tax professional before making a wraparound commitment.

1. Is wraparound financing a first trust or a second trust? It is sometimes argued that a wraparound has the effect of a first trust, but others maintain that it is nothing more than a glorified second trust. The difference can be important for two reasons:

   First, many states have different usury limits for first mortgages and second trusts. How a wraparound mortgage is defined can determine whether usury statutes are being violated.

   Second, what is the order of re-payment in the event of default? In the example above, there are liens on the property for both the original first trust and the wraparound financing, a total of $170,000. What if the buyer gets still another loan secured by the property? Is it a second claim? A third claim?

2. What happens if the buyer wants to get additional financing above the $50,000 remaining from the original loan. How does this affect the wraparound lender's security?

3. What if a payment on the original loan is missed? If the wraparound lender fails to make a payment on the first trust, it is possible that the original lender can foreclose, in which case the borrower can lose his home and both the buyer and the seller can lose some or all of their equity.

   One way to resolve the missed payment problem is to have the buyer issue separate checks each month, one to the first trust holder and a second to the wraparound lender for the balance due. Another approach is to deposit payments with a local lender who then pays the original lender and the holder of the wraparound note. This approach insures that a precise record of all payments will be made and avoids the potential problem of payments lost or delayed in the mail.

4. What about property taxes? Both the original financing and the wraparound note will be recorded liens against the property—a total of $170,000 in our illustration even though the actual sales value was only $150,000. An unsympathetic assessor can read such numbers and assign a higher value to the property for tax purposes than might otherwise be warranted. Check with local assessors to find out how such matters are handled.

5. Is a wraparound mortgage an *installment loan*, a loan where a purchaser does not get title until some or all payments are made? If yes, consult with an attorney to evaluate such financing and determine buyer rights in the community where the property is located.

6. Is a wraparound a good deal? To analyze this question, one must consider alternative monthly costs and potential interest expenses.

For sellers, holding a wraparound becomes attractive if such financing provides an equal or better rate of return than alternative investments of similar risk. Also, wraparounds may be extremely attractive in those situations where market interest levels are high and few buyers qualify for financing. In such circumstances, no financing means few sales and so a seller who can hold financing has a decided marketing advantage.

Questions to Ask

What is the current interest rate for conventional financing?

What is the remaining loan balance on the property?

Is the current loan freely-assumable?

How many years remain on the original loan?

Will the seller hold wraparound financing?

How much cash down is required if a wraparound is to be used to buy property?

Do commercial lenders in the jurisdiction where the property is located make wraparounds?

What are the precise terms of the proposed wraparound? How much are the monthly payments, what is the interest rate, how long will the loan last?

How does a wraparound deal compare with assuming the first trust and getting a second mortgage to acquire or refinance a property?

For the purpose of defining usury limits, is a wraparound regarded in your jurisdiction as a first trust or as a second trust?

Is the wraparound loan an installment mortgage?

Who gets to deduct property tax and interest payments?

If the house burns down, who gets the insurance benefit?

Zero-Interest (ZIP) Mortgages

By definition, the idea of a no-interest mortgage seems to be a contradiction in terms. Is a loan without interest a gift? How can a lender profit if there is no interest? Who will make an interest-free loan?

With an $85,000 zero-interest (ZIP) loan the payments for a $127,500 house look like this: one-third down ($42,500) plus 60 monthly installments of $1,416.67. That's it.

In comparison, with 20 percent down ($25,500), a 30-year $85,000 conventional mortgage at 7 percent interest will have 360 payments of $565.51 and a total interest cost over 30 years of $118,580. If 28 percent of an individual's income can be devoted to principal and interest ($565.51 in this case), insurance (let's say $40 a month), and property taxes (say, $60 a month), then PITI equals $665.51, and a qualifying income of $28,522 would be required for an $85,000 loan.

Why no interest? The answer lies elsewhere. Buried in the deal is a higher price for the property, a bigger down payment, and the world of discounted loans.

Suppose a property is marketed for $106,250. With 20 percent down there will be an $85,000 mortgage. The builder, paying some closing fees, will net in the area of $100,000.

ZIP Versus Conventional Financing		
	ZIP	**Conventional**
Sale Price	$127,500.00	$106,250.00
Down Payment	$42,500.00	$25,500.00
Loan Size	$85,000.00	$85,000.00
Interest Rate	$0.00	7 Percent
Monthly Payment	$1,416.67	$565.51
Income Required	$60,714.00	$28,522.00
Number of Payments	60	360
Total Payments	$85,000.00	$203,584.00
Total Interest	$0.00	$118,580.00

If the same property is sold with a ZIP loan, the price will be higher, say $127,500. Here, the buyer will put down $42,500 and get an $85,000 zero-interest mortgage for the balance.

In many cases, it is the builder who first holds the zero-rate mortgage. Because the builder wants cash from the loan, he'll sell the note to an investor. The investor will see that the note has a term of five years, a $1,416.67 monthly payment and an $85,000 face value. If the investor wanted a 9 percent return he will buy the $85,000 mortgage at discount and pay $68,246 in cash to the builder. (Alternatively, a lender can make a zero-rate loan if a builder pays points up front. This arrangement has the same effect as an investor buying the loan at discount.)

The builder has now collected $42,500 from the buyer and $68,246 from the investor, or a total of $110,746 for his property—a few thousand dollars more than the property could be sold with conventional financing.

The note holder—whether builder, lender, or investor—will view zero-rate financing as a low-risk loan. Such mortgages have short terms, usually five to seven years, and represent only a fraction of the property's market value, 80 percent or less.

Because ZIP loans have limited risk, qualification standards for such mortgages are generally far more liberal than the guidelines used for conventional financing. With a ZIP loan perhaps one-third of an individual's gross income can be applied to principal, interest, taxes, and insurance payments, up from 25 to 28 percent with conventional mortgages.

ZIP loans, as good as they seem, raise four issues for borrowers.

First, is it worth paying a premium purchase price to obtain zero-rate financing? In this example, the buyer has paid $42,500 up front to save as much as $118,580 in future interest payments. If you've got the cash, there are few investments of equal risk (very small) or economic potential (savings are not income and are therefore not taxed). However, it should be noted that the borrower does pay a higher cost up front and loses potential income that the larger cash down payment might have earned.

Second, some borrowers will be bothered by the apparent lack of interest payments. With no interest payment, there can be no tax deduction. However, the IRS may allow an *imputed* rate of interest as a tax deduction. (*Imputed* interest is the fair market interest for a loan—whether or not money is collected. Since interest is income to lenders, it's possible to have a tax on imputed interest even though such interest has been neither paid nor received.) To find the latest IRS rulings with regard to zero-interest loans and to determine the size of any possible imputed interest claim, check with a CPA, enrolled agent, or tax attorney before buying property with a zero-interest mortgage format.

Of course, if borrowers can deduct imputed interest, then lenders must receive imputed interest, money on which they should pay taxes even though they have not actually received spendable cash. The concept of paying tax on theoretical interest is not one that thrills many lenders.

Third, resale profits over a short period of time may be hindered by ZIP financing. Prices for properties of equal size, location, and quality will have to rise substantially before the market value of a property with ZIP financing exceeds its purchase price.

Fourth, because ZIP financing is generally associated with premium prices, borrowers might pay higher taxes when local assessors check selling prices.

Although zero-interest loans are generally available only through new home builders, a seller can conceivably take back a zero-interest loan directly from a purchaser. This can be an attractive sales tool, particularly if combined with a premium price and down payment. However, be aware that there may be income tax to pay on the imputed interest credited to the seller but not actually received. Again, see a tax specialist for current advice before making commitments.

Although premium prices are associated with ZIP financing, there is no rule that requires owners to raise asking values. In a buyer's market where property is not selling well, it may be possible to get both ZIP financing and a normal price—a deal that effectively offers a steep discount. In any case, buyers would be well advised to negotiate.

ZIP loans are clearly designed for people who can afford to put a significant sum of money down and pay large monthly costs for a few years thereafter. Even with premium property prices, ZIP loans deserve careful consideration by qualified borrowers, particularly if an imputed tax benefit is available. If you are a buyer without sufficient down payment dollars to afford ZIP financing on your own, a shared-equity arrangement can help get the cash you need—but watch out for those steep monthly costs and high purchase prices.

Questions to Ask

What is the interest rate for conventional financing?

What is the price for comparable properties financed conventionally?

How much cash down is required for a ZIP loan?

What are the monthly payments?

Can you claim a tax deduction for imputed interest? If so, at what rate?

If you hold ZIP financing, will you pay a tax on interest not actually received? If so, what portion of the loan is regarded as taxable income?

2 1

LOANS TO AVOID

A VAST ARRAY of loan choices are available to the public at any time, and yet borrowers are frequently lured into transactions that are implausible if not unworkable. Often these arrangements are described in glowing terms as "too good to be true," a literally correct phrase in too many instances.

Different arrangements work for different borrowers, so with the exception of fraudulent transactions, there are few strategies not right for someone. The problem is that a given strategy that is "right" for one person may be "wrong" for virtually everyone else. Here are several loans that should be viewed with great caution, if not total avoidance, by borrowers.

125–150 Percent Financing

We usually think of loan programs as conservative arrangements well-secured by property and personal pledges. But of late there is a new trend in real estate finance, what might be called the movement to *debt replacement* or *debt repositioning* mortgages.

To see how such programs work, imagine that a home is valued at $100,000. There are now lenders who will lend more than the value of this property, perhaps $125,000 in this example.

Huh? What about those sacred loan-to-value ratios?

Adventuresome lenders have tossed out the old loan standards (as well as the lessons of a lifetime of borrowing) and now offer programs that greatly expand consumer opportunities to be deeply in debt.

In the $100,000 home above, it may well be that $25,000 in capital improvements would bring the home up to par in a neighborhood of $150,000 homes. So rather than getting one loan to acquire the property and a second loan to fix it up, a borrower gets a single loan.

This type of debt replacement mortgage greatly resembles the FHA 203(k) plan. Part of the loan is used to acquire the home, and part is held in reserve. As approved improvements are made, the lender releases funds so the work can be paid off.

A second type of debt repositioner loan works like this: the Belmonts want to buy a $100,000 home but have $25,000 in credit card debt. Normally the Belmonts, who earn about $80,000 a year, might be seen as undesirable borrowers given their level of credit debt. But, suppose the credit debt was consolidated into a single loan secured by the property? The interest rate would be far lower and the monthly payments would be radically reduced. Combine such financing with a family budget and the termination of all but one credit card, and suddenly the Belmonts' financial picture is much brighter.

There are other uses for debt replacement loans as well. A mammoth balloon loan, a medical emergency, or the re-payment of a loan to yourself from a 401K retirement account might—in theory—justify a debt replacement loan.

But although there is a limited place for debt replacement loans, there are some cautions that should be mentioned.

- If the home is sold, the value of the property may be less than the debt. This means an owner will have to come up with cash at closing to settle the house—perhaps a lot of cash when marketing expenses, closing costs, and unpaid mortgage debt are considered. Some lenders have a built-in provision to work around this problem: if you move, any excess debt is converted into a personal loan. This sounds great—at least until you apply for another mortgage and your prospective new lender sees a huge amount of personal debt.

• With debt replacement financing, owners will have problems if property values decline and there is a need to sell. Declining values are not an issue if the borrower remains at the property and continues to make full and timely payments.

• If a debt repositioning mortgage is used for capital improvements, borrowers may pay interest on funds not actually released. In the example above, $25,000 was borrowed to make capital improvements such as the addition of a great room or the construction of a garage. Although the $25,000 was "borrowed" as of the day of closing, it may be held by the lender for several months until construction is completed. In the meantime, borrowers are paying interest.

• A debt replacement borrower who does not adopt a budget or continues to use credit cards freely may well wind up in horrible financial shape—big credit card balances coupled with debt replacement financing is a sure path to financial disaster.

• Debt repositioning mortgages imply substantial risk for lenders; thus, borrowers pay premium interest rates. Such rates apply to the entire loan amount, not just the amount above the value of the home.

Suppose a $100,000 loan is available today at 8 percent interest. Suppose, also, that a debt replacement loan for $125,000 is available at 11 percent interest.

Conventional Versus Debt Replacement Financing

	Conventional	Debt Replacement
Loan Amount	$100,000.00	$125,000.00
Term	30 Years	30 Years
Additional Capital	$0.00	$25,000.00
Interest Rate	8 Percent	11 Percent
Monthly Payment, Principal, and Interest	$733.76	$1,198.40
Interest, Year 1	$7,970.00	$13,722.00

What is the interest rate on the additional $25,000?

The first $100,000 can be expected to have an interest rate of, well, 8 percent. But because the $100,000 is buried within 125 percent financing it has an 11 percent interest rate. In the first year, the additional cost is about $3,000 (the difference between 8 percent and 11 percent interest).

The extra $25,000 has an interest rate of 11 percent. In the first year, the interest cost to borrow the additional $25,000 will be $2,750.

So, to get the extra $25,000 we must first pay a $3,000 premium on $100,000. Add the $3,000 premium with the $2,750 first-year interest cost for the first loan and the total is $5,750—23 percent of $25,000 and the real cost of borrowing the additional money.

Not only is the effective interest cost for debt replacement financing steep, but high rates plus a larger debt cause monthly payments to soar—in this example from $733 a month for principal and interest to $1,196. Given such numbers, borrowers need to consider if there might be better ways to obtain extra capital—or spend less money.

With debt replacement financing, the loan value may exceed the adjusted cost basis of the home when we sell. For instance, suppose a house was bought for $100,000. There were $5,000 in settlement expenses to purchase and $7,000 in costs to sell, a total of $12,000. The adjusted basis of the property is thus $88,000 ($100,000 less $12,000).

But, if the outstanding loans on the property total $125,000, the government may consider the difference between $88,000 and $125,000 as *excess mortgage*—money that may be taxable when the property is sold.

A second taxing catch works like this: mortgage interest is deductible to the extent that it's secured by real property. By definition, a loan amount equal to 125, 130, or 150 percent of a property's value includes funding that is not secured by real estate—and thus there can be no interest deduction on the excess amount borrowed.

The bottom line: see a tax professional for current information regarding the tax implications associated with debt replacement loans.

The use of anything over 100 percent financing to *reduce credit debt* should be seen as a red flag suggesting a need to budget, reduce debt, and look at other credit sources. Lenders certainly see it that way—one reason rates for excess mortgage loans are so high.

Questions to Ask

What is the current interest rate for conventional financing?

Is debt replacement or debt repositioning mortgage financing available from local lenders?

How much can you borrow?

What is the interest rate?

What is the term of the loan?

What credit is required to qualify?

What alternative loans are available?

Do you need to refinance credit cards? Have you reached credit card limits? Do you have—and keep—a budget?

If you have 125 percent financing and need to move, how do you pay the lender?

What is the tax impact of 125 percent financing?

Balloon Loans

Balloon loans are a form of financing with a hook: loans where you end up in debt.

With most loans in this category, a single large payment—the *balloon*—remains even after all monthly payments have been made. If the remaining payment was a few dollars or not much more than a regular monthly payment, then balloon financing would not be a concern. Unfortunately, some balloon notes have final payments that are nearly as large—and sometimes larger—than the original loan.

In general terms, four types of balloon mortgages can be found.

1. **Short-Term Balloons.** These are loans specifically designed to include a balloon payment. For example, if you have a $25,000 loan at 7 percent it would take monthly payments of $166.33 to re-pay the note over 30 years. If the loan only lasted five years, there would be a balloon payment of $23,523.57.

2. **Short-Payment Balloons.** Another way to create an intentional balloon note is to make monthly payments that are not large enough to re-pay the loan. If you have a $50,000 mortgage due in 10 years at 7 percent interest, it will take monthly payments of $580.55 to re-pay the loan. If monthly payments are only $500, then at the end of the loan term, a balloon payment of $13,940.68 will be due to the lender.

3. **Sometime Balloon Notes.** In this case, there are times when the amount owed can exceed the amount borrowed. For instance, in the early years of a graduated-payment mortgage (GPM), the principal amount will grow because monthly payments are small. If the mortgage continues past the balloon period, then the amount owed will decline and at the end of the loan, nothing will be owed to the lender—the loan becomes self-amortizing over time.

4. **Borrower-Created Balloon Notes.** Borrowers can make their own balloon notes—just don't make monthly payments and the entire debt will be owed, due, and payable.

Caution: Not all potential balloon notes are clearly identified. We now have loans with fixed rates for 3, 5, 7, and 10 years. After the initial fixed-rate period, the loan converts to an adjustable-rate mortgage (ARM).

The trick is that not all two-part loans convert *automatically* to long-term ARMs. Some loan documents provide in tiny print that if rates rise 5 percent or more, or if a borrower is not "financially qualified," or if a second loan has been placed on the property, then the lender has the right to end the loan once the fixed-rate period is over. By any standard, such loans are nothing more than potential balloon notes with all the risks such financing implies.

A Short-Payment Balloon Versus a Self-Amortizing Loan

	Self-Amortizing	Balloon
Loan Amount	$50,000.00	$50,000.00
Interest Rate	7 Percent	7 Percent
Loan Term	10 Years	10 Years
Monthly Payment	$580.55	$500.00
Final Loan Balance		
Year 1	$46,420.00	$47,418.21
Year 2	$42,581.19	$44,649.78
Year 3	$38,464.86	$41,681.22
Year 4	$34,050.98	$38,498.08
Year 5	$29,318.02	$35,084.81
Year 6	$24,242.90	$31,424.80
Year 7	$18,800.92	$27,500.22
Year 8	$12,965.52	$23,291.92
Year 9	$6,708.27	$18,779.41
Year 10	$0.00	$13,940.68

Lenders sometimes argue that they will continue balloon notes providing the borrower has made timely payments. Even in the best circumstances, however, lender assurances should *not* be seen as a substitute for the certainty of a self-amortizing loan.

Whenever balloon loans are discussed, great attention should be paid to the risks such financing represents. Borrowers who fail to make large final payments will likely lose their property through foreclosure.

Also, although it may be true that a qualifying borrower can refinance a balloon, not all borrowers are qualified, and refinancing will involve another loan application and another closing—two inconvenient and expensive events. No less important, who can tell where interest levels will be in 5 or 10 years? If rates are sufficiently high, then obtaining a new loan to replace balloon financing may be better than foreclosure, but it may also mean huge monthly payments.

The balance between the risk and benefit of a balloon payment must be carefully weighed by individual purchasers and lenders. Buyers without adequate financial means, discipline, or planning should stay away from balloon loans. As to those who do use balloon loans, such borrowers must develop a rational re-payment strategy, possibly one listed here.

1. **Seek a Long Loan Term.** In general, borrowers should seek the longest possible term when using balloon financing. More years mean more potential opportunities to renegotiate loans, refinance property, or sell real estate to cover the debt.

Having the longest possible term does not mean borrowers should wait to the last minute before refinancing. As time passes, interest charges accrue and balloon payments grow. More dollars, even dollars devalued by inflation, will be required to satisfy the note, and so an effort to refinance should be considered as soon as possible.

2. **Refinance in Part.** In those situations where the first mortgage has a balloon payment, it may be possible to raise needed cash by obtaining a second mortgage, hopefully a loan without a balloon requirement.

3. **Get a New Balloon Note.** This will not resolve the ultimate problem of a balloon payment, but at least it defers the issue for a while. Try to get a longer note, lower interest, or better monthly payments when refinancing.

4. **Refinance Completely.** If you have been making regular payments on your current mortgage and have a good credit record, you may be able to replace your balloon note with a new, self-amortizing loan from a commercial lender.

5. **Get an Extension.** If you have a good payment record, a lender may want to continue the loan, particularly if the rate of return is at or above current market levels. Warning: even if you have a great payment record and offer an insanely high interest level, a lender is not required to continue the loan.

6. **Sell Part of the Property.** It may be possible to subdivide your property and sell off some portion to meet a balloon payment. For instance, you have a $100,000 first trust and a $50,000 second loan with a balloon payment. The property consists of two lots. If you sell one lot, you can re-pay the balloon note. The catch? Both

lots secure both loans. To sell one lot you will need permission (a release) from the first lender because the value of their security (your property) is being reduced. If the first lender will not provide a release, you may want to consider a sale of the lot and a simultaneous refinancing. See brokers, lenders, and an attorney for details.

7. **Sell an Interest in the Property.** Enter into an equity-sharing arrangement with a cash-rich buyer. This will raise cash to pay off the balloon note but will also dilute your interest in the future profits, benefits, and losses associated with the property. Again, you will need a lender release or new financing.

8. **Sell the Property.** Investment buyers will frequently acquire property financed with a balloon note with the intention of selling before the balloon payment is due. The proceeds from the sale can then be used to pay off all liens against the property, including the balloon note. In considering this approach, one must wonder what happens if the property's value does not appreciate or the cost of marketing eliminates all profit.

Questions to Ask

How large is the balloon payment? (Always get an amortization schedule to determine principal and interest costs.)

What is the rate of interest?

When is the balloon payment due?

How long will it take to refinance? Be certain to allow extra time in case an application is delayed or rejected and additional weeks or months are needed to process a new or revised application.

What are the tax implications of subdividing property, particularly land that is part of a personal residence? What are the tax implications of entering into a shared-equity arrangement? Speak to a tax consultant for specific advice.

Can you subdivide property while keeping the first trust? What if a first lender will not provide a release allowing division?

Credit Card Financing: Plastic Mortgages for Everyone?

If they could, most people would reduce credit card debt, a sensible idea because many credit cards charge anywhere from a "modest" 20 percent to rates best associated with large, well-armed personal lenders willing to hold a borrower's knees as collateral.

A second problem for people who use credit card "money" to finance a car, boat, vacation, pool table, or refrigerator is that Uncle Sam will say thanks for boosting the national economy, but forget about deducting that personal interest at tax time.

But if you borrow money with a credit card and use it to buy a car, boat, or whatever, and then secure that credit card with your home, the rules change. You now have "real estate" debt, and for most of us the interest is entirely deductible.

Given that a car is a car and a vacation is a vacation, by playing the definition game one can quickly and easily cut financing costs merely by placing debt in the right column. Pay for that trip to Bora Bora with "secured real estate" debt rather than "personal" debt and your interest costs suddenly become deductible.

If you're in the 15 percent federal tax bracket, writing off interest worth $1,000 will effectively place $150 in your pocket. If you're among the rich and famous and suffer with a 39.6 percent rate, then you're ahead by $396 dollars if your $1,000 in interest is deductible. No less interesting, if you also pay state income taxes, that too makes deducting interest attractive.

The catch to all of this—and you knew there would be one—is that using credit cards secured by real estate is risky, costly, and generally not advised. To see why, consider the nature of home-equity credit cards.

To create a home-equity credit card, we first need a home-equity loan, generally a second trust with a revolving line of credit. Such financing is commonly available with little cost up front and rates that are marginally higher than traditional first mortgages. Money from a typical home-equity line of credit can usually be obtained by just writing a check. As the loan is repaid, the line of credit is restored so that continued borrowing power is assured.

With typical credit cards there is also a revolving line of credit. However, credit cards routinely represent high rates of interest, plus annual fees, low monthly payments (which happen to draw out re-payment schedules), and special charges in the event cash is withdrawn.

Combine home-equity loans with credit cards and suddenly one has two forms of borrowing that do not mix particularly well.

A typical credit card may have a credit limit of several thousand dollars, but with a home-equity card, huge volumes of credit may be available, perhaps $25,000 to $50,000—or more.

The very size of such credit lines coupled with the easy and instant access represented by credit cards may create an illusion of vast wealth, at least until the credit limit is reached.

Borrow $1,000 with a credit card and the monthly payments can be as little as $25 or $30. Borrow $25,000 and suddenly the minimum monthly bill can total $625 to $750—enough to sink many households. In comparison, a $25,000 mortgage at 8.75 percent will cost $238.91 per month over 15 years, or $183.44 monthly over 30 years.

Fail to re-pay a credit card with $1,000 outstanding and the credit card lender is apt to be fairly peeved. You will surely receive a steady stream of letters and calls to resolve the matter, and perhaps a court date as well.

But if the credit card is secured by your home, the lender has enormous leverage. Unpaid real estate debt, even $1, can lead to foreclosure, the loss of years of equity, a woefully flawed credit history, and financial ruin.

If your mailbox and e-mail accounts are like mine, there is no shortage of credit card companies that would like your business. And as long as that business is not secured by your home, then fine; have as much plastic as makes financial sense.

But when it comes to credit cards secured with real estate, beware. Big numbers can produce big problems, easy access to credit cannot continue indefinitely, and if complications arise, they are unlikely to be either minor or marginal.

So although writing off credit card interest seems appealing and logical, there can be enormous costs for the unwary, the unsophisticated, and the irresponsible.

If you want a line of credit secured by real estate, stop by any mortgage source and look into a plain and simple home-equity loan with a revolving line of credit. Compare deals in terms of closing costs, interest levels, re-payment terms, and annual fees.

But also think about this: if you have a credit card secured by real estate can you also get additional personal credit cards? In other words, what is to prevent a borrower from running up more debt in addition to what they now owe on the house? And at what point is debt so great that bankruptcy looms?

Land Contracts

We usually think of real estate financing as part of a transaction that results in a change of ownership at the time a loan is created. You go to closing, sign lots of paper, create debt, but also get title to the property.

Land contracts work differently. With land contracts a borrower makes monthly payments but title (ownership) does not transfer until a certain number of payments—sometimes all payments—have been made.

This arrangement—also called an "installment contract," "bond for deed," "installment sale," "contract for deed," or a "conditional sales agreement"—is used in several situations:

- Recreational land sales and timeshare purchases are often financed with land contracts. The logic is that developers have many, many small units to sell, and the cost of foreclosing on tiny loans is prohibitive. With a land contract, the developer can take the property back and quickly re-sell it because a foreclosure is not required—since the buyer doesn't have title, there is nothing to foreclose.
- Properties are sometimes sold to purchasers with weak credit and thus little chance of borrowing from commercial lenders. In such cases, a seller may take back financing until the buyer can build up credit and refinance.

- A seller wants a higher rate of interest than might otherwise be available and so offers a land contract to a purchaser. Because there are no points or complex applications, such an arrangement can be appealing to buyers.

With land contracts, a buyer has an "equitable" interest in the property until title is changed. In the event a single payment is missed, the borrower can lose the property, the down payment, and all accumulated equity because title is in the seller's name. In effect, all payments are nothing but rent.

Although title does not change hands immediately when land contracts are employed, borrowers should ask if the deal will at least be filed in public records, a requirement in a growing number of jurisdictions. Recordation alerts the public to the title holder's claims and the existence of any rights a borrower may have to the property.

It sometimes happens that a home is sold with a loan that cannot be assumed. To get around the assumption ban, buyer and seller may try to use a land contract because such arrangements are sometimes not recorded in public records. On paper, it looks as though the house still belongs to the seller.

The seller in such cases continues to make monthly mortgage payments to the original lender, while the buyer pays the seller on a monthly basis. The buyer gets to record title when the property is refinanced or the debt is paid off.

Some attorneys argue that a land contract does not violate assumption bans, so-called due-on-sale clauses. Other lawyers strenuously disagree because they contend that the seller has no intention of regaining occupancy and has effectively given up possession.

In those situations where the loan is assumable, it makes far more sense for the buyer to assume the loan, get a second trust or wraparound note, and get title at closing.

If the original loan is not assumable, then one has to ask if the purpose of an unrecorded transaction, where the original mortgage is not paid off, is to deny the rights of a lender.

In discussing land contracts there has, as yet, been no mention of interest rates or terms. The reason is that any loan format can be the basis of a land-contract arrangement as long as title does not pass to the borrower when the loan starts.

Although they may sound similar, a land contract is entirely different from a land lease, or a ground lease. A *land lease* is an arrangement in which ground and improvements are owned separately. For instance, Mr. Hubbard can erect an apartment building on ground owned by Mrs. Thornton. Thornton can rent the use of the land for a given period, say 75 years, at which point Hubbard's rights as a renter will end and Thornton or, more likely, Mrs. Thornton's heirs, will then own the building. The benefit of a land lease for buyers is that a home is less costly because the property (land) is not being purchased.

From the questions that follow, it should be clear that land contracts raise a variety of basic issues not found in other financing arrangements. If, for some reason, a land contract seems enticing, at least have a knowledgeable real estate attorney review the deal *before* signing a sale agreement or any other papers.

Questions to Ask

If a payment is late, is there a grace period?

What are the borrower's rights if a payment is missed entirely?

What are the rights and credits, if any, if the borrower misses one or more payments?

Because he or she is not an owner of record, what right does the borrower have to modify the property? Must the title holder give permission before the property is painted or the hot water heater is upgraded?

What right, if any, does the buyer have to raise capital by getting a second trust? What lender will make such loans to someone without actual title?

Can the land contract be assumed or pre-paid without penalty?

What right does the borrower have to sell the property?

In those jurisdictions that have rent control, is the borrower a tenant under such regulations? If so, what rights and obligations are created?

What are the buyer's rights and remedies if the seller fails to pay the original lender?

Who pays for fire, theft, and liability insurance, the borrower or the seller? (Lenders often find out about unrecorded land contracts when they receive annual renewal notices from insurers. When the names of the owner of record and the insured don't match, lenders will ask why.)

If the property burns down, who gets the insurance money? The owner of record (the seller)? The borrower? Neither? Both? If both, who gets what portion?

Who pays property taxes? If you are not an owner, can you get a tax deduction? Speak to a CPA, enrolled agent, or tax attorney for advice.

What are the state rules regarding installment sales? A number of states have created regulations that greatly protect buyer/borrowers under land contract arrangements.

Pre-Payment Penalty Mortgages

Like some bad dream, pre-payment penalties are back—this time dressed-up as a "benefit" to consumers.

Some 20 years ago, pre-payment penalties were fairly common. The argument was that big investors such as insurance companies would not buy mortgages if an assured rate of return could not be established. To be certain that borrowers would not refinance too often—and thereby reduce investor returns—pre-payment penalties were found in many loans.

The argument was and is faulty—there is little doubt that big investors had (and have) a very precise idea of what returns to expect because they employ large numbers of actuaries and economists to make such projections.

But what really caused pre-payment penalties to be disliked was their combination with due-on-sale clauses. In this situation, a borrower faced a huge extra cost merely by selling a home and paying off the loan. Because lenders, and investors, knew (and know) that few loans last 30 years, pre-payment penalties represented hidden profits in addition to interest and fees.

The latest crop of pre-payment penalties is less onerous than the old variety—many pre-payment loan programs (but not all) restrict penalties to refinancing situations and not home sales, a substantial concession. But still, a penalty is a penalty, and one should not accept such arrangements without a substantial benefit in return.

Here's how such programs work.

A lender will generously knock off .125 to .25 percent on a fixed-rate loan, but if you refinance within the loan's first three to five years there's a penalty to pay. How much of a penalty? Say, six months' interest on the outstanding loan amount. Or 1.5 percent of the original mortgage balance.

Let's run the numbers. Say you can borrow $100,000 at 8 percent. But, for a lower rate, you agree to a pre-payment penalty. Your rate will drop and your annual cost will fall by $125 to $250. Over five years you save roughly $625 to $1,250.

But, a year later you see a chance to refinance from 7.875 percent to 7 percent. Your payments would fall from $725 to $665 a month—about $720 a year in savings. But, there is that pesky pre-payment penalty. Six months' interest is about $4,000. Or 1.5 percent of the original loan amount, $1,500.

Now, in addition to the cost of refinancing, consumers with penalty loans must also look at the expense to pay off the old loan. In many cases, consumers will not refinance because they lack the cash to cover the pre-payment penalty—precisely what the lender wants.

Why are lenders once again interested in pre-payment penalties?

Well, sure, more profit is one obvious and overt answer. But the real problem is loan churning.

Loans are now available with little down. More importantly, refinancing is now available with few costs up front and sometimes almost none. Think of so-called no-cost refinancing loans.

Lenders are absolutely joyous when consumers elect to refinance. You want to refinance with Smith Lending? That's great, says Mr.

Smith. But, if refinancing means moving loans from Smith Lending to Jones, Mr. Smith becomes very dour.

The problem for lender Smith is that he may have made a no-cost loan. Such financing has costs, but instead of being paid at closing they are instead included in a larger loan amount or in the form of a higher interest rate.

If Smith has made a no-cost loan with a higher interest rate, it will take some time for him to recapture his up-front expenses. If a borrower quickly repays the Smith loan, guess who loses money and guess why Smith wants a pre-payment penalty in his no-cost loan . . .

The catch is that if you have few costs up front to refinance, or maybe no costs, then why not refinance when rates fall even a little? After all, if lenders think it is a big deal to lower rates by 1/8th or 1/4th of a percent, why shouldn't consumers think it's worthwhile to refinance when rates fall just a touch—especially if there is virtually no cost at closing?

One can readily understand that lenders want to recover the costs associated with loans that require few consumer dollars up-front. But, to be polite, negligible rate reductions are simply not enough to accept many pre-payment loan arrangements.

Conversely, if you think rates are likely to remain stable or to rise in the next few years, or if a marginally lower rate will help you qualify, then the latest bunch of loans with pre-payment penalties may be acceptable. If you are considering a pre-payment penalty mortgage, at least make sure that it offers three concessions:

1. Partial pre-payments are allowed without penalty—say, as much as 20 percent of the loan amount each year.
2. There is no pre-payment penalty if the home is sold.
3. The pre-payment penalty is automatically waived if you refinance with the same lender.

Questions to Ask

What is the prevailing rate for conventional loans?

What is the interest rate for a specific loan product with a pre-payment penalty and without one?

Are you allowed to make some pre-payments without penalty?

Is the pre-payment penalty automatically waived in a sale situation?

Is the pre-payment penalty automatically waived if you refinance with the same lender?

Section 32 Mortgages

For a long time, the lending industry has had to contend with rogue mortgage sources offering rates and terms so unfair that the entire industry has been scandalized.

No one argues that lenders should not make a profit from the services they provide, but in the course of commerce we limit profits derived from increased human misery. We do not, for example, try to cheat people out of their homes with the provision of financing that realistically cannot be re-paid.

All of which brings us to the Home Ownership and Equity Protection Act of 1994 (HOEPA), a law that makes a serious effort to limit scam mortgages.

HOEPA impacts federal Truth-in-Lending rules through what is called Section 32 of Regulation Z, a regulation that outlines mortgage disclosure standards. Because of where the HOEPA rules are located in the federal guidelines, mortgages covered under HOEPA are known generally as *Section 32 mortgages*.

Section 32 sets up a series of disclosure requirements for lenders so that borrowers must be clearly informed when certain loan terms have been proposed. In essence, Section 32 identifies what anyone would consider high-cost financing: home-equity installment loans and mortgage refinancing with rates at least 10 percentage points above the rate for Treasury notes of similar length—and/or points and fees equal to 8 percent or more of the amount borrowed or $400, whichever is larger. (The dollar figure changes each year with inflation.)

If a Section 32 mortgage is proposed, several rules immediately swing into play:

- Balloon payments are generally prohibited for loans with terms of five years or less.
- Negative amortization is banned.
- Most pre-payment penalties are forbidden.
- Lenders are prohibited "from engaging in a pattern or practice of extending credit to consumers based on the consumer's collateral without regard to the consumer's re-payment ability, including the consumer's current and expected income, current obligations, and employment." In English, if someone has a $100,000 home and no income, a lender cannot provide Section 32 financing with the hope that a foreclosure will soon follow.
- Borrowers must have three business days to review Section 32 disclosures. The loan can be rejected during this three-day period. Written disclosures from the lender, and another three-day period, are required if loan terms are changed.
- Consumers must be notified that "you are not required to complete this agreement merely because you have received these disclosures or have signed a loan application. If you obtain this loan, the lender will have a mortgage on your home. You could lose your home, and any money you have put into it, if you do not meet your obligations under this loan."

Although Section 32 is written with the best of intentions, and although it is a great improvement over past regulations, it does not go far enough. Among the notable exceptions:

- It does not apply to most reverse mortgages.
- Balloon payment prohibitions do not apply to bridge loans (this is not unreasonable because most bridge loans assume that a balloon payment will be made, but consumers should be aware of this exception).
- It is does not apply to purchase money mortgages—the loans used to acquire real estate.

- It does not apply to home-equity lines of credit. A line of credit is similar to a credit card. Section 32 does apply to home-equity installment loans—second trusts with a set term and no ability to borrow funds again once a portion of the debt has been repaid.
- The three-day waiting period can be waived by consumers. This is a substantial problem because a borrower may not understand the impact of a waiver.
- It doesn't ban lousy loans—deals 9 percentage points above Treasury notes.
- It doesn't ban loans with rates 15 percentage points above Treasury notes—it just says hapless consumers must be notified and have a three-day waiting period.

We are each ultimately responsible for ourselves, and there are limits beyond which government cannot go to protect us. But, clearly, Section 32 financing is most likely to impact those people least able to defend their own interests. Common decency suggests that predatory loans should not be proposed and thus there should be no need to regulate such financing—but the world obviously doesn't work the way it "should."

If it happens that someone proposes a Section 32 loan, no matter how dressed up or appealing such a loan might seem, realize that in essence it's probably a raw deal that will only add to borrower woes.

Short Sale "Financing"

People sometimes forget that real estate is a commodity, and like all commodities, values can both rise and fall. We like the happy news associated with booming markets, but the bottom-line reality is that property prices do not always go up.

Stagnant and falling prices that occur from time to time have given rise to a new concept, the so-called *third-party short sale*. The idea works like this:

When home values rise, borrowers keep all the benefits. When home values fall, lenders are supposed to forgive debts, hide negative credit, not foreclose, and otherwise share losses.

Imagine that a condo was bought for $150,000 with a spiffy 90 percent loan from a local lender. The property is now three years old and prices have plunged—the condo is only worth $120,000 today. If it costs $10,000 for marketing and closing costs, and if the loan now has an outstanding balance of $132,000, the owner will owe the lender $22,000 at closing.

Some owners, wanting to move and looking at the projected bottom line, think they can avoid all problems by simply transferring title to a third party. Such owners, being both depressed and foolish, incorrectly equate giving up title with selling the home and settling with the lender.

Not surprisingly, there are third parties out there who will gladly accept title to your home if *you* will pay them to do so—say 1 percent of the outstanding loan amount.

In this case, the condo owner will pay a $1,320 fee to a third party, and the third party will "buy" the condo for $132,000. The third party is now in the interesting position of holding title to the condo but not owing a dime to the lender because the loan has not been assumed with the lender's permission. Also interesting is how the money moves: in a typical sale situation the buyer pays and the seller gives up title. With this arrangement, the seller pays *and* gives up title in exchange for, er, what is it that the seller is getting?

The title holder will now try to sell the property. If there is a sale, the loan will be paid off at closing if the purchase price is high

---

Short Sale Economics

Purchase Price	$150,000
Amount Down	$15,000
Original Loan Amount	$135,000
Current Property Value	$120,000
Selling Cost	$10,000
Current Loan Balance	$132,000
Net Position	−$22,000

enough. But what if no buyer is interested? What if no buyer will purchase the property for enough to pay off the loan balance?

At this point, the third-party title holder goes to the lender and offers to negotiate a *short sale*, meaning that the lender should accept less than the $132,000 owed on the loan.

From start to finish, such a deal is a sham:

- The property isn't worth $132,000. If it was worth $132,000, then why not sell it to a buyer—someone who pays the owner?
- There was never an intention to pay the full sale price.
- If the ultimate sale price is less than the mortgage amount, it's the original borrower who remains liable to the lender.
- The third-party short sale buyer never paid a dime for the property.

Lenders—even if they must foreclose and face losses—routinely hold the line against third-party short sales in three ways:

1. Lenders and private mortgage insurers will seek deficiency judgments against the original borrower if possible. In California (and possibly elsewhere) this is a problem because lenders may not be able to get a deficiency judgment against a defaulting borrower if the financing involved was a *purchase money mortgage*—a loan used to acquire a home. If the property has been refinanced, however, then lenders are free and clear to pursue borrowers. Please see an attorney or tax professional for specifics.
2. Lenders will post the largest, blackest mark they can find on borrower credit reports, thereby making it difficult to borrow for years.
3. Lenders will invoke due-on-sale clauses at the first sign of a third-party short sale.

When times are tough, everyone suffers. Lenders, being rational, want to avoid or limit losses. Indeed, it is sometimes possible to work with lenders to extend loans, modify terms, postpone payments, refinance, and otherwise contain both lender damage and borrower suffering.

If not third-party short sales, what about a short sale between a borrower and a lender?

In this situation the borrower (or, more likely, the borrower's attorney) goes to the lender and says, "Look, I've got to sell the house. The property is worth less than the debt. What can we do?"

The lender will plainly want to know about the borrower's income and assets. Maybe some of the debt can be converted into a personal loan. Maybe some of the debt can be forgiven. Perhaps the lender will want all the money borrowed—if you were the lender would you want less? Maybe the lender knows a broker or buyer with an interest in the property.

Borrowing money and not re-paying may create "imputed income." In the case above, if the lender settles for under the $132,000 mortgage balance, the original borrower owes less. Say the lender agrees to a $100,000 pay-off. The result is a $32,000 gain for the borrower.

Is the $32,000 taxable? In most cases the lender will promptly file a form 1099C with the IRS to show that the owner has received imputed income worth $32,000.

However, some experts say there may be an exception. Suppose the loan was a "purchase money" mortgage in California or where a lender has agreed to "non-recourse" financing (fat chance of finding a lender who would offer such financing voluntarily). The lender cannot seek a deficiency judgment with such financing, and thus the borrower's debt is satisfied by giving title back. In this situation, it is argued that any unpaid debt cannot be "income" because in creating the loan the lender effectively agreed that getting title would satisfy the note.

Sound tricky? Sound complex? Sure. Be certain to speak with a tax attorney, CPA, or enrolled agent for specifics.

Questions to Ask

Has anyone offered to buy your home for the outstanding loan amount, or less?

Has anyone offered to buy your home if you will pay *them* to take title?

Has anyone said your liability to a lender can be relieved by transferring title, even if the loan is not assumable or requires lender approval for an assumption?

Has anyone said you will not face a tax obligation if your loan was paid off with something less than the full amount owed? What does your tax professional say?

What will happen to your credit in a third-party short sale?

What does the attorney general in your state say about third-party short sale "buyers"?

Does the third-party short sale buyer claim to be able to negotiate with your lender? If anyone can negotiate with your lender, why can't you?

Have you spoken with your lender regarding a strategy to minimize losses to everyone in the case of a difficult situation? Have you first spoken with an attorney before contacting your lender?

Rather than selling, would it make any sense to rent the property?

The 40-Year Mortgage

Whenever money is tight, some bright person comes up with this thought: monthly mortgage payments will be lower if loan terms are stretched from 30 to 40 years. If monthly payments are lower, more people can qualify for financing. Therefore, why not have more 40-year loans? Here's why:

Suppose you want to borrow $150,000 at 7.5 percent. A 30-year note for this sum will require monthly payments of $1,048.82, while a 40-year loan will have monthly installments of $987.11. However, for the monthly saving of $61.71, a small figure in the context of this loan, the 40-year note will require 120 additional monthly payments and nearly $100,000 in excess interest.

Conventional Loan Costs by Term			
Loan Size	$150,000.00	$150,000.00	$150,000.00
Loan Term	15 Years	30 Years	40 Years
Interest Rate	7.5 Percent	7.5 Percent	7.5 Percent
Number of Payments	180	360	480
Monthly Payment	$1,390.52	$1,048.82	$987.11
Monthly Cost Difference	+$341.70	$0.00	−$61.71
Potential Interest Cost	$100,293.10	$227,577.41	$323,800.98

Huge potential interest costs plus marginal monthly savings suggest that longer loans are simply unfavorable to most buyers. If in the context of a $150,000 mortgage it's important to save $62 per month, both buyer and lender will be better off if the purchaser bought a smaller, more affordable property.

Alternatively, a 40-year loan may make sense if it leads to home ownership at a time when other financing is not available and property values are increasing. In a few years, borrowers can either refinance the property or—if there is no pre-payment penalty—make larger monthly payments.

Questions to Ask

What is the monthly cost of a 30-year mortgage?

What is the monthly cost of a 40-year loan?

How much cash is required for a down payment with 40-year financing?

What is the possible interest cost for a 30-year loan? (To find the total potential interest cost of a 30-year mortgage, multiply 360 times the value of the monthly payment and subtract the loan's original face value.)

What is the potential interest cost of a 40-year mortgage? (Multiply 480 times the monthly payment and subtract the loan's original face value.)

22

Budget Refinancing

Many people believe that once a mortgage has been made, its terms are set in stone. Year after year they make regular payments without a thought to restructuring their loans, and as a result, they fail to quickly and easily cut interest costs by thousands of dollars.

That said, refinancing is not always easy. Lenders, for example, won't refinance everyone at every moment. If you have too little equity or recently refinanced and took cash out of your property, many lenders will ask that you go elsewhere. If you have a loan that requires a pre-payment penalty, you need to check costs before looking at new mortgages.

But in general, refinancing should be seen as a live option at all times—especially today when it's possible to refinance with little cash up front.

Taxes and Refinancing

In basic terms, singles and married couples can deduct interest payments on loans worth up to $1 million ($500,000 if married and filing separately), providing such financing is used to acquire or improve a prime residence or a second home. They can also deduct up to $100,000 for a second trust, home-equity loan, or for a refinanced loan that exceeds the current mortgage amount by up to $100,000. In total, interest on loans worth as much as $1.1 million may be fully deductible.

The catch comes with refinancing. Suppose a home was purchased 10 years ago for $100,000 and has a $75,000 balance. This is called *home acquisition debt*. Suppose also that the property value has risen and that the owners, Mr. and Mrs. Connors, decide to obtain a $120,000 second trust. This new loan is considered home-equity debt.

At this point the Connorses have a $75,000 first trust balance plus a second trust worth $120,000, a total debt of $195,000. Interest on the $75,000 current loan balance is deductible because it represents home acquisition debt—money used to acquire the property. As to the $120,000 second trust, interest on $100,000 is deductible, but interest on the $20,000 balance is not deductible. As the IRS says, "Interest on amounts over the home equity debt limit generally is treated as personal interest and is not deductible."

Because deductibility can be based on the current loan balance, capital improvement costs, plus $100,000, those who buy property for cash or who pay off loans may find that future deductibility is limited.

Points are another tax issue to consider when refinancing. In general terms, points used to *acquire* real estate are deductible in the year paid, but points paid to *refinance* must be deducted over the loan term. For example, you pay one point worth $1,000 to refinance your home with a new 30-year mortgage. Each year you may deduct $33.33. If the loan is repaid or the home sold in 10 years, the remainder of the deduction can then be claimed at once.

Not only are there federal taxes, but local jurisdictions may charge recording fees to place documents in public files; others actually tax new financing. Costs vary considerably but could amount to hundreds or thousands of dollars, depending on where the property is located and the size of the new loan.

Interest deductions and points are major issues that should concern property owners who refinance. Before you refinance, check first with a CPA, enrolled agent, or tax attorney for the latest rules, regulations, and interpretations.

The 2 Percent Myth

The public is forever told that refinancing makes sense only when the difference between today's interest rate and the old rate is at least 2 percent. Such advice is quick, convenient, and expensive.

Imagine there is an owner with 9 percent financing and a five-year-old $100,000 mortgage balance. Monthly payments for principal and interest total $804.62. If the owner refinances the outstanding balance ($95,880.34 after five years) at 7 percent, the monthly payments over 25 years will be $677.66, a savings of $126.96 per month.

Let us also imagine that to close this loan the owner will pay 2 points ($958.88 × 2) plus $1,500 in taxes, fees, and other expenses. All told, our owner must shell out $3,417.76 to refinance. If the owner keeps the property for at least 27 months, he or she will come out ahead ($3,417.76/$126.96).

So far it looks as though the 2 percent rule makes sense, but suppose interest rates only fall 1 percent? In such circumstances, can refinancing be a good deal?

If our owner refinances $95,880.34 at 8 percent over 25 years, then regular mortgage expenses will drop to $740.02 for principal and interest, a savings of $64.60 per month. If it still costs $3,418 to close the deal, then it will take another 53 months of ownership—

Refinancing Choices

	Interest Rate	Monthly Payment	Loan Term	Monthly Savings
Current Loan				
$100,000	9 Percent	$804.62	30 Years	None
New Loan Number 1				
$95,880.34	7 Percent	$677.66	25 Years	$126.96
New Loan Number 2				
$95,880.34	8 Percent	$740.02	25 Years	$64.60

Restructuring Versus Refinancing

There are differences between *restructuring* and *refinancing* that are important to borrowers.

With *restructuring*, you take the loan you now have and revise the payment schedule to reduce interest costs. The loan remains in place, so there are no costs for a new closing, lender fees, title searches, state stamp taxes, and so forth.

If you *refinance*, you replace one loan with another. Refinancing requires a new closing, and a new closing can mean big costs up front for legal fees, title insurance, title searches, state taxes, points, lender fees, and other costs.

a little more than four years—to recover up-front costs with monthly savings.

Clearly, saving 2 percent is better than saving 1 percent, but the oft-forgotten point is this: saving 1 percent is not shabby. For those who intend to hold their property for a sufficient term, even a 1 percent interest differential can make sense.

In fact, in an era when lenders offer refinancing that does not require cash to close up front, refinancing can make sense even when rates are reduced less than 1 percent.

The catch to deals that require no money for closing—incorrectly described as "no-closing cost" and "zero-cost" loans—is this: the money paid by a consumer can be found in the form of a somewhat higher rate, a larger loan amount, or both. There *is* a cost to refinance—it just comes elsewhere in the process instead of being paid at closing.

Rather than relying on the mystical 2 percent solution, owners should refinance when visible economic returns are available over a reasonable term. A basic formulation would work like this:

First, what is the cost for principal and interest today?

Second, what is the cost for principal and interest at new and lower rates if all closing costs are paid up front?

Third, how many months does the owner intend to hold the property?

Fourth, divide the monthly savings created by a new and lower monthly payment into the cost of refinancing.

Fifth, if the number found in item four is smaller than the number of months shown in item three, then consider refinancing.

Pre-Payments

If you now have a loan with a low interest rate, and if a loan can be pre-paid in whole or in part without penalty, then a loan can be effectively and inexpensively refinanced by making larger monthly pre-payments—the monthly payments go up but there is no cost for a new loan application, closing costs, taxes, or other fees.

For example, Mr. Conrad has a 30-year $125,000 mortgage at 8 percent interest. After five years, the principal balance is down to $118,836.96.

Rather than make 300 more payments (25 years) of $917.21, Conrad decides to pay off the loan in 20 years. He does this by increasing his remaining monthly payments to $994.00, an increase of $76.79 a month. The result is that over 20 years he makes additional payments of $18,429.60 (240 months × $76.79). He saves $55,032.60 (60 months × $917.21). His net benefit is $36,603 ($55,032 less $18,429.60).

Saving Through Pre-Payments

Original Loan Amount	$125,000.00
Current Balance	$118,836.96
Interest Rate	8 Percent
Remaining Term	25 Years
Monthly Cost	$917.21
New Term	20 Years
Monthly Cost	$994.00
Interest Savings	$36,603.00

Before mortgages can be revised, a borrower must first find out about pre-payment rules and penalties.

Pre-payment penalties are fees and charges designed to stop or discourage borrowers from making early re-payments. Lenders, however, cannot always charge pre-payment fees, because they are regulated in many jurisdictions and with certain types of loans.

For example, there is no pre-payment penalty with FHA loans, provided the pre-payment is not less than the monthly installment. In some jurisdictions there is no pre-payment penalty if a loan is more than three years old or if the pre-payment is above a certain size, say, $10,000 in the first year. Moreover, it should be said that in many cases lenders will wave penalties to rid their books of an unwanted (read *low yield*) mortgage. ARM financing typically excludes pre-payment penalties.

Conceivably, if a loan is silent on the matter of pre-payments or permits the borrower to re-pay the note at any time in whole or in part without penalty, a borrower has the right to restructure a loan at will as long as monthly payments do not drop below required monthly minimums.

To restructure a loan, one must first examine the lowly *amortization statement*, a table showing monthly mortgage payments, payment allocations for interest and principal, and the mortgage balance. Today, such tables can be created with cheap or free computer programs or generated online at websites.

Except for adjustable-rate loans, where future monthly payments, interest rates, and principal balances cannot be guaranteed, amortization schedules demonstrate how various mortgage formats compare. They also illustrate how rapid re-payment strategies can produce tremendous mortgage savings.

With a 30-year $125,000 conventional mortgage at 8 percent interest, the payments will be $917.21 per month for 360 months. Yet although the payments are equal, the pace of amortization is not.

1. In the first month, only $83.88 goes to reduce the principal balance. In fact, in the first year the total principal reduction is just $1,044.29, and interest payments amount to $9,962.23.

2. At the end of the 10th year, payment number 120, the mortgage balance is $109,654.98—despite total payments of $110,065.20 (120 × $917.21).
3. At the end of the 15th year, payment number 180, the mortgage balance drops to $95,975.27—after total payments of $165,097.80 (180 × $917.21).
4. In the 29th year, interest totals just $461.94, and the principal reduction amounts to $10,537.50.

The nature of mortgage amortization shows that pre-payments at the beginning of the mortgage term have greater financial impact than those made as the loan matures. The reason is that pre-payments made up front reduce outstanding principal balances early in the loan term. Less debt translates into less interest, and less debt early in the loan term means big interest savings.

Pre-Payment Strategies

Pre-paying can be an effective and attractive way to reduce overall mortgage costs, providing your loan has an attractive interest rate and there are no pre-payment penalties.

Here are four pre-payment strategies for a 30-year $100,000 mortgage at 7.5 percent interest.

Program One: The Steady Payment Approach

Prior to settlement, you see that your $100,000 mortgage requires monthly payments of $699.21. However, if the same loan is re-paid over a 15-year period, the payments increase to $927.01—a difference of $227.80 per month. Because you anticipate a rising income, you elect to spend a week of vacation at home in the coming year to raise the additional $2,735 needed for the first 12 monthly payments. Future pay raises will cover the additional cost in the following years.

Potential Savings: You pay an additional $227.80 for 180 months, or $41,004 over 15 years. You save $84,853.80 (180 payments × $699.21 equals $125,857.80 that you don't have to pay, less $41,004).

Program Two: The Double-Up Plan

You check the amortization schedule and see that in the first month the payment is $699.21, but only $74.21 goes to reduce principal. In the second month you see that the same payment is made but the principal balance drops by the munificent sum of $74.67. You decide to go from payment 1 to payment 3. When it comes time to make your first payment, you write out a check for $773.88 ($699.21 plus $74.67). The principal balance has now been reduced by both $74.21 and $74.67—and you are ahead one month on the amortization schedule.

Double-Up Impact			
	Principal	**Interest**	**Balance**
Month 1	$74.21	$625.00	$99,925.79
Month 2	$74.67	$624.54	$99,851.12
Month 3	$75.14	$624.07	$99,775.98

Potential Savings: You effectively move down the amortization schedule from month 1 to month 3 and therefore do not pay $624.54 in interest for month 2. However, you do make your regular payment in the second month and in all following months. If you hold the loan to maturity there will be one less payment to make. Do it enough and you can cut years off your mortgage.

Program Three: The Lump-Sum Rapid Reduction

Lenders are sometimes not too pleased about an advance payment of $75 or so. Suppose your lender requires pre-payments of at least a full month's usual payment, or $699.21 in this case.

At the end of the first year you have made 12 payments and the mortgage balance is reduced to $99,078.17. By making an additional payment of $699.21 you reduce the loan balance to $98,379.02. Had you followed the usual amortization program you would not have reached this level until payment 21.

Potential Savings: You have skipped ahead nine payments, worth $6,292.89. To achieve this advantage you spent $699.21. Your maximum potential net benefit is $5,593.68 ($6,292.89 less $699.21).

	Principal	Interest	Balance
Lump-Sum Rapid Reduction Plan			
Payment #12	$79.48	$619.74	$99,078.17
Payment #21	$84.06	$615.15	$98,340.12

Program Four: The Large Lump-Sum Rapid Re-Payment

You see from the amortization statement that the principal balance of the loan will be $75,426.67 after 15 years of payments—a drop of $24,573.33. The first year you get the mortgage, you decide to postpone the purchase of a new car and instead get a $25,000 personal loan from a local lender at 11 percent interest. The loan must be re-paid over four years with monthly payments of $646.14, or a total cost of $31,014.74. (Alternatively, you receive a gift of $25,000 from a relative, sell stock, or whatever.) You take the $25,000 and now the loan can be repaid in 178.1 payments.

Potential Savings: You spend $31,014.63 but save $127,186.30 (181.9 × $699.21). The maximum net benefit is $96,171.67 ($127,186 less $31,014.63).

The benefits of these strategies can be measured within two boundaries. If you hold a mortgage through its full term, you get the total benefit cited in each example. If, however, you sell or refinance a property before the mortgage is paid off, your minimum benefit will be the interest not paid and a smaller loan balance to pay off.

Large Lump-Sum Re-Payment Plan	
Personal Loan Principal	$25,000.00
Monthly Payment	$646.14
Number of Payments	48
Mortgage Principal	$100,000.00
Monthly Mortgage Payments	$699.21
Mortgage Interest Rate	7.5 Percent
Number of Payments	360
Mortgage Less Personal Loan	$75,000.00
Number of Remaining Payments	178.1
Eliminated Payments	181.9
Net Interest Savings	$96,171.67

In addition to saving money, each of these mortgage-reduction strategies offers a series of important advantages:

First, each program is at your option.

Second, in each case 100 percent of the principal is being re-paid. Because there is no discount, there is no imputed income to tax.

Third, all property owners should periodically review the mortgage market to see if an interest-reduction program is appropriate. Deals that may not have been possible at the time property was acquired or refinanced may arise in later years.

Fourth, many people view a home mortgage as a discomforting burden that should be re-paid even if rapid re-payments are not the best financial choice. Interest-reduction programs are especially valuable for such individuals.

Questions to Ask

Can you re-pay present financing in whole or in part at any time and without penalty?

If there is a penalty, what is it?

Will the lender waive the penalty if you agree to higher but steady payments?

What is the current interest rate on your mortgage?

What is the prevailing, post-tax return on alternative investments such as money market funds, savings accounts, or government securities?

Should you refinance or is your money better invested elsewhere? What about reducing credit card balances or paying off car loans?

What are the tax consequences of your prospective new financing?

Full Curtailments: Paying Off Loans at Discount

If that stock market hunch finally paid off or Uncle Jasper left you with a large chunk of cash, you may want to examine the idea of re-paying your current mortgage with a single lump sum, a process known as a *full*, or *total*, *curtailment*.

First, the loan is paid off at one time.

Second, a full curtailment often involves a principal discount. Part of the loan debt is usually forgiven in exchange for the pre-payment, particularly when the lender wants to close an unprofitable loan.

Suppose you can get 8 percent interest from a mutual fund. Suppose also that you have a 7 percent mortgage with a remaining balance of $45,000 and 15 years left on the loan.

At 7 percent, $45,000 will earn $3,150 a year in simple interest. If you can get 8 percent, a savings account with $39,375 will yield the same $3,150.

Clearly, you would do better to leave your money in the savings account rather than pay off the remaining loan balance. But what would happen if the lender said, "Look, give us the $39,375 and we'll consider the loan fully paid." Would you take a cash discount of $5,625?

Although the lender obviously prefers to get the entire $45,000, a curtailment may be a better deal than another 15 years of low-interest payments. For the lender, getting back a little more than $39,000 means getting rid of your old loan and putting more cash in the vault, money that can be re-loaned as new, higher-rate financing with up-front points and fees.

Loan curtailments are possible at any time, but discounts are unlikely when your home is on the market. If the lender is aware that you are selling property, he or she is also aware that your loan is likely to be re-paid in full at settlement—particularly if the loan value is a small portion of the total sales price. For this reason, borrowers looking for a curtailment should approach lenders well before placing their homes for sale.

Caution: The value of a mortgage discount, that is, the difference between the remaining principal balance and the cash used to re-pay the loan, may be regarded as regular income for tax purposes. Thus, a discount may raise your taxable income, so when calculating the value of a discount, attention must be paid to the possible tax costs involved, taxes that will reduce the benefit of any discount you obtain.

In contrast, lower interest costs are merely a "savings" and therefore not taxable.

For current information about curtailment tax angles, speak to a tax attorney, CPA, or enrolled agent.

Questions to Ask

What is the interest rate on your current financing?

What is the rate of return on alternative conservative investments such as savings accounts or money market funds?

Full Curtailment	
Remaining Loan Balance	$45,000
Loan Interest Rate	7 Percent
Annual Yield	$3,150
Alternative Rate	8 Percent
Alternative Principal	$39,375
Differential	$5,625

How much cash do you have available for a curtailment?

What deal can you make with a lender?

If you pay off an FHA mortgage where the insurance premium was prepaid, how much of the premium will be refunded? When can you expect a refund? Speak to the lender who services the mortgage for details.

What are the tax consequences of a curtailment?

Cash-Out Refinancing

One of the great benefits of falling interest rates is that budgets go further. Although $500 a month at 8 percent interest is enough to cover principal and interest costs for a loan worth $68,142, the same amount of money can be used to borrow $75,154 at 7 percent.

Although a calculator can quickly tell you how lower interest rates will boost your borrowing power, there is an institutional problem to consider: although lenders are elated to provide a *rate and term* refinancing—a deal where you replace a current loan with a new one of equal size but a lower rate—they have traditionally shied away from *cash-out refinancing*, loans that allow you to walk away from the closing table with a fat check.

The problem is that lenders have long been convinced that if vast numbers of people refinance and have cash, suddenly such borrowers will head to Rio while leaving massive unpaid debts behind. The historic view, however, has begun to change, especially as lenders look for additional business, fees, and income.

Cash-out refinancing can occur in two situations. In one case, you replace a current loan with a bigger mortgage and walk away with the difference; or you keep the old loan and use your property to secure additional financing.

To make a cash-out work, you need an excellent credit history, solid real estate equity, and a local real estate market where values are rising. Given such circumstances, most lenders have historically been willing to provide financing for as much as 75 percent of a home's value. (For investor properties, think in terms of cash-out loan-to-value ratios of 65 percent.)

In recent years, however, some lenders have become more liberal. After all, if lenders will finance mortgages equal to 125 or 150 percent of a property's value, why worry if some consumer wants to get a few dollars from his or her property and not much equity remains? Just swallow the risk and charge higher rates.

To see how cash-out refinancing works, consider the Kemp property. The Kemps bought 20 years ago for $35,000. Their property today is worth $175,000. They refinanced 10 years ago, and their current mortgage balance is $40,000.

How much can the Kemps borrow? Seventy-five percent of $175,000 is $131,250. That amount, less $40,000, means they can borrow $91,250 in the usual case.

To get either a full or a partial cash-out refinancing will require a complete loan application, closing, and the usual array of costs and charges. In addition, the lender will be keenly interested in why you want cash-out refinancing.

Desirable reasons—at least from the lender's perspective—include a plan to fix up your property, expand it, or otherwise add value. Such improvements increase the property's worth and thus reduce the lender's risk. Other reasons for cash-out refinancing that will attract lender interest include paying off debt (this reduces the lender's risk because the borrower's financial security is improved), buying a business (or expanding one), or using the money to underwrite a college education.

Questions to Ask

Do you have equity that can be used to obtain cash-out financing?

Are real estate prices in your community generally rising at the rate of inflation or above?

Do local lenders make cash-out loans? If so, what loan-to-value ratios do they use for prime residences? For investment property?

Are there local lenders who will make cash-out loans based on the value of your property after improvements have been made?

What rate of interest do lenders seek for cash-out refinancing? How many points? What are the rates and terms for investment properties?

What are the tax implications of a cash-out refinance?

Streamline Refinancing

Streamline deals are quicker and less costly than new loans, especially if you work with your current lender. The idea of a streamline loan is to take the loan you now have and replace it with a new loan of equal size but lower rates, payments, or both.

Streamline refinancing is usually quick because lenders have fewer requirements—they already know you, your credit, and your payment history.

In many cases, streamline refinances will offer these eight benefits:

1. New financing without a new appraisal
2. No income, asset, or debt qualifications under some programs
3. A shorter loan term. For example, if you have 25 years remaining on your current mortgage, then under a streamline refinance a new loan can also be 25 years in length. This is a good deal for borrowers because excess interest costs are reduced.
4. An easy way to move from an ARM to fixed-rate financing if you do not have a conversion clause
5. The ability to go from a fixed-rate loan to an ARM, but only if the new rate is 2 percent less than the old mortgage and the loan is for an owner-occupied property
6. No face-to-face interview

7. New borrowers may be added to the loan.
8. No-cost refinances—plans under which the lender pays some or all of the borrower's closing costs in exchange for a marginally higher interest rate

You'll want to check with lenders for the latest streamline possibilities, but here are options we've seen:

Fannie Mae

Under Section 103 of the Fannie Mae guidelines, streamline refinancing that does not pay cash to the borrower is available for both prime residences (up to 90 percent of the property's value) and second homes (up to 70 percent of the property's value).

Speak to your lender to obtain a streamline refinance for a loan held by Fannie Mae. The general requirements are that the lender must obtain a loan application, credit report, and a pay statement from those who are employed or the most recent tax return for a self-employed borrower. An appraisal may not be required if the refinancing is done through the original lender.

The lender must review the credit report to ensure that general bills are being paid in a timely manner and that no mortgage payments were more than 30 days late during the past year. The lender must also assure Fannie Mae that the property has sufficient value to justify a new loan, a requirement meaning that in communities where values are steady or falling lenders are likely to ask for a new appraisal.

With a Fannie Mae streamline refinance, monthly mortgage costs may rise by as much as 15 percent, a situation that could arise if someone went from 30-year to 15-year financing.

Freddie Mac

Under the Freddie Mac program, borrowers need a solid re-payment history to qualify for a streamline refinance: no defaults, no payments more than 30 days late, and no pattern of late charges. Income must be steady or increasing, and the new mortgage payment cannot be 15 percent greater than the old cost for principal and interest.

The money available under the Freddie Mac streamline program can be used to pay off a first mortgage, junior liens that are at least a year old, and closing costs.

To start the streamline process, a borrower will need a new property appraisal, credit report, and a payroll stub if employed or a complete tax return if self-employed.

For a prime residence, as much as 90 percent of a property's value can be financed with a no-cash-out loan but only 75 percent if the deal involves more than 1 percent of the loan amount going to the borrower.

FHA

FHA allows streamline refinances without an appraisal for rate-and-term refinancing—in other words, where the size of the mortgage is not being increased to take cash out of the property. Streamline refinancing is available for second homes and investment properties; however, the new loan documents must conform to FHA's present policies, which means the new loan cannot be assumed by an investor or someone who intends to use the property as a second home.

Under FHA rules, streamline refinancing is available with an appraisal, in which case there is no requirement to complete application questions concerning income, assets, or debts.

Borrowers may refinance 30-year loans under the streamline program to a shorter term, say 20 years or 15 years, providing that monthly payments do not rise by more than $50.

VA

The VA offers an aggressive streamline program, the theory being that as monthly costs decline, the agency has less risk.

No property appraisal or credit underwriting is required for a VA streamline refinance, but certain baseline conditions must be met.

For instance, the new loan must be secured by the same property as the old financing, the vet must own the property, and in all cases the new loan must have a lower interest rate than the original mortgage.

Under a May, 1999, rule a VA interest rate reduction loan must generally result in a lower monthly payment. Loans more than 30 days overdue require prior VA approval to refinance. The loan amount is limited to the outstanding balance of the old loan, plus allowable closing costs and no cash can be paid to the vet.

In the case of assumptions, loans can be refinanced under the streamline program, but only if a vet substitutes his or her entitlement for the entitlement of the original vet borrower.

One unusual concept adopted by the VA concerns death and spouses. VA rules provide that if a vet dies, his or her spouse is regarded as a vet for purposes of the refinance program. The surviving spouse must own the property being refinanced.

In addition to the formal programs mentioned above, a growing number of lenders offer streamline refinancing for their *portfolio loans*, mortgages they keep and service as opposed to loans they make and then sell to outside investors. The rules for streamline deals vary among lenders, but the basic point is that borrowers with solid payment histories can obtain lower rates with less time and trouble than a new loan might require.

Questions to Ask

Do you offer a streamline refinance program? If so, what steps must I take to refinance and what will it cost? (Note: always ask your current lender about streamline refinancing before you contact other loan sources.)

Do you require a new appraisal?

Must I re-qualify for financing by showing my income, assets, and debts?

Can I move from an ARM to fixed-rate financing under your streamline program?

Can I move from a fixed-rate loan to an ARM under your streamline program?

Do you have a no-cash program that will pay all of my closing costs? If so, what is your current rate?

Must I pay escrow fees for insurance and taxes at closing? (If you have a streamline refinance with the lender who holds your current loan, then escrow money is already in hand and additional funds should not be required. If you are refinancing with a new lender, however, you may need to pay escrow charges at closing. Money from your current escrow account will be returned by your present lender after closing and the old loan is paid off.)

What paperwork do you require for a streamline refinance?

ARM Conversions

ARMs have always represented more risk for borrowers than fixed-rate financing. Although ARM rates can drop, and although ARM rates have largely fallen during the past decade and thus represented a good financing choice, it is equally possible for ARM rates to rise.

Many borrowers inherently dislike ARMs (even as they use them to finance home purchases), so to overcome public apprehension lenders have tried to make ARMs more appealing through the use of low start rates, liberal qualification rates, caps on payment hikes and interest rates, as well as the use of loan conversion clauses.

In a typical situation, an ARM can be converted to fixed-rate financing within the first five years after origination. The fixed rate is determined by a pre-arranged formula, perhaps the current required Freddie Mac net yield plus five-eighths of a percent rounded to the next highest quarter. Converting to plain language, this means if the base rate is 7 percent then the lender adds .625 percent for a total of 7.625 percent. The combined figure is then rounded to the next highest quarter, 7.75 percent in this example.

The cost for an ARM conversion is generally cheap, say $250 to $500 for loans of $500,000 or less. There are usually no appraisals involved, no additional closing costs, and no qualification headaches. Paperwork requirements may amount to one or two forms in most cases.

By any standard ARM conversion options are quick, easy, and simple, but conversions may be unavailable if not made within the contractual time frame, say five years after the loan was first originated. For complete information, review mortgage documents with care and speak with your lender for details.

Questions to Ask

Do you have an ARM conversion option?

How is a fixed-rate computed?

What is the conversion cost?

Must the conversion occur within a given time frame? If so, when will the conversion option end?

Don't Forget Refinancing Costs

When considering either a partial or complete refinancing, borrowers should be concerned with more than interest rates.

Because of the many expenses involved, the full cost of refinancing is often concealed in a maze of charges, fees, and accounting concepts that can easily distort the advantages of lower rates.

Here are some of the charges to anticipate for a $100,000 refinance, items that alone may seem small, but when added together seriously affect the true cost of borrowing.

• **Points (Loan Discount Fees).** A point is equal to 1 percent of the value of a mortgage. Unlike a sales situation where buyer and seller may split the cost of financing, with a refinancing situation there is no one with whom the fee can be divided. Cost: 1 percent or more of the mortgage, or $1,000.

- **Loan Origination Fee.** Essentially a charge by the lender to grant the loan. Cost: 1 percent of the loan, or $1,000 in this example.

- **Appraisal.** An appraisal will be required by the lender to establish the property's value. Cost: could be as little as $50 for a "drive-by" valuation, $200 or more for a full appraisal.

- **Credit Report.** A lender will examine your finances and charge a credit report fee. Cost: $25 to $50.

- **Application Fee.** A payment to the lender for processing the loan. Cost: varies and may be waived when refinancing with the lender who holds the current mortgage.

- **Pre-Payment Penalty.** A charge established in the original mortgage to discourage early re-payment. Such charges are limited in many jurisdictions and in some cases may be waived by lenders. Cost: from zero to a fixed percentage of the remaining mortgage balance or the value of interest for a certain period, perhaps six months. Ask your lender for details before refinancing.

- **Survey.** A lender may require a new survey to assure there have been no encroachments or other location problems since the home was last financed. Cost: varies considerably.

- **Termite Inspection.** May be required by lenders. Cost: $50 to $100.

- **Title Insurance.** Lenders will commonly require title insurance up to the value of their loan. In the event the title is faulty, "lenders" title insurance ensures that the party making the mortgage will be re-paid. Cost: varies by jurisdiction and according to the size of the new mortgage. Suggestion: see if you qualify for a "re-issue" rate. In cases where there has been a title search in the past 5 to 10 years, many insurers offer a discounted rate and you may save 10 to 20 percent.

- **Legal Fees.** New financing requires a new title search, document preparation, and other legal and paralegal services. Cost:

expect to pay for specific services according to local regulations and the requirements of the lender.

Time is also important when refinancing. If you expect to hold property for a relatively short period, it may actually pay to keep current, high-interest loans. The reason: the benefit of low-interest financing may be offset by high non-interest expenses. To make the best decision, check with local lenders for rates, terms, and costs.

Then Again, Maybe You Shouldn't Refinance

The idea of refinancing assumes there is some benefit for the borrower—usually lower monthly costs or reduced interest expenses. These are surely items not to overlook, but if we are going to look at financial matters then we should also have a wider vision.

For instance, given a choice of spending $1,000 to reduce the balance on a 9 percent mortgage or a 14 percent credit card, it may be best to pay down the credit debt.

Or, if one has $1,000, perhaps the money can be better invested in stocks, bonds, retirement accounts, or other financial options. The catch here is that alternative investments may represent more risk than a simple mortgage debt reduction—something to consider because markets do not always rise, nor do individual stocks, bonds, or investment choices.

Alternatively, if you collect the change from your pocket or purse each night, you will perhaps accumulate enough in the course of a month to make regular mortgage pre-payments. And such money, unless otherwise saved, would likely not be spent as well.

23

CHEAP REFINANCING

FEW MATTERS IN life are more enjoyable for real estate owners than the vision of plummeting interest rates. As rates fall, the results are lower monthly costs for owner-occupants and reduced expenses for investors.

Unfortunately, it's not always easy to obtain those good-looking lower rates. Stories abound regarding owners who refinance once, twice, and even three times in the span of a year or two, each time paying points, closing costs, and taxes to reach the promised land of lower rates.

But refinancing is not the only path to lower rates. Rather than a formal refinancing ordeal with points and heavy closing costs, many borrowers obtain lower rates by simply *modifying* current loan terms—in effect, a cheap form of refinancing.

To see how this is done, imagine that Mr. Graves borrows $100,000 with an ARM. The initial interest rate is 4 percent, but the rate can change by as much as 2 percent annually. In addition, the loan has a cap that prohibits monthly payment costs from going up or down more than 7.5 percent annually.

The ARM obtained by Mr. Graves permits *negative amortization,* a phrase that means that if loan costs rise faster than monthly payments, the difference is added to the loan amount. Because of negative amortization, it is possible that the $100,000 originally borrowed by Graves could actually rise to $103,000, $105,000, or such amount as circumstances might direct. In addition, the Graves ARM allows the mortgage term to be extended from 30 years to as much as 40 years if the loan amount increases because of negative amortization.

What makes the Graves loan interesting is that although monthly payments, interest rates, term, and the amount owed can rise up or down, there has been only one settlement. In effect, Graves and his lender have a loan that is automatically modified year after year.

But where is the rule that says loan modifications are restricted to ARMs? Is it not possible to modify a fixed-rate loan after closing and thus avoid the expense and irritation of additional settlements?

You bet.

As an example of how loan modifications work, consider this experience: I have, or had, a three-year $65,000 balloon note on an investment property—not the type of mortgage most consumers should consider because the failure to re-pay the balloon could result in foreclosure.

Several months before the loan was due I went to the lender (a private pension in this case) and made a proposal: because all payments have been paid in full and on time, since the value of the property greatly surpassed the loan amount, and because a full re-payment of the loan will only mean that lender funds will have to be reinvested somewhere else, would you consider a five-year loan extension at 8.5 percent?

At the time, 8.5 percent was a somewhat higher rate than residential borrowers were paying, but this was financing for an investment property and no points were involved. More importantly, 8.5 percent was substantially more interest than the pension could obtain from low-risk alternative investments such as top-grade bonds. The lender liked my proposal.

The next step was to change the loan agreement. We had recorded the original loan, conducted a title search, and obtained title insurance to protect the lender. I called my attorney and asked how the loan could be changed.

One choice would be to pay off the old loan and have settlement on a new one, an option that made little financial sense. A second alternative, said my attorney, was a simple letter to the lender outlining the new terms. By signing and dating the letter, the lender could accept the loan modifications and the matter would be finished.

I wrote a basic letter to the lender (a trustee for the pension, in this case) that described the old loan terms and suggested new ones. The letter also stated that other than changes in the interest rate, monthly payment, and loan term, all other conditions would remain in effect.

I faxed a copy to my attorney for review, and then mailed a copy to the lender along with a copy of the original note and an amortization statement showing payments to date. A few days later my letter—appropriately countersigned—was returned and my note was fully refinanced. The cost to refinance a $65,000 mortgage: $35 in legal fees and a few pennies in postage.

The alternative to my loan modification was a full or partial refinancing, a process that would have required application forms, paperwork, fees, appraisals, title searches, title insurance, points, origination fees, taxes, and a vast amount of bother, aggravation, and cash—perhaps several thousand dollars in the case of my $65,000 loan.

Modification Strategies

Although lenders understand the concept of modifying an ARM, they are reserved when it comes to changing the rate and terms of a fixed-rate loan—especially when *changing* means lowering, reducing, and consumer savings.

Why would a lender modify a loan?

If you have been a good borrower—someone who makes complete and timely payments over a period of years—a lender knows that holding your mortgage is a mechanical process with few problems. The lender would like to keep your business, and it thus becomes possible to speak to the lender in these terms:

"I'd really like to stay with you folks, but I can get a 7 percent loan anywhere. It would be much more interesting for everyone if we took the loan we now have and simply modified the rate.

"Suppose, for example, we agreed to modify the loan on this basis: instead of 7 percent I'll pay 7.25 percent [or whatever number]."

Or . . .

"I'm willing to pay 1 point on the outstanding balance [not the original amount] if the loan can be modified.

"As a lender, you know that a loan modification is quick, easy, devoid of most paperwork, and continues your servicing income. Without a modification, I'll be forced to go elsewhere, and you'll have to get another borrower and have all the expenses and headaches associated with a new loan."

If a loan officer cannot help, speak with the manager of the loan department. If the manager cannot help, ask for the name of his or her boss and continue up the corporate ladder. This may take some time, but considering the values involved, it can be a worthwhile effort.

A more complex situation involves the institutions we view as "lenders." For instance, if Michaels sends a mortgage check each month to Smith Mortgage and Finance, Michaels is likely to believe that Smith is his lender. But Smith may have obtained the loan for Michaels and they may collect a monthly check, but they may also have sold the loan to an investor. Whoever holds the loan is now the "lender," and Smith is merely the servicing agent. Thus, Smith may not have the right to change the loan terms, even if it wanted to change them.

But many investors—the people and institutions who actually own home mortgages—will go along with loan modifications under certain conditions.

• **Disasters.** When hurricanes, floods, tornadoes, and other natural disasters hit, lender protection plummets. Having a $100,000 mortgage secured by a property that is currently underwater does little good for anyone. Compelling owners to make mortgage payments when their homes and jobs are entirely disrupted is a great way to earn long-term public enmity.

Thus, when disaster strikes, major lenders routinely modify mortgage terms, but only on a case-by-case basis. Typical approaches follow:

• **Allowing Late Payments.** If the mortgage payment is due on the 10th, a lender might allow a later payment, say, the 20th or 25th, for a period of one to several months. This is also known as a *temporary indulgence*.

- **Waiving Late Payment Fees.** In disaster situations, it is likely that local lender facilities are closed and that postal operations are curtailed; thus, it makes sense to waive late payment fees.

- **Credit Report Waivers.** Because a disaster will delay payments, lenders commonly do not report late or missed payments to credit reporting agencies, the theory being that late and unpaid mortgage bills are not within the borrower's control.

- **Payment Deferrals.** Lenders who offer deferrals allow borrowers to suspend monthly payments for two or three months. The unmet payments are then paid back with somewhat larger future payments, say a payment-and-a-quarter or a payment-and-a-half until the lost payments are made up. In extreme cases, lenders may use payment deferrals to reorganize the loan—for example, allowing a borrower to skip three payments now but then adding three payments to the end of the mortgage. Temporary payment deferrals are also known within the mortgage industry as *special forbearance*.

- **New Terms.** It is sometimes possible to adjust mortgage terms in a way that benefits everyone. For instance, suppose you have an ARM and rates have been dropping steadily. Payments, however, have only decreased 7.5 percent a year, and the result is overly large monthly principal reductions. In this situation, a lender might accept lower monthly payments because such payments will be more tolerable to the borrower and because interest is being earned on all outstanding principal.

- **Foreclosure Freeze.** For those facing foreclosure, a disaster can bring relief of sorts. Lenders commonly halt foreclosure actions because foreclosures may be impossible to schedule and properties may be impossible to sell. Lenders want to avoid foreclosures in disaster areas—especially if a large number of properties must be foreclosed—because mass sales will depress values at the very time lenders are trying to recapture their money and local property sales are already questionable.

- **Reduced Monthly Payments.** In this situation, the borrower has income and can make monthly payments but not all monthly charges. A lender might allow the borrower to make smaller payments for several months, say, $500 a month rather than $750, with the difference paid out on top of future payments (say, an extra $100 a month) or added to the mortgage balance.

- **Refinancing.** Rather than continue with a current loan, lenders may encourage refinancing to reduce monthly costs. Refinancing, however, may be enormously difficult if the value of the underlying security—the home—is greatly diminished. Those protected with proper and appropriate insurance are usually able to repay some or all mortgage claims and start over with a clean financial statement.

- **Operation of Law.** Mortgages are contracts, and as a matter of public interest government may regulate the formation of agreements. The classic case involves the state of Iowa, which declared a one-year foreclosure moratorium for farmers in 1985.

- **Widespread Loss of Income.** In cases where entire communities face severe economic conditions, lenders may agree to loan modifications. For instance, a town depends on the local wicker furniture plant for 60 percent of all jobs. The plant burns down and the owners cannot re-open. Suddenly unemployment is rampant, the town cannot collect taxes, merchants have no markets, and the entire community is in deep financial trouble. In such instances, lenders may modify loans by offering to replace contract mortgage rates with current interest levels, if lower.

- **Preforeclosure Sale.** It sometimes happens that people have both general misfortunes and a property with some economic worth. If the situation persists, the owners are likely to go bankrupt and the property will probably be foreclosed. In this situation, a lender may agree to reduce or suspend monthly mortgage payments, providing the property has value and is actively marketed.

The attraction of this scenario is that with reduced monthly costs the owners may be able to solve some of their financial problems. For lenders, forbearance can be attractive if it means avoiding a lengthy bankruptcy proceeding and the cost of a foreclosure. All missed payments will be recaptured when the property is sold.

• **Hardship.** On a case-by-case basis, some lenders (but not all) will modify loan terms in hardship situations such as a major accident or medical disability. In hardship cases, owners will be asked to provide extensive and compelling documentation to justify a loan modification.

Two-Way Street

A mortgage is a contract, and as a contract it can only be modified with the agreement of both lender and borrower. Although loan modifications sound wonderful when rates are falling, imagine the hue and cry if lenders sought to modify interest levels when rates were rising.

In fairness to lenders, it must be said that loan modifications are not always attractive. Suppose you're a lender with a 9 percent loan in a 7 percent market and a borrower asks you to modify the loan. From the borrower's perspective, a lower rate is certainly a great idea, but perhaps as a lender you can get 7.5 percent elsewhere. Thus, as a lender you might offer to modify the loan to 7.5 percent (or more) or you might simply ask the borrower to refinance and pay off the debt.

Moreover, it should be said that a large proportion of all mortgage debt is obtained in the open market through the sale of Ginnie Mae, Fannie Mae, and Freddie Mac financial paper. Those who invest in such securities expect a given rate of return and a given level of risk. If pro-borrower loan modification clauses are included in fixed-rate mortgages, then investors may want more interest or they may simply invest in other market instruments. If enough investors leave the mortgage arena, mortgage rates will rise because the supply of investment funds will dwindle.

The point is that loan modifications should not be seen as a one-way street. As long as a loan is in place, lenders have a right to receive the contractual interest rate and all other benefits to which they are entitled as part of the original bargain.

Then again, if you ask a lender to modify a loan, they can always say no. Asking—in and of itself—hurts no one and from time to time can lead to significant financing benefits.

Modification Versus Refinancing

So far we have seen that loan modifications are quick, cheap, and easy when compared to refinancing, facts that raise a question: if loan modifications are such a good idea, how come we don't see them more often?

One answer is that circumstances are not always right for a loan modification. It takes the agreement of both borrower and lender to modify a mortgage, and such agreement is not always possible.

A second problem is that because loan modifications are quick, cheap, and easy, they can reduce the income enjoyed by many players in the real estate financing game. Thus, if you were in the lending business or the closing industry you would have little incentive to suggest loan modifications.

But although these two problems stand out, the case for loan modifications is compelling in certain situations.

If you are a lender, and borrower Hansen is about to refinance a 9 percent mortgage for 7 percent, he will either refinance with you or refinance elsewhere. If he refinances with you, your stream of income declines because of the lower interest level but you get the benefit of additional fees and charges. If Hansen refinances elsewhere, you still get a stream of income because you'll loan the money to someone else and in today's 7 percent market, that's all that is available.

The bottom line is that whether Hansen refinances with his current lender or goes elsewhere, the result for the lender is largely the same.

But suppose we had a lender with a different perspective. Suppose we had a lender who thought like this:

"It's in my interest to originate as many loans and service as many mortgages as possible. If I say to people that the only way to obtain a lower rate is to refinance, some will go elsewhere. I can replace those folks with new borrowers, but my share of the marketplace may not hold steady or increase.

"As an alternative—and knowing that it will not be possible in all cases—what about this idea: a loan modification instead of full refinance.

"The great advantage for me, the lender, is that it will allow me to keep current borrowers. I can still charge points and fees, but because the borrower will not have to pay for a new title search (the old loan is still in place) or a new closing (there is nothing to close), the borrower can save thousands of dollars."

In addition to marketplace advantages, loan modifications offer another benefit as well.

Suppose the Grafton house is financed with two loans, a $150,000 first trust and a $20,000 second trust. When the Graftons refinance the first trust, they pay $150,000 to the old lender to settle that debt, and they then place a new loan on the property for $150,000.

The moment the original first trust is paid off, the former second trust—the $20,000 loan—becomes the new first trust. The new $150,000 mortgage becomes a huge second trust.

Why is the new loan a second trust? Because it was placed on the public record *after* the $20,000 note. Is it important to be a first trust or first mortgage? You bet.

If there is a foreclosure, the first lien holder must be paid in full before a dime is paid to second trust lenders. Thus, a second trust has more risk than a first trust, and more risk means more interest. Because of the risks involved, it is very important for lenders to keep their place in line as creditors.

With a loan modification, the original loan stays in place and that means the lender's position in the event of default is as safe as possible.

Mortgage Assignments

In many jurisdictions, local governments earn extra dollars by taxing homeowners who refinance. In some jurisdictions, ingenious attorneys are sometimes able to help clients avoid the tax.

There are two approaches. One strategy is to modify a current mortgage. In this case, the old mortgage remains on the books and thus there are no new papers to file or tax. This can work when borrower and lender agree to change the interest rate, monthly payment, or loan term. Enlarge the loan amount, however, and problems can arise.

A second approach is to assign the mortgage. In this case we have a lender with an existing loan on the property and a second lender who is providing refinance money. The first lender assigns the loan to the second lender; the second lender then changes the terms—except that in no case can the loan amount be increased.

For details, speak with an attorney in the community where you are refinancing.

Questions to Ask

What is the current interest rate on your mortgage?

What is today's interest rate?

Do you have a loan modification program?

Is your loan held by an investor, such as Fannie Mae or Freddie Mac? If not, who or what actually holds the loan at this time?

If a modification program is available, what are the costs and conditions required to modify your loan?

Do you need to enter the loan modification agreement in local property records?

What closing costs, if any, can you expect with a loan modification?

What are the legal and tax implications? Ask an attorney and tax professional for specific advice.

Skip-a-Payment Financing

The usual relationship between borrowers and lenders is best described as *adversarial*, an expression that also works nicely when picturing two countries locked in combat.

Borrowers and lenders—to judge from much of human history—are at odds over just about everything. Lenders want more interest; borrowers want less. Lenders want more paperwork; borrowers believe entire forests could be saved if only loan applications were less complex. Lenders believe that borrowers should pay their debts in a timely manner, but borrowers—like Einstein—sometimes feel that time is a relative concept.

But despite the vast gulf that separates their interests, borrowers and lenders are tied together by mutual need. Borrowers want cash, lenders have cash, and so with a little bartering back and forth, everyone's wants can be satisfied.

All of which brings us to the world's strangest letter, a missive from one of my lenders that said, in so many words, that if at some point during the next several months I didn't feel like making a mortgage payment, forget it. No problem. We'll just up the loan balance by the interest not paid. *In effect, a loan modification proposed by a lender!*

The mortgage in question is an ARM secured by an investment property. Skipping a payment would add about $700 to the loan balance. Because the loan rate was roughly 7 percent at the time of the lender's offer, skipping a payment would increase future mortgage costs by roughly $4.75 per month if loan rates remain stable.

In looking at the skip-a-payment proposal, one must admire its simplicity and elegance. Rarely can one find a deal that better serves both borrowers and lenders at the same time.

From the borrower's perspective, the ability to defer a payment means that debt can be shifted from high-cost, short-term obligations to long-term, low-interest debt. For example, in the case above, the payment is equal to the monthly interest cost ($700 in this case) plus the monthly amortization, say, about $135. In total, $835 not paid to a mortgage lender can be used by the borrower for whatever purpose makes sense.

Let's say that the borrower elects to pay off a credit card bill with a nominal interest rate of 18 percent. Skipping a payment and adding $835 to the mortgage creates additional debt at 7 percent interest, a full 11 percent less than the credit card company charges. In terms of cash costs, the additional mortgage payment will total about $4.75 instead of credit card payments of $25 to $42 monthly, depending on individual re-payment schedules.

A savvy borrower will take the skip-a-payment deal, pay off or reduce credit card debt, and then apply the monthly cash savings to the mortgage. Adding $20 to $40 a month to a mortgage payment may not seem significant, but the savings can be impressive. For instance, going from $835 a month to $855 monthly for a $125,500 mortgage at 7 percent interest will reduce the number of payments from 360 to 333½. That's a potential interest saving of $22,127, assuming a borrower starts higher payments as soon as the loan is established. If the payment increases to $875 a month, interest worth as much as $40,497 can be saved over the loan term.

It may seem surprising that lenders would favor a program that offers the possibility of substantially lower interest costs, but the skip-a-payment concept also generates a host of lender benefits.

To create business, lenders must advertise, fund offices, pay loan officers, and so forth. With the skip-a-payment program, lenders can forget such expenses and instead invest in postage and printing.

Suppose a lender sends out 250,000 skip-a-payment letters. In a typical direct mailing, a 1 to 2 percent response is often regarded as successful, but here we have a letter from a known party (the lender) about a matter most borrowers would find enticing (not making a mortgage payment). It's just speculation, but it's hard to imagine that a lender could get less than a 10 percent response.

If the average outstanding loan balance is worth $80,000 and a typical payment is $597 at 8 percent interest, then an everyday monthly interest bill is $533. If 25,000 people elect to skip a payment, then the lender has increased its loan volume by $13.3 million for the price of a mailing and a little paper shuffling.

No less important for both lender and borrower, the skip-a-payment program is done without a title search (the loan is already in place), closing costs (the loan is already closed), or massive paper-work (my loan required a half-page form). In effect, the skip-a-payment concept is nothing more than a shrewd mortgage modification plan, one with obvious advantages for everyone.

There is some expectation that skip-a-payment programs may become more common. One can easily imagine a shrewd lender offering loans with an automatic skip-a-payment feature. A loan could be structured so that after an initial period, say, two years without a late or missed payment, a borrower would have an automatic right to skip one payment a year as long as all other payments are timely.

To use the skip-a-payment feature, the borrower would notify the lender on or before the payment due date. Notices received after the due date would be regarded as late and subject to a penalty. The *due date* would be defined not as the contractual date when a payment is due, but the end of the grace period that follows the contractual payment date.

Skip-a-payment loans have an undeniable popularity, and for those with the willingness and discipline to save, a skip-a-payment feature offers great value from time to time.

Questions to Ask

If you now have financing, does your lender offer a skip-a-payment program?

If you are looking for financing, do lenders have loans that include a skip-a-payment feature?

Does it make sense for you to skip a payment? That is, if you do not pay the lender, how will the unspent mortgage payment be used?

INDEX

ABOUT THE AUTHOR

PETER G. MILLER, widely known as OurBroker,® is an Internet real estate columnist with *Realty Times* (www.realtytimes.com), the author of several highly-regarded books in the field, and a Web pioneer who established one of the first realty sites on the Internet. Mr. Miller has been featured on numerous radio and television programs, including *Oprah*, *Today*, CBS *Morning News*, and CNN.